Using Corpora

Discourse Analysis

Bloomsbury Discourse Series

Series Editor: Professor Ken Hyland, Institute of Education, University of London.

Discourse is one of the most significant concepts of contemporary thinking in the humanities and social sciences as it concerns the ways language mediates and shapes our interactions with each other and with the social, political and cultural formations of our society. The *Continuum Discourse Series* aims to capture the fast-developing interest in discourse to provide students, new and experienced teachers and researchers in applied linguistics, ELT and English language with an essential bookshelf. Each book deals with a core topic in discourse studies to give an in-depth, structured and readable introduction to an aspect of the way language is used in real life.

Other titles in the series

Metadiscourse
Ken Hyland

Discourse Analysis: An Introduction
Brian Paltridge

Spoken Discourse: An Introduction (forthcoming)
Diana Slade and Helen de Silva Joyce

Historical Discourse: The Language of time, Cause and Evaluation
Caroline Coffin

Using Corpora in Discourse Analysis

Paul Baker

BLOOMSBURY

LONDON • NEW DELHI • NEW YORK • SYDNEY

Bloomsbury Academic
An imprint of Bloomsbury Publishing Plc

50 Bedford Square	175 Fifth Avenue
London	New York
WC1B 3DP	NY 10010
UK	USA

www.bloomsbury.com

First published in 2006 by the Continuum
International Publishing Group Ltd
Reprinted 2007, 2008, 2009, 2010, 2011
Reprinted by Bloomsbury Academic 2013

British Library Cataloguing-in-Publication Data
A catalogue record for this book is available from the British Library.

ISBN: HB: 978-0-8264-7724-8
PB: 978-0-8264-7725-5

Library of Congress Cataloging-in-Publication Data
A catalog record for this book is available from the Library of Congress.

Typeset by Fakenham Photosetting Limited, Fakenham, Norfolk

Acknowledgements

Thanks to Susan Hunston for providing inspiration and for her detailed comments on a draft of this book, to Ken Hyland and Jennifer Lovel for their patience and suggestions, Tony McEnery for being a sounding-board, Mike Scott for inventing WordSmith and his supportive email advice over the years, Paul Rayson for help with WMatrix, Hans Martin Lehmann for affording me access to BNCweb, Elena Semino and Veronika Koller for their advice on corpus-based metaphor analysis and Ruth Wodak for her encouragement and comments on discourses of refugees.

Contents

1 Introduction

This book is about a set of techniques of analysing language for a particular purpose. Or more precisely, it is about using *corpora* (large bodies of naturally occurring language data stored on computers) and corpus processes (computational procedures which manipulate this data in various ways) in order to uncover linguistic patterns which can enable us to make sense of the ways that language is used in the construction of *discourses* (or ways of constructing reality).

It therefore involves the pairing of two areas related to linguistics (corpora and discourse) which have not had a great deal to do with each other for reasons I will try to explain later in this chapter. This book is mainly written for 'linguists who use corpora' (Partington 2003: 257), rather than explicitly for corpus linguists, although hopefully corpus linguists may find something of use in it too.

This chapter serves as an overview for the rest of the book. A problem with writing a book that involves bridge-building between two different disciplines, is in the assumptions that have to be made regarding a fairly disparate target audience. Some people may know a lot about discourse analysis but not a great deal about corpus linguistics. For others the opposite may be the case. For others still, both areas might be equally opaque. So, for the sake of completeness and inclusiveness, I will try to cover as much ground as possible and hope that readers bear with me or can skim through the parts that they are already familiar with. I will begin by giving a quick description of corpus linguistics, followed by one of discourse.

Corpus Linguistics

Corpus linguistics is 'the study of language based on examples of real life language use' (McEnery & Wilson, 1996: 1). However, unlike purely qualitative approaches to research, corpus linguistics utilizes bodies of electronically encoded text, implementing a more quantitative methodology, for example by using frequency information about occurrences of particular linguistic phenomena. As Biber (1998: 4) points out, corpus-based research actually depends on both quantitative *and* qualitative techniques: 'Association patterns represent quantitative relations, measuring the extent to which features and variants are associated with contextual factors. However functional (qualitative) interpretation is also an essential step in any corpus-based analysis.'

Corpora are generally large (consisting of thousands or even millions of words), representative samples of a particular type of naturally occurring language, so they can therefore be used as a standard reference with which claims about language can be measured. The fact that they are encoded electronically means that complex calculations can be carried out on large amounts of text, revealing linguistic patterns and frequency information that would otherwise take days or months to uncover by hand, and may run counter to intuition.

Electronic corpora are often annotated with additional linguistic information, the most common being part of speech information (for example, whether something is a noun or a verb), which allows large-scale grammatical analyses to be carried out. Other types of information can be encoded within corpora – for example, in spoken corpora (containing transcripts of dialogue) attributes such as sex, age, socio-economic group and region can be encoded for each participant. This would allow language comparisons to be made about different types of speakers. For example, Rayson *et al* (1997) have shown that speakers from economically advantaged groups use adverbs like *actually* and *really* more than those from less advantaged groups, who are more likely to use words like *say*, *said* and *saying*, numbers and taboo words.

Corpus-based or equivalent methods have been used from as early as the nineteenth century. The diary studies of infant language acquisition (Taine 1877; Preyer 1889), or Käding's (1897) frequency distribution of sequences of letters in an 11 million word corpus of German focused on collections of large, naturally occurring language use (in the absence of computers, the data was painstakingly analysed by hand). However, up until the 1970s, only a small number of studies utilized corpus-based approaches. Quirk's (1960) *Survey of English Usage* began in 1961, as did Brown and Kucera's work on the Brown corpus of American English. It was not until the advent of widely available personal computers in the 1980s that corpus linguistics as a methodology became popular. Johansson (1991) shows that the number of such studies doubled for every five year period between 1976–1991.

Corpus linguistics has since been employed in a number of areas of linguistic enquiry, including dictionary creation (Clear *et al* 1996), as an aid to interpretation of literary texts (Louw 1997), forensic linguistics (Wools and Coulthard 1998), language description (Sinclair 1999), language variation studies (Biber 1988) and language teaching materials (Johns 1997). The aim of this book, however, is to investigate how corpus linguistics can enable the analysis of discourses. With that said, the term *discourse* has numerous interpretations, so the following section explains what I mean when I use it.

Discourse

The term *discourse* is problematic, as it is used in social and linguistic research in a number of inter-related yet different ways. In traditional linguistics it is defined as either 'language above the sentence or above the clause' (Stubbs 1983: 1), or 'language in use' (Brown and Yule 1983). We can talk about the discourse structure of particular texts. For example, a recipe will usually begin with the name of the meal to be prepared, then give a list of ingredients, then describe the means of preparation. There may be variants to this, but on the whole we are usually able to recognize the discourse structure of a text like a recipe fairly easily. We would expect certain lexical items or grammatical structures to appear at particular places (for example, numbers and measurements would appear near the beginning of the text, in the list of ingredients, e.g. '4 15ml spoons of olive oil', whereas imperative sentences would appear in the latter half, e.g. 'Slice each potato lengthwise.'). The term *discourse* is also sometimes applied to different types of language use or topics, for example, we can talk about political discourse (Chilton 2004), colonial discourse (Williams and Chrisman 1993), media discourse (Fairclough 1995) and environmental discourse (Hajer 1997). A number of researchers have used corpora to examine discourse styles of people who are learners of English. Ringbom (1998) found a high frequency of lexis that had a high generality (words like *people* and *things*) in a corpus of writings produced by learners of English when compared to a similar corpus of native speakers. Ringbom suggests that this results in learner English having a vague style. Similarly, Lorenz (1998) found that learners modify adjectives frequently, giving their discourse a sense of overstatement 'The sea was very clean', whereas Flowerdew (2000) showed that learner discourse contained an under-use of hedging devices (words like *perhaps* and *possibly*), making their writing appear overly direct. So this is a conceptualization of discourse which is linked to genre, style or text type. And throughout this book we will be examining a range of different discourses: tourist discourse in Chapter 3, news reporting discourse in Chapters 4 and 7, and political discourse in Chapter 6. However, discourse can also be defined as 'practices which systematically form the objects of which they speak' (Foucault 1972: 49) and it is this meaning of discourse which I intend to focus on in this book (although in practice it is difficult to consider this meaning without taking into account the other meanings as well).

In order to expand upon Foucault's definition, discourse is a 'system of statements which constructs an object' (Parker 1992: 5) or 'language-in-action' (Blommaert 2005: 2). It is further categorized by Burr (1995: 48) as 'a set of meanings, metaphors, representations, images, stories, statements and so on that in some way together produce a particular version of events ... Surrounding any one object, event, person etc., there may be a variety of different discourses, each with a different story to tell about the world, a different way of representing it to the world.' Because of Foucault's notion of practices, discourse therefore becomes a countable noun: *discourses* (Cameron 2001: 15). So around any given object or concept there are likely to be multiple ways of constructing it, reflecting the fact that humans are diverse creatures; we tend to perceive aspects of the world in different ways, depending on a range of factors. In addition, discourses allow for people to be internally inconsistent; they help to explain why people contradict themselves, change position or appear to have ambiguous or conflicting views on the same subject (Potter and Wetherell 1987). We can view cases like this in terms of people holding competing discourses. Therefore, discourses are not valid descriptions of people's 'beliefs' or 'opinions' and they cannot be taken as representing an inner, essential aspect of identity such as personality or attitude. Instead they are connected to practices and structures that are lived out in society from day to day. Discourses can therefore be difficult to pin down or describe – they are constantly changing, interacting with each other, breaking off and merging. As Sunderland (2004) points out, there is no 'dictionary of discourses'. In addition, any act of naming or defining a discourse is going to be an interpretative one. Where I see a discourse, you may see a different discourse, or no discourse. It is difficult, if not impossible, to step outside discourse. Therefore our labelling of something as a discourse is going to be based upon the discourses that we already (often unconsciously) live with. As Foucault (1972: 146) notes, 'it is not possible for us to describe our own archive, since it is from within these rules that we speak.'

To give a couple of examples, Holloway's (1981, 1984) work on heterosexual relations produced what Sunderland (2004: 58) refers to as a 'male sexual drive' discourse, one which constructs male sexuality as a biological drive – men are seen as having a basic need for sex which they cannot ignore and must be satisfied. Such a discourse could be used in law courts to ensure that male rapists receive lighter sentences. Similarly, Sunderland (2004: 55) identifies a discourse of *compulsory heterosexuality*, based on Rich's critical essay 'Compulsory Heterosexuality and Lesbian Existence' (1980). This discourse would involve practices which involve overlooking the existence of gay and lesbian people by assuming that everyone is heterosexual. Traces of this discourse could be found in a wide range of language contexts – for example, at a (traditional) wedding when relatives tell single people 'It'll be your turn next!', in adverts for perfume or lingerie, where it is almost always a man who is shown buying gifts for his female partner or in medical, scientific or advisory texts (which may focus on male-female penetrative (missionary position) intercourse as the only (or preferred) way of conceiving a child or achieving orgasm). Discourses of compulsory heterosexuality could also be shown by the *absence* of explicit references to heterosexuality in speech and writing, effectively normalizing or unproblematizing the concept. For example, we would expect the terms *man, gay man* and *heterosexual man* to occur in general language usage in the order of frequency that I have just listed them in. *Man* is generally taken to mean *heterosexual man*, which is why the latter term would appear so rarely. *Gay man* – being the marked, 'deviant' case would therefore appear more frequently than *heterosexual man*, but not as often as *man*.[1]

Therefore, one way that discourses are constructed is via language. Language (both as an abstract system: phonetics, grammar, lexicon, etc. and as a context-based system of communication) is not the same as discourse, but we can carry out analyses of language in texts in order to uncover traces of discourses.

So bearing this linguistic dimension of discourse analysis in mind, to what extent have corpora been utilized in studies of discourse analysis?

The shift to post-structuralism

Discourse analysts have used corpora in order to analyse data such as political texts (Flowerdew 1997; Fairclough 2000; Piper 2000; Partington 2003), teaching materials (Stubbs and Gerbig 1993; Wickens 1998), scientific writing (Atkinson 1999) and newspaper articles (van Dijk 1991; Morrison and Love 1996; Caldas-Coulthard and Moon 1999; Charteris-Black 2004). Such studies have shown how corpus analysis can uncover ideologies and evidence for disadvantage (see Hunston 2002: 109–23 for a summary).

In addition, corpus-based techniques have been employed in studies which have attempted to analyse differences in language usage based on identity (most notably gender). For example, Shalom's study of men's and women's personal adverts (1997), McEnery *et al*'s (2000) work on swearing and demographic categories in the British National Corpus and Schmid and Fauth's (2003) exploration of gender differences in the ICE corpus. Rey (2001) performed a corpus-based study of dialogue spoken in the television series *Star Trek* looking for differences between male and female language use, while Biber and Burges (2001) looked at changing gender differences in dramatic dialogue using the ARCHER corpus of dramatic texts from the seventeenth to the twentieth century. Holmes (2001) looked at the frequencies of sexist and non-language in a corpus of New Zealand English while Sigley and Holmes (2002) carried out an analysis of frequencies and collocations of the terms *girl(s)* and *boy(s)* in five corpora of British English, concluding that adult females are linguistically constructed as immature with emphasis on their appearance, dependence, domesticity and submissiveness. Finally, Stubbs' (1996) analysis of the ways that gender is constructed within two of Robert Baden-Powell's speeches to boys and girls highlights the fact that ideological issues can be present even around a fairly innocuous word like *happy*. Stubbs showed that Baden-Powell (the founder of the Boy Scouts Association) instructed girls to make other people happy whereas boys were simply instructed to live happy lives.

So while there are a small number of researchers who are already applying corpus methodologies in discourse analysis, this is still a cross-disciplinary field which is somewhat under-subscribed, and appears to be subject to some resistance. Some researchers may acknowledge that theoretically it is a good idea, but continue with mainly qualitative analyses of single texts (or not employ texts at all). Others are more vociferously opposed to corpus-based analysis of discourses. In the process of going to international conferences in various areas of linguistics over the past few years, I have heard interest, disinterest and hostility towards using corpora to analyse discourse in about equal amounts. Part of the problem is perhaps to do with either misconceptions about what corpus analysis actually involves or a dislike of, or unfamiliarity with, computers. Another, more valid issue, which I address below, involves some quite strong (and seemingly incompatible) differences about what counts as 'good' research in both corpus linguistics and discourse analysis. Therefore, it can be difficult to merge both sets of research ideologies.

And while I find corpus-based discourse analysis to be a worthwhile technique, I do not wish to be blindly evangelical about it.

All methods of research have associated problems which need to be addressed and are also limited in terms of what they can and can not achieve. One criticism of corpus-based approaches is that they are too broad – they do not facilitate close readings of texts. However, this is akin to complaining that a telescope only lets us look at faraway phenomena, rather than allowing us to look at things close-up, like a microscope (Partington 1998: 144). Kenny (2001) argues that in fact, the corpus-based approach is more like a kaleidoscope, allowing us to see textual patterns come into focus and recede again as others take their place. Acknowledging what a corpus-based approach can do and what it cannot do is necessary, but should not mean that we discard the methodology altogether – we should just be more clear about when it is appropriate to use it or employ some other method.

Other researchers have problematized corpora as constituting *linguistics applied* rather than *applied linguistics* (e.g. Widdowson 2000). Widdowson claims that corpus linguistics only offers 'a partial account of real language' (2000: 7) because it does not address the lack of correspondence between corpus findings and native speaker intuitions. Widdowson also questions the validity of analysts' interpretations of corpus data and raises questions about the methodological processes that they choose to use, suggesting that the ones which computers find easier to carry out will be chosen in preference to more complex forms of analysis. Additionally, Borsley and Ingham (2002) criticize corpus-based approaches because it is difficult to make conclusions about language if an example does not appear in a corpus. They also argue that language is endowed with meaning by native speakers and therefore cannot be derived from a corpus. See Stubbs (2001a, 2002) for rejoinders to these articles. A related criticism is by Baldry (2000: 36) who argues that corpus linguistics treats language as a self-contained object, 'abstracting text from its context'. And Cameron (1997), in an article about dictionary creation using corpus-based methodologies warns that corpus linguists have had a tendency to over-rely on newspapers and synchronic data, at the expense of charting the historical origins surrounding words and their changing meanings and usages over time. Such criticisms are worth bearing in mind, although should not prevent researchers from using corpora, rather, they should encourage corpus-based work which takes into account potential problems, perhaps supplementing their approach with other methodologies. For example, there is no reason why corpus-based research on lexical items should not use diachronic corpora in order to track changes in word meaning and usage over time and several large-scale corpus building projects have been carried out with the aim of creating historic corpora from different time periods.[2]

Corpus linguistics also tends to be conceptualized (particularly by non-corpus researchers) as a *quantitative* method of analysis: something which is therefore at odds with the direction that social inquiry has taken since the 1980s. Before the 1980s, corpus linguistics had struggled to make an impact upon linguistic research because computers were not sufficiently powerful enough or widely available to put the theoretical principles into practice. Ironically, by the time that computers had become widely available to scholars, there had already occurred a shift in the social sciences in the accepted ways that knowledge was produced via research methodologies. For much of the nineteenth and twentieth centuries, knowledge had been gathered by taking approaches which have been variously called scientific, positivist, essentialist, empirical or structuralist. Such approaches viewed the universe as containing facts or truths that could be discovered by objective researchers working under experimental conditions. They emphasized measurement and categorization – for example, the classification of different species of plants or animals into related groups or the measurement of human characteristics such as height, weight or IQ in order to discover averages or norms. Researchers would form hypotheses and test them under strict experimental conditions. While this approach is often still associated with the natural, physical and biological sciences, it was also used in the social sciences – particularly in sociology, psychology and linguistics where phenomena such as personality, IQ, attitudes and accents were examined.[3] However, social psychologists in the 1960s and early 1970s argued that the discipline was implicitly voicing the values of dominant groups (see Harré and Secord 1972; Brown 1973; and Armistead 1974). Additionally, Gergen (1973) argued that all knowledge is historically and culturally specific and that it isn't possible to look for definitive accounts of people and society, because social life is continually changing. Quantitative research was also criticized as being a form of social regulation in itself (e.g. Hacking 1990) or a way of controlling and predicting (Buchanan 1992), while other researchers (e.g. Cicourel 1964) have argued that quantitative researchers tend to fix meanings in ways that suit their preconceptions.

By the 1980s, an alternative means of producing knowledge had become available, roughly based around the concept of *post-modernism* and referred to as post-structuralism or social constructionism. As Denzin (1988: 432) writes:

> Gone are words like theory, hypothesis, concept, indicator, coding scheme, sampling, validity, and reliability. In their place comes a new language: readerly texts, modes of discourse, cultural poetics, deconstruction, interpretation, domination, feminism,

genre, grammatology, hermeneutics, inscription, master narrative, narrative structures, otherness, postmodernism, redemptive ethnography, semiotics, subversion, textuality, tropes.

While Denzin optimistically suggested that now researchers had a *choice* (1988: 432) I would agree with Swann, in her assessment of recent language and gender research, who notes that 'On the whole ... there does seem to have been a shift towards more localised studies' and 'far less reliance is placed on quantifiable and/or general patterns' (2002: 59). So corpus linguistics largely became viable as a methodology at a point where this epistemological shift had already occurred, and its grounding in quantification has not made it attractive to social scientists. Both McEnery and Wilson (1996: 98) and Biber *et al* (1998) also note that the amount of corpus-based research in discourse analysis has been relatively small.

Post-structuralists have developed close formulations between the concepts of language, ideology and hegemony, based on the work of writers like Gramsci (1985) and Bahktin (1984). And the move towards deconstructionism in the social sciences over the past 20 years or so has tended towards research into language and identities that could be particularly associated with people who are viewed as holding or sympathetic towards problematic, contested or powerless identities (for example, gay men and lesbians, women, deaf people, people from non-white ethnic groups, etc). Such people are likely to be aware of the oppression of such groups and therefore hold with forms of analysis that are associated with questioning the *status quo* – e.g. queer theory, feminist linguistics and critical discourse analysis rather than reiterating and reinforcing a list of ways in which people speak, think or behave differently from each other. Burr (1995: 162) refers to this as *action research*, forms of research which have change and intervention rather than the discovery of 'facts' as their explicit aim. Corpus research then, with its initial emphasis on comparing differences through counting, and creating rather than deconstructing categories, could therefore be viewed as somewhat retrograde and incompatible with post-structuralist thinking. Indeed, one area that corpus linguistics has excelled in has been in generating *descriptive* grammars of languages (e.g. Biber *et al* 1999) based on naturally occurring language use, but focusing on language as an abstract system.

Finally, another reason why language and identity researchers have shied away from corpora is due to practical, rather than ideological, considerations. Researchers have argued that discourse analysis is very labour intensive (e.g. Gill 1993: 91) and therefore 'discourse analysis, as with many other varieties of qualitative research is usually *more* difficult than positivist number crunching' (Parker and Burman 1993:

9

156). However, I would argue that a corpus linguistics approach can be perceived as equally time consuming. Large numbers of texts must first be collected, while their analysis often requires learning how to use computer programs to manipulate data. Statistical tests may be carried out in order to determine whether or not a finding is significant, necessitating the requisite mathematical know-how (or access to a good statistics department). Gaining access to corpora is not always easy – and large corpus building projects can be very time consuming and expensive, sometimes requiring the acquisition of research grants in order to be carried out successfully. No wonder then, that it is often simply less effort to collect a smaller sample of data which can be transcribed and analysed by hand, without the need to use computers or mathematical formulae.

As I stated at the beginning of this section, criticisms of a corpus-based approach are useful in that they make us aware of limitations or potential pitfalls to be avoided. However, having come this far, it seems fair to consider an alternative perspective – what can be *gained* from using corpora to analyse discourse?

Advantages of the corpus-based approach to discourse analysis

Reducing researcher bias

While older, empirical views of research were extremely concerned with the removal of researcher bias in favour of empiricism and objectivity, newer, more post-modern forms of research have argued that the unbiased researcher is in itself a 'discourse of science through which a particular version ... of human life is constructed' (Burr 1995: 160). Burr argues that objectivity is impossible as we all encounter the world from some perspective (the 'objective' stance is still a stance). Instead researchers need to acknowledge their own involvement in their research and reflect on the role it plays in the results that are produced. However, not all discourse analysts are inclined to take this view of objectivity. Blommaert (2005: 31–2) points out, in relation to critical discourse analysis that 'The predominance of biased interpretation begs questions about representativeness, selectivity, partiality, prejudice, and voice (can analysts speak for the average consumer of texts?)'.

It *is* difficult if not impossible to be truly objective, and acknowledging our own positions and biases should be a prerequisite for carrying out and reporting research. However, this perspective assumes a high degree of researcher self-awareness and agency. The term *critical realism* (Bhaskar 1989) is useful, in that it outlines an approach to social research which accepts that we perceive the world from a particular viewpoint, but the world acts back on us to constrain the ways that we can perceive it. So we need to be aware that our research *is* constructed, but we shouldn't deconstruct it out of existence.

Also, we may be biased on a subconscious level which can be difficult to acknowledge. At other times, we may not want to acknowledge our position for various reasons (concerns, for example, that our findings may be played down because they were published by someone who holds a particular identity, or we may desire to protect or conceal some aspect of our own identity such as sexuality, gender or ethnicity for other reasons). And a lot of academic discourse is written in an impersonal, formal style, so introducing some sort of personal statement may still seem jarring, particularly in some disciplines.

And ultimately, even if we declare our personal circumstances and their relationship to our research, we may still end up being biased in ways which have nothing to do with who we are but are more concerned with the way that human beings process information. A famous study by psychologists Kahneman and Tversky (1973) showed that people (105 out of 152 to be exact) tend to think that in a typical sample of text in the English language the number of words that begin with the letter 'k' is likely to be greater than the number of words that have 'k' as the third letter. In reality, there are about twice as many words that have 'k' as their third letter than there are words that begin with 'k'. Yet we tend to index on the first letter because we can recall such words more easily. We also tend to succumb to other cognitive biases. Mynatt *et al* (1977) showed that in a variety of settings, decision makers tended to notice more, assign more weight to, or actively seek out evidence which confirmed their claims, while they tended to ignore evidence which might discount their claims (*confirmation bias*). Related to this is the *hostile media effect* (Vallone *et al* 1985) which shows that ideological partisans tend to consistently view media coverage as being biased against their particular side of the issue (a phenomenon that perhaps we should attend to when carrying out action research). People also tend to focus more on information that they encounter at the beginning of an activity (the *primacy effect*). The presence of such cognitive biases can be particularly problematic when carrying out discourse analysis. For example, we may select a newspaper article which 'confirms' our suspicions, but ignore other articles which present a different perspective. There is nothing essentially 'wrong' about that, but it may mean that we need to be careful in terms of any generalizations we make beyond the article itself.

Additionally, we may only focus on aspects of a text which support our initial hypotheses, while disregarding those which present a more complex or contradictory picture.

By using a corpus, we at least are able to place a number of restrictions on our cognitive biases. It becomes less easy to be selective about a single newspaper article when we are looking at hundreds of articles – hopefully, overall patterns and trends should show through.

Of course, we cannot remove bias completely. Corpus researchers can theoretically be just as selective as anyone in choosing which aspects of their research to report or bury. And their interpretations of the data they find can also reveal bias. For example, in Chapter 5 of this book I look at the terms *bachelor* and *spinster*, in order to argue that there are strong differences in the ways that meanings and connotations surrounding these words are constructed in a large corpus of general language use. An initial finding in Chapter 5 is that *bachelor* (and its plural form) occur more often than *spinster(s)*. The actual figures are 506 vs. 175. This may lead us to conclude that unmarried men are discussed more in general English than unmarried women, which could be part of a larger trend whereby male terms are more frequent than female terms – an overfocus on men at the expense of women in actual language use. However, a closer look at the data reveals that in some cases *bachelor* actually refers to women. We would also need to take into account the fact that in about 61 cases *bachelor* refers to a type of degree rather than an unmarried man (although we could argue that historically, the two meanings are connected). There are also other cases where *bachelor* refers to proper nouns, e.g. the name of a horse. Again, we may argue that in itself, it is of note that things are named after bachelors but not after spinsters. And we may also decide to focus on words that regularly co-occur with *bachelor*, that tend to index positive attitudes, such as *eligible*, but overlook other, less positive words that also co-occur with *bachelor*, such as *lonely*. With corpus analysis, there are usually a lot of results, and sometimes, because of limitations placed on researchers (such as word length restrictions of journal articles), selectivity does come into play. But at least with a corpus, we are starting (hopefully) from a position whereby the data itself has not been selected in order to confirm existing conscious (or subconscious) biases. One tendency that I have found with corpus analysis, is that there are usually exceptions to any rule or pattern. It is important to report these exceptions alongside the overall patterns or trends, but not to over-report them either.

12

The incremental effect of discourse

As well as helping to restrict bias, corpus linguistics is a useful way to approach discourse analysis because of the *incremental* effect of discourse. One of the most important ways that discourses are circulated and strengthened in society is via language use, and the task of discourse analysts is to uncover how language is employed, often in quite subtle ways, to reveal underlying discourses. By becoming more aware of how language is drawn on to construct discourses or various ways of looking at the world, we should be more resistant to attempts by writers of texts to manipulate us by suggesting to us what is 'common-sense' or 'accepted wisdom'.

So a single word, phrase or grammatical construction on its own may suggest the existence of a discourse. But other than relying on our intuition (and existing biases), it can sometimes be difficult to tell whether such a discourse is typical or not, particularly as we live in 'a society saturated with literacy' (Blommaert 2005: 108). By collecting numerous supporting examples of a discourse construction, we can start to see a cumulative effect. In terms of how this relates to language, Hoey (2005) refers to the concept of *lexical priming* in the following way: 'Every word is primed for use in discourse as a result of the cumulative effects of an individual's encounters with the word.' As Stubbs (2001b: 215) concludes 'Repeated patterns show that evaluative meanings are not merely personal and idiosyncratic, but widely shared in a discourse community. A word, phrase or construction may trigger a cultural stereotype.' Additionally, Blommaert (2005: 99) notes that a lot of human communication is not a matter of choice but is instead constrained by normativities which are determined by patterns of inequality.

And this is where corpora are useful. An association between two words, occurring repetitively in naturally occurring language, is much better evidence for an underlying hegemonic discourse which is made explicit through the word pairing than a single case. For example, consider the sentence taken from the British magazine *Outdoor Action*: 'Diana, herself a keen sailor despite being confined to a wheelchair for the last 45 years, hopes the boat will encourage more disabled people onto the water.' We may argue here that although the general thrust of this sentence represents disabled people in a positive way, there are a couple of aspects of language use here which raise questions – the use of the phrase *confined to a wheelchair*, and the way that the co-ordinator *despite* prompts the reader to infer that disabled people are not normally expected to be keen sailors. There are certainly traces of different types of discourses within this sentence, but are they typical

13

or unusual? Which discourse, if any, represents the more hegemonic variety?

Consulting a large corpus of general British English, we find that the words *confined* and *wheelchair* have fairly strong patterns of co-occurrence with each other. The phrase *confined to a wheelchair* occurs 45 times in the corpus, although the more neutral term *wheelchair user(s)* occurs 37 times. However, *wheelchair bound* occurs nine times. We also find quite a few cases of *wheelchair* appearing in connection with co-ordinators like *although* and *despite* (e.g. *despite being restricted to a wheelchair he retains his cheerfulness; despite confinement to a wheelchair, Rex Cunningham had evidently prospered; although confined to a wheelchair for most of her life, Violet was active in church life and helped out with a local Brownie pack*). While this isn't an overwhelmingly frequent pattern, there are enough cases to suggest that one discourse of wheelchair users constructs them as being deficient in a range of ways, and it is therefore of note when they manage to be cheerful, prosperous or active in church life! The original sentence about Diana the keen sailor certainly isn't an isolated case, but conforms to an existing set of expectations about people in wheelchairs. Thus, every time we read or hear a phrase like *wheelchair bound* or *despite being in a wheelchair*, our perceptions of wheelchair users are influenced in a certain way. At some stage, we may even reproduce such discourses ourselves, thereby contributing to the incremental effect without realizing it.

Resistant and changing discourses

As well as being able to establish that repeated patterns of language use demonstrate evidence of particular hegemonic discourses or majority 'common-sense' ways of viewing the world, corpus data can also reveal the opposite – the presence of counter-examples which are much less likely to be uncovered via smaller-scale studies. And if a resistant discourse *is* found when looking at a single text, then we may mistake it for a hegemonic discourse.

Discourses are not static. They continually shift position – a fact that can often be demonstrated via analysis of language change. There is little agreement among linguists about whether language reflects thought or shapes thought or whether the relationship constitutes an unending and unbroken cycle of influence. Whatever the direction of influence, charting changes in language is a useful way of showing how discourse positions in society are also in flux. What was a hegemonic discourse ten years ago may be viewed as a resistant or unacceptable discourse today. At the most basic level, this can

Introduction

be shown by looking at changing frequencies of word use in a diachronic (or historical) corpus, or by comparing more than one corpus containing texts from different time periods. For example, if we compare two equal sized corpora of British English[4] containing written texts from the early 1960s and the early 1990s we see that in the 1990s corpus there are various types of words which occur much more frequently than they did in the 1960s corpus: e.g.: lexis which reflect the rise of capitalist discourses: *initiatives, strategies, capitalist, customer, resources, privatisation, market*; and lexis which reflect 'green' discourses: *environmental, global, environment, worldwide, conservation*. In addition, we find that certain terms have become less frequent: *girl* and titles like *Mr* and *Mrs* were more popular in 1960s British English than they were in the 1990s, suggesting that perhaps sexist discourses or formal ways of addressing people have become less common.

However, we could also compare the actual contexts that words are used in over different time periods as it may be the case that a word is no more or less frequent than it used to be, but its meanings have changed over time. For example, in the early 1960s corpus the word *blind* almost always appears in a literal sense, referring to people or animals who cannot see. The term *blind* is not significantly more frequent in the 1990s corpus, although in about half its occurrences we now find it being used in a range of more metaphorical (and negative) ways: *turn a blind eye, blind ambition, sheer blind anger, blind panic, blind patriotism, the blind lead the blind, blind to change*. We could say that *blind* has expanded semantically, to refer to cases where someone is ignorant, thoughtless or lacks the ability to think ahead. As Hunston (1999) argues, this non-literal meaning of *blind* could constitute a discourse prosody which influences attitudes to literal blindness (although it could also be argued that the separate meanings exist independently of each other). What the corpus data has shown, however, is that the negative metaphorical meaning of *blind* appears to have increased in written British English over time – it is not a concep-tualization which has always been as popular.[5]

Triangulation

As described earlier in this chapter, the shift to post-structuralist methods of thought and research has served to de-emphasize the focus on more quantitative, empirical methods. However, another aspect of post-structuralism may actually warrant the inclusion of corpus-informed research. One of the main arguments of social constructionism is to question and 'deconstruct' binary arguments that have served the

15

basis of western thinking for thousands of years, such as 'nature or nurture' (Derrida 1978, 1981).

Such oppositions are typical of ideologies in that they create an inherent need to judge one side of the dichotomy as primary and the other as secondary, rather than thinking that neither can exist without the other. Instead, Derrida recommends that we reject the logic of *either/or* of binary oppositions, in favour of a logic of *both/and*. The same could be said for the split between *quantitative/qualitative* or *structuralism/post-structuralism*. Indeed, post-structuralism favours a more eclectic approach to research, whereby different methodologies can be combined together, acting as reinforcers of each other. It is not the case that corpus linguists should view corpora as the only possible source of data; 'Gone is the concept of the corpus as the sole *explicandum* of language use. Present instead is the concept of a balanced corpus being used to *aid* the investigation of a language' (McEnery and Wilson 1996: 169).

Tognini-Bonelli (2001) makes a useful distinction between *corpus-based* and *corpus-driven* investigations. The former uses a corpus as a source of examples, to check researcher intuition or to examine the frequency and/or plausibility of the language contained within a smaller data set. A corpus-driven analysis proceeds in a more inductive way – the corpus itself is the data and the patterns in it are noted as a way of expressing regularities (and exceptions) in language. In this book (apart from in Chapter 7), the case studies I describe are corpus-driven analyses – each one uses a particular corpus as the main or only source of data. However, there is no reason why corpora cannot take more of a corpus-based role in discourse analysis either.

As McNeill (1990: 22) points out, *triangulation* (a term coined by Newby 1977: 123), or using multiple methods of analysis (or forms of data) is now accepted by 'most researchers'. Layder (1993: 128) argues that there are several advantages of triangulation: it facilitates validity checks of hypotheses, it anchors findings in more robust interpretations and explanations, and it allows researchers to respond flexibly to unforeseen problems and aspects of their research. Even when discourse analysts do not want to have to go to the trouble of building a corpus from scratch, they could still gainfully use corpora as a reference, to back up or expand on their findings derived from smaller-scale analyses of single texts (something which I will look at in Chapter 7). For example, Sunderland (2004: 37–8) looked at a newspaper article which publicized a 'fairytale' venue for marriage ceremonies. She argued that the article focused on the bride as the bearer of the (stereotypically) male gaze (due to phrases such as 'its flying staircase down which the bride can make a breathtaking entrance'). An analysis of the words which *bride* tends to collocate (co-occur) with most often in a large corpus of naturally occurring language revealed terms to do with appearance like *blushing, dress, wore, beautiful* and *looked*. On the other hand, *bridegroom* and *groom* tended to collocate with mainly functional words (pronouns, conjunctions, prepositions, etc.), suggesting that the constructions of brides in the article were 'loaded' in a way which did not apply to bridegrooms. So while the main focus of Sunderland's analysis was a single news article, a general corpus proved to be useful in confirming suspicions that what she was seeing *was*, in fact, a hegemonic discourse. In such cases it only takes a couple of minutes to consult a reference corpus, showing such a corpus-based method to be an extremely productive means of triangulation.

Some concerns

While in the last section I have hoped to show how corpus linguistics can act as a useful method (or supplementary method) of carrying out discourse analysis, there are still a few concerns which are necessary to discuss, before moving on.

First, corpus data is usually only language data (written or transcribed spoken), and discourses are not confined to verbal communication. By holding a door open for a woman, a man could be said to be performing a communicative act which could be discursively interpreted in numerous ways – a discourse of 'the gallant man', of 'male power imposing itself on women' or a non-gendered discourse of 'general politeness in society' for example. In a similar way, discourses can be embedded within images – for example, pictures of heterosexual couples often occur in advertising, helping to normalize the discourse of compulsory heterosexuality, while photo-spreads of women in magazines aimed at (heterosexual or bisexual) men reveal dominant discourses about what constitutes an attractive woman by male standards. Caldas-Coulthard and van Leeuwen (2002) investigate the relationship between the visual representations of children's toys (in terms of design, colour and movement) such as The Rock and Barbie and texts written about them, suggesting that in many cases discourses can be produced via interaction between verbal and visual texts.

The fact that discourses are communicated through means other than words indicates that a corpus-based study is likely to be restricted – any discourses that are uncovered in a corpus are likely to be limited to the verbal domain. Some work has been carried out on creating and encoding corpora of visual materials, e.g. Smith *et al*'s corpus of children's posters (1998), although at the moment there does not appear to be a standardized way of encoding images in corpora.

In addition to that, issues surrounding the social conditions of production and interpretation of texts are important in helping the researcher understand discourses surrounding them (Fairclough 1989: 25). Questions involving production such as who authored a text, under what circumstances, for what motives and for whom, in addition to questions surrounding the interpretation of a text: who bought, read, accessed, used the text, what were their responses, etc. can not be simply answered by traditional corpus-based techniques, and therefore require knowledge and analysis of how a text exists within the context of society. One problem with a corpus is that it contains decontextualized examples of language. We may not know the ideologies of the text producers in a corpus. In a sense, this can be a methodological advantage, as Hunston (2002: 123) explains '. . . the researcher is encouraged to spell out the steps that lie between what is observed and the interpretation placed on those observations.'

So we need to bear in mind that because corpus data does not interpret itself, it is up to the researcher to make sense of the patterns of language which are found within a corpus, postulating reasons for their existence or looking for further evidence to support hypotheses. Our findings *are* interpretations, which is why we can only talk about restricting bias, not removing it completely. A potential problem with researcher interpretation is that it is open to contestation. Researchers may choose to interpret a corpus-based analysis of language in different ways, depending on their own positions. For example, returning to a study previously mentioned, Rayson *et al* (1997) found that people from socially disadvantaged groups tend to use more non-standard language (*ain't, yeah*) and taboo terms (*fucking, bloody*) than those from more advantaged groups. While the results themselves aren't open to negotiation, the reasons behind them are, and we could form numerous hypotheses depending on our own biases and identities, e.g. poor standards of education or upbringing (lack of knowledge), little exposure to contexts where formal language is required or used (no need to use 'correct' language), rougher life circumstances (language reflecting real life), the terms helping to show identity and group membership (communities of practice), etc. Such hypotheses would require further (and different) forms of research in order to be explored in more detail. This suggests that corpus analysis shares much in common with forms of analysis thought to be qualitative, although at least with corpus analysis the researcher has to provide explanations for results and language patterns that have been discovered in a relatively neutral manner.

18

Also, a corpus-based analysis will naturally tend to place focus on patterns, with frequency playing no small part in what is reported and what is not. However, frequent patterns of language do not always necessarily imply underlying hegemonic discourses. Or rather, the 'power' of individual texts or speakers in a corpus may not be evenly distributed. A corpus which contains a single (unrepresentative) speech by the leader of a country or religious group, newspaper editor or CEO may carry more weight discursively than hundreds of similar texts which were produced by 'ordinary people'. Similarly, we should not assume that every text in a corpus will originally have had the same size and type of audience. General corpora are often composed of data from numerous sources (newspaper, novels, letters, etc.) and it is likely to have been the case that public forms of media would have reached more people (and therefore possibly had a greater role to play in forming and furthering discourses) than transcripts of private conversations. We may be able to annotate texts in a corpus to take into account aspects of production and reception, such as author occupation/status or estimated readership, but this will not always be possible.

In addition, frequent patterns of language (even when used by powerful text producers) do not always imply mainstream ways of thinking. Sometimes what is *not* said or written is more important than what is there. A hegemonic discourse can be at its most powerful when it does not even have to be invoked, because it is just taken for granted. For example, in university prospectus discourse we would expect to find a term like *mature student* occurring more often than a term like *young student*. However, we should not assume that there are more mature students than young students, as the term *student* implicitly carries connotations of youth and does not need to be expanded upon, hence there is little need for a marked opposite equivalent of *mature student* (*immature student*?). Similarly, a hegemonic discourse can be at its most powerful when it does not even have to be invoked, because it is just taken for granted. A sign of true power is in *not* having to refer to something, because everybody is aware of it. Prior awareness or intuition about what is possible in language should help to alert us to such absences, and often comparisons with a larger normative corpus will reveal what they are.

We also need to be aware that people (as suggested earlier in this chapter) tend to process information rather differently to computers. Therefore, a computer-based analysis will uncover hidden patterns of language. Our theory of language and discourse states that such patterns of language are made all the more powerful because we are not aware of them; therefore we are unconsciously influenced. However, it can be difficult to verify the unconscious. For example, in Chapter 4 I show how refugees are characterized as out-of-control water, with phrases like *flood of refugees*, *overflowing camps*, *refugees streaming home*, etc. being used to describe them. I (and other researchers) have interpreted this water metaphor as being somewhat negative and dehumanizing. However, would we all interpret *flood of refugees* in the same way? Hoey (2005: 14) points out that we all possess personal corpora with their own lexical primings which are 'by definition irretrievable, unstudiable and unique'. If we were very concerned about the ways that refugees are represented, then we may have already consciously noticed and remarked on this water-metaphor pattern. But what if English was not our first language? Would we be less or more likely to notice and understand the metaphor? And if we were someone who didn't approve of refugees, we may even interpret the word *flood* as being too 'soft', preferring a less subtle negative description. Also, did the person who wrote *flood of refugees* actually intend this term to be understood in a negative sense, or were they simply unthinkingly repeating what has now become a 'naturalised' (El Refaie 2001: 366) way of writing about refugees (as Baker and McEnery 2005 point out, even texts produced by The Office of the United Nations High Commissioner for Refugees, a body aimed at helping refugees, contain phrases using the water metaphor). As Partington (2003: 6) argues, 'authors themselves are seldom fully aware of the meanings their texts convey'. Perhaps conscious intention is more crucial to the *formation* of discourses and reliance on subconscious repetition and acceptance is required for their *maintenance*. See also Hoey (2005: 178–88) for further discussion.

And words do not have static meanings, they change over time. They also have different meanings and triggers for different people. Some people, for example, tend to get annoyed by a recent development of the word *gay* to refer to things that people disapprove of – e.g. 'this exam timetable is so gay' (Baker 2005: 1). However, from talking to people who use the word in this way, many of them do not intend it to be homophobic (some of them are gay themselves) and some (much younger users) are not aware that the word *gay* refers to same-sex attraction or even understand what same-sex attraction is. Corpus analysis needs to take into account the fact that word meanings change and that they can have different connotations for different people.

Therefore, a corpus-based analysis of language is only one possible analysis out of many, and open to contestation. It is an analysis which focuses on norms and frequent patterns within language. However, there can be analyses of language that go against the norms of corpus

20

data and in particular, research which emphasizes the interpretative repertoires (Gilbert and Mulkay 1984) that people hold in relationship to their language use can be useful at teasing out the complex associations they hold in connection to individual words and phrases.

Corpus linguistics does not provide a single way of analysing data either. As the following chapters in this book show, there are numerous ways of making sense of linguistic patterns: collocations, keywords, frequency lists, clusters, dispersion plots, etc. And within each of these corpus-based techniques the user needs to set boundaries. For example, at what point do we decide that a word in a corpus occurs enough times for it to be 'significant' and worth investigating? Or if we want to look for co-occurrences of sets of words, e.g. how often do *flood* and *refugees* occur near each other, how far apart are we going to allow these words to be? Do we discount cases where the words appear six words apart? Or four words? Unfortunately there aren't simple answers to questions like this, and instead the results themselves (or external criteria such as word count restrictions on the length of journal articles) can dictate the cut-off points. For example, we may decide to only investigate the ten most frequently occurring lexical words in a given corpus in relation to how discourses are formed. However, while these words tell us something about the genre of the corpus, they may be less revealing of discourses. So we could expand our cut-off point, to investigate the top 20 words. This is more helpful, but then we find that we have too much to say, or we are repeating ourselves by making the same argument, so we make a compromise, only discussing words which illustrate different points.

Again, these concerns should not preclude using corpus data to analyse discourse. But they may mean that other forms of analysis should be used in conjunction with corpus data, or that the researcher needs to take care when forming explanations about her or his results.

Structure of the book

This book has two main goals: to introduce researchers to the different sorts of analytical techniques that can be used with corpus-based discourse analysis, and to show how they can be put into practice on different types of data. Because I feel that people understand better when they are given real life examples, rather than discussing ideas at an abstract level, I have included a range of different case studies in the following chapters in the book (see Table 1.1 for a summary). Chapter 2 looks at issues to do with data collection and corpus building, in order to address questions such as how large a corpus should be and the best ways to collect and annotate data. Chapter 3 uses a small corpus of holiday leaflets written for young adults in order to examine how some of the more basic corpus-based procedures can be carried out on data and their relevance to discourse analysis. It includes looking at how frequency lists can be used in order to provide researchers with a focus for their analyses and how measures such as the type token ratio help to give an account of the complexity of a text. It also shows how the creation of dispersion plots of lexical items can reveal the development of discourses over the course of a particular text.

Chapter 4 investigates the construction of discourses of refugees in newspaper data and is concerned with methods of presenting and interpreting concordance data. It covers different ways of sorting and examining concordances as well as introducing the concept of semantic and discourse patterns. Chapter 5 uses a large corpus of general British English in order to consider differences in discourses surrounding never-married men and women. Collocations of the words *bachelor* and *spinster* are examined. This chapter explores different ways of calculating collocation and the pros and cons associated with each. It shows how reference corpora can be used to uncover hidden meanings within words or phrases, and how collocational networks can reveal strong associations between central concepts in a text.

Chapter 6 examines different discourse positions within a series of debates on fox-hunting which took place in the British House of Commons. In order to achieve this, we look at the concept of keywords, lexical items which occur statistically more frequently in one text or set of texts when compared with another (often a larger 'benchmark' corpus). However, this chapter expands the notion of keywords to consider key phrases (e.g. multiword units) and key semantic or grammatical categories – which necessitates prior annotation of a text or corpus.

Chapter 7 considers how the corpus approach can be employed in order to examine linguistic phenomena that occur beyond the lexical level, by looking at patterns of nominalization, attribution, modality and metaphor. Using a single news article which contains reference to *allegations of rape*, I use a reference corpus to examine typical language patterns surrounding this term and its related forms in order to show whether the language of the news article is typical or not. Finally, Chapter 8 concludes the book and re-addresses some of the concerns that have been first raised in this chapter.

However, before moving on to look at the different techniques that can be used in order to carry out corpus-based discourse analysis, we first need a corpus. Chapter 2 therefore explores issues connected to obtaining data, building and annotating a corpus.

Table 1.1 Texts, topics and methods of analysis used in this book

Chapter	Text type	Topic	Main Techniques covered
3	Holiday leaflets	Young people/ use of alcohol	Frequency lists, clusters, dispersion plots
4	Newspaper articles	Refugees	Concordances
5	General Corpus	Never-married people	Collocations
6	Political debate	Fox-hunting	Keywords
7	General Corpus	Allegations of rape	Analysis of nominalization, modality, attribution and metaphor

Notes

1. In fact, in the 100 million word British National Corpus, *gay man* appears 17 times, *homosexual man* occurs 6 times and *heterosexual man* appears once. *Straight man* appears 20 times, of which only two occurrences refer to sexuality (the others mainly refer to the 'straight man' of a comedy duo). *Man* (without these sexuality markers) occurs 58,834 times.

2. For example, the Helsinki Corpus of English Texts: Diachronic Part consists of 400 samples of texts covering the period from 750 to 1700 (Kytö and Rissanen 1992).

3. For example, in psychology, researchers had created the notion of different 'personality' traits or scales such as Eysenk's introversion/extroversion scale (1953) which could be quantified via asking subjects a list of questions such as 'Do you enjoy going on roller-coasters?', and then calculating a score based on their answers. However, an extreme social constructionist viewpoint would argue that the concept of personality is unreal because people behave differently in a range of contexts (e.g. depending on whether they are at work or with their parents or different groups of friends). Ironically, psychologists labelled people's ability to adjust their behaviour according to social context as being yet another quantifiable personality trait – *self monitoring* (Snyder and Gangestad 1986). Personality inventories therefore assume that there must be an essential identity, an 'inner me' or true personality, which social constructionists would dispute. In a similar way, Potter and Wetherell (1987: 43–55) questioned the notion of quantitative questionnaire-based 'attitude' research (e.g. Marsh 1976) by carrying out a qualitative analysis of interviews that attempted to elicit attitudes about immigrants. They found that the analyst's categories did not match the participant's terms, elicited attitudes were often contradictory and that defining the status of the object under discussion was problematic.

4. The Lancaster-Oslo/Bergen (LOB) and the Freiberg Lancaster-Oslo/Bergen (FLOB) corpora respectively.

5. The reasons why these changes in uses of *blind* over time have appeared is another matter. Perhaps the more negative idiomatic metaphoric uses of *blind* have always existed in spoken conversation, but were censored in written texts because editors required authors to use language more formally. What is interesting though, is that there has been a shift in written discourse which has resulted in *blind* being conceptualized in a very different way over a 30 year period.

2 Corpus Building

Introduction

As discussed in Chapter 1, one of the potential problems with using corpora (as our only source of data) in the analysis of discourse is that we are dealing with decontextualized data. A corpus is a self-contained entity – issues to do with production and reception can be difficult to ascertain from looking at a frequency list (see Chapter 3) or a concordance (see Chapter 4). In addition, relationships between different texts in a corpus or even between sentences in the same file may be obscured when performing quantitative analyses.

A possible step towards countering some of these concerns would be for the researcher to familiarize him/herself with the corpus. Both Hardt-Mautner (1995a: 8) and Partington (2003: 259) suggest that some form of prior interaction with the texts in a corpus, e.g. reading transcripts or listening to spoken files, will ensure that the discourse analyst does not commence from the position of *tabula rasa*. One means of familiarization would be to actually build a corpus from scratch, choosing which texts are to go in it. The process of finding and selecting texts, obtaining permissions, transferring to electronic format, checking and annotating files will result in the researcher gaining a much better 'feel' for the data and its idiosyncrasies. This process may also provide the researcher with initial hypotheses as certain patterns are noticed – and such hypotheses could form the basis for the first stages of corpus research.

This chapter covers issues relating to choosing or building a corpus to carry out discourse analysis on. In terms of corpus building I address questions to do with corpus size and representative, as well as considering some concerns related to different text types (written, spoken or computer-mediated). I also look at issues pertaining to permissions, annotation and validation. Finally, I consider the fact that many researchers do not need to build corpora from scratch – they can simply choose from a range of pre-built corpora. Therefore, I address a number of considerations connected to choosing a pre-existing corpus, and how they are obtained and exploited.

Some types of corpora

Before thinking about how one would go about building a corpus, it is useful to know a little about the ways that different corpora can be categorized into types. While the term *corpus* merely refers to a body of electronically encoded text, it is not the case that a corpus consists of any collection of texts, picked at random. Instead, researchers have produced a range of recognizably different types of corpora, depending on the sorts of research goals that they have had in mind.[1]

The first, and perhaps most important type of corpus (in terms of discourse analysis) is called a *specialized corpus*. This would be used in order to study aspects of a particular variety or genre of language. So for example, we might just be interested in the language of newspapers, or the language used in academic essays, or in spoken conversations between men and women. So it would make sense then to only collect texts that conform to this specialized criteria. We may also place restrictions on the corpus in regard to time or place. A good example of a specialized corpus would be the Michigan Corpus of Academic Spoken English; the texts in this corpus consisting of transcripts of spoken language recorded in academic institutions across America.

We could specialize even further than this, for example, by only choosing texts which refer to a specific topic. For example, Johnson *et al* (2003) built a corpus of British newspaper texts that contained references to the concept of political correctness. The criteria for inclusion in this corpus was that each article had to contain a phrase like *politically correct*, *PC* or *political incorrectness*.

It may be useful at this point to make a distinction between *corpora* and *text archives* or *databases*. An archive is generally defined as being similar to a corpus, although with some significant differences. Leech (1991: 11) suggests that 'the difference between an archive and a corpus must be that the latter is designed for a particular "representative" function'. An archive or database, on the other hand is simply 'a text repository, often huge and opportunistically collected, and normally not structured' (Kennedy 1998: 4). Corpora therefore tend towards having a more balanced, carefully thought-out collection of texts that are representative of a language variety or genre. Archives or databases may contain all of the published work of a single author, or all of the editions of a newspaper from a given year. More care is therefore taken when selecting texts to go in a corpus, although even so, there is usually a degree of opportunism or compromise in terms of what the builder would like to include and what is available. The hard theoretical distinction between *corpus* and *text archive* is therefore sometimes blurred in practice, and the desire to fulfil the criteria of 'standard reference' is what needs to be kept in mind when building corpora.

Another aspect of traditional corpus building is in sampling. Many corpora are composed of a variety of texts, of which samples are taken. For example, if we were building a corpus of English literature, we may choose to take the first 2,000 words of *Pride and Prejudice*, or 2,000 words from the middle chapters of *Wuthering Heights*. This technique of sampling is in place to ensure that the corpus is not skewed by the presence of a few very large single texts taken from the same source. We try to take samples from a range of different places in texts to ensure that our corpus is not comprised of only the first 2,000 words of texts (unless we are only interested in the language used at beginnings of texts, e.g. introductions, prologues, prefaces, etc).

If we use equally sized samples, we are more likely to be able to claim that our corpus is representative. However, for the purposes of discourse analysis, it may not be such a good idea to build a corpus which includes samples taken at different points from complete texts. We may be more interested in viewing our texts as having beginnings, middles and ends and tracking the ways that language is used at different points within them (see the section on dispersion in Chapter 3). Of course, it is important to bear in mind the types of research questions that we want to ask, and if we are only building a small corpus or utilizing a few texts, there may be no need for sampling in any case. However, an awareness of the issue of sampling and the possible restrictions it can place on certain forms of analysis are worth considering.

For the purposes of discourse analysis, many of the chapters in this book utilize some form of specialized corpus, e.g. a corpus of holiday leaflets (Chapter 3), a corpus of newspaper articles about refugees (Chapter 4) or a corpus of political debates on fox-hunting (Chapter 6). These were corpora which I built myself, they are reasonably small (none of them are over 200,000 words in size), and did not take a great deal of time to assemble. My corpora all included complete texts, rather than samples.

One question which beginning corpus builders often ask is 'how large should my corpus be?' There is no simple answer unfortunately, although there are a few points that are worth bearing in mind. For many (non-discourse oriented) corpus-based studies, a million words of one variety of language, e.g. British English, Indian English, collected in a relatively short time period, is viewed as adequate for comparative work (e.g. Leech's (2003) study of modal verbs across the Brown family of corpora). Perhaps most importantly, the size of the corpus should be related to its eventual uses. Will it be used in order to derive simple frequencies, collocations or word meanings from concordances? Kennedy (1998: 68) suggests that for the study of prosody 100,000 words of spontaneous speech are adequate, whereas an analysis of verb-form morphology would require half a million words. For lexicography, a million words is unlikely to be large enough, as up to half the words will only occur once (and many of these may be polysemous). However, Biber (1993) suggests that a million words would be enough for grammatical studies.

Regarding using corpora for discourse analysis, it *is* possible to carry out corpus-based analyses on much smaller amounts of data. For example, Stubbs (1996: 81–100) compared two short letters from Lord Baden-Powell, consisting of approximately 330 and 550 words each. Even within these two short texts he was able to show that there were repetitive differences in the ways that certain words were used.

If we are interested in examining a particular genre of language, then it is not usually necessary to build a corpus consisting of millions of words, especially if the genre is linguistically restricted in some way. Shalom (1997) analysed a corpus of personal advertisements sent to a lonely-hearts column in a London-based magazine. She collected a total of 766 adverts, which probably puts her corpus size at between 15,000 and 20,000 words. With this relatively small sample, Shalom was able to demonstrate a range of lexical and grammatical patterns, for example, frequent co-occurrences of words like *slim* and *attractive*.

So data that are made up of small 'colony texts' (Hoey 1986) do not need to be millions of words in length. An average personal advert is only about 20 to 30 words long. Each advert represents an individual text, and a page of adverts would be a colony text, the order in which the texts are placed would not alter the meaning of an individual advert. Other corpora of colony texts that are found in newspapers or magazines might include letters to problem pages, recipes or horoscopes.

One consideration when building a specialized corpus in order to investigate the discursive construction of a particular subject is perhaps not so much the size of the corpus, but how often we would expect to find that subject mentioned within it. For example, if we are interested in studying, say, discourses of unmarried mothers in newspapers, which of the following two corpora would be most useful to us? One which has ten million words but mentions unmarried mothers 30 times in total, or one which has fifty thousand words but mentions unmarried mothers 600 times? The first corpus may be useful as a reference (see below), but the second is likely to tell us more about unmarried mothers due to the higher frequency of occurrences of this topic within it. Therefore, when building a specialized corpus for the purposes of investigating a particular subject or set of subjects, we may want to be more selective in choosing our texts, meaning that the quality or content of the data takes equal or more precedence over issues of quantity.

An aspect of corpus-based analysis that can often be extremely useful in terms of analysing discourses is the process of checking changes over time. Although discourses are not static, one technique of discourse maintenance is by implying or stating that 'things have always been this way'. Discourses therefore may have the appearance of having been written in stone, for example, being cemented by phrases like 'It is a truth universally acknowledged that ...' or 'since time immemorial ...'. However, discourses are *not* static, and one way of investigating their development and change is to use a diachronic corpus.

A *diachronic corpus* is simply a corpus which has been built in order to be representative of a language or language variety over a particular period of time, making it is possible for researchers to track linguistic changes within it. For example, the Helsinki Corpus of English Texts: Diachronic Part consists of 400 samples of texts covering the period from AD 750 to 1700 (Kytö and Rissanen 1992). A diachronic specialized corpus was used by Rey (2001) who collected scripts from the television series *Star Trek* and two related spin-off series *Star Trek the Next Generation* and *Star Trek: Deep Space Nine*, dating from 1966 to 1993. By analysing the language used in the scripts, she concluded that 'female language has shifted away from highly involved linguistic production toward more informational discourse, while at the same time male language has shifted away from highly informational language toward more involved discourse' (2001: 155).

The use of a diachronic corpus can therefore enable researchers to address the criticism that corpus users tend not to take into account the fact that as society changes language changes with it. Clearly though, a diachronic corpus may not be able to fully take into account language change. For example, a corpus which consists of newspaper texts taken at regular intervals across a 20 year period, e.g. from 1980 to 2000, will only reveal changes in language from that period – researchers will still have to undertake other forms of analysis if they want to investigate how particular words were used before and after that point. However, a diachronic corpus can introduce a more dynamic aspect into corpus-based analysis, although this can also result in issues connected with over-focusing on change and reifying difference (a point which is addressed in more detail in Chapter 6).

A final type of corpus which is often extremely useful for discourse analysis, although it may not incorporate the main research focus is a *reference corpus*. A reference corpus is what purists would generally refer to when they use the term *corpus*. It consists of a large corpus (usually consisting of millions of words from a wide range of texts) which is representative of a particular language variety (often but not always linked to a national language). For example, the British National Corpus (BNC) is a reference corpus consisting of approximately one hundred million words of written and spoken data. Its 4,124 texts were mainly produced in the late 1980s and early 1990s, although about 5.5 million words were first published between 1960 and 1984. The written texts consist of extracts from regional and national newspapers, specialist periodicals and journals, academic books and popular fiction, published and unpublished letters and school and university essays. The spoken part includes a large number of unscripted informal conversations, recorded by volunteers selected from different age, regional and socio-economic groups, together with language collected in different contexts, ranging from formal business or government meetings to radio programmes and phone-ins. A similar project, based at Vassar, has created the American National Corpus, which was released in 2005. Other types of reference corpora include the Bank of English (BoE) launched in 1991 by COBUILD (a division of HarperCollins publishers) and The University of Birmingham. The BoE consisted of 450 million words of spoken and language in January 2002. This breaks down to approximately 7 per cent spontaneous speech from casual conversations, 42 per cent of scripted radio and television broadcasts and 51 per cent written texts. The majority of texts reflect British English but approximately 25 per cent are from American sources and a further 5 per cent from other native varieties of English. The BoE is also a *monitor corpus*, in that texts are contin-ually being added to it, allowing for diachronic change to be studied.

The Brown 'family' of corpora are also used as reference corpora, although individually each one is much smaller than the BNC or BoE. The original Brown Corpus consists of approximately one million words of written American English dating from 1961. It contains 500 samples of text, each of about 2,000 words from 15 different genre categories including press, religion, mystery and detective fiction, science fiction, love story and humour. Its creation has spawned a number of similarly structured corpora: the Lancaster-Oslo/Bergen (LOB) corpus, (one million words of 1960s British English); the Freiberg Lancaster-Oslo/Bergen (FLOB) corpus (1990s British English);

and the Freiberg-Brown (FROWN) corpus (1990s American English), with plans in place to create further corpora for other varieties of English.

Capturing data

So returning to the question of how large a corpus should be – the answer very much depends on the type of language that is being investigated. The more specific the use of language, the less need there is to collect millions of words of data. On the other hand, if you are intending to study language use in a relatively general context, it might be a good idea to make use of an existing reference corpus, rather than undertake the time consuming task of creating one yourself. Very large reference corpora are likely to be good sources for uncovering discourses pertaining to an extremely wide range of subjects, simply because of their large size. They also have the advantage of containing texts from many sources, which may result in a more interesting and varied set of discoveries, than, say, just looking at a corpus of newspapers. The section on *Using a reference corpus* below discusses using reference corpora in more detail.

However, there are also good reasons for building a specialized corpus: reference corpora may not contain enough of the text types you are interested in examining or may not have enough references to the subject(s) you want to investigate. And the data may already be too old (one potential problem with many reference corpora is that they take so long to build that by the time they are completed they resemble historical documents, useful for diachronic analysis, but perhaps not directly valuable in revealing much about current discourses).[2]

As with other methodologies, when building a corpus from scratch, it is often useful to carry out a pilot study first in order to determine what sort of texts are available, how easy they are to obtain access to and convert to electronic form.

One of the easiest ways to collect corpus texts is to use data which already exist in electronic format. Due to the proliferation of internet use, many texts which originally began life in written form can be found on websites or internet archives. Exploiting this can make the job of the corpus builder much less arduous than in earlier decades. For example, the websites Newsbank[3] and LexisNexis[4] contain the full-text content (minus the advertising and visuals) from a range of newspapers (both broadsheet and tabloid). Articles are stored as individual texts and a searchable interface allows the user to bring up all the articles which contain a specific word or phrase, restricted to a certain newspaper or a particular time period. The United Kingdom Parliament website[5] contains full transcripts of daily debates from the British House of Lords and House of Commons, whereas the search engine Google contains searchable archives of Usenet discussion forums[6] and millions of other web pages.[7] Other archives include Bibliomania[8] which contains free online literature from 2,000 classic texts, the Oxford Text Archive[9] which contains 2,500 resources in over 25 languages, and the Electronic Text Centre[10] which contains humanities texts in 13 languages. It is often the case that when looking for particular texts, placing a well-thought out phrase into an internet search engine will result in the appearance of some relevant data.

Once a relevant internet archive is found, there then comes the matter of downloading the texts. Depending on how many web pages there are to download, this may be a simple matter of saving the web pages as text files; for example, in Internet Explorer (version 6) select File | Save As and choose Text file from the 'Save as Type' menu. This will effectively strip all of the images and formatting styles from the page (which may be a problem if you want to take into account images and font style). It is also possible to save files in other formats which retain the images, styles and layout of the page. However, this may make carrying out corpus-based searches difficult – as concordance programs (the software used to carry out the analysis of corpora, see Chapter 4) usually function best when working with plain text files. Saving a version of the file which contains the html (hypertext markup language) code may be of use, as this means that file is still in text only format, but contains annotations that indicate formatting like bullet points, paragraphs, etc. which we can usually specify concordance programs to ignore if necessary (see the section on annotation below).

Sometimes, internet text is not encoded in html/text format, but is instead represented in other formats, such as bitmap, jpg or gif files or as pdf documents. In the latter case, it may be necessary to obtain software which converts the pdf document back to plain text (or otherwise be prepared to do a lot of cutting, pasting and editing to make the document readable). When text is represented as a graphics file, then it will either need to be keyed in by hand or scanned in, there is no point in simply saving the graphics files – current concordance programs will not be able to recognize the text within them. An additional problem with saving files as plain text is that we need to assume that all of the language data we are collecting is going to be recognizable in plain text, which is not always the case. At the most simple level, this may mean that speech marks like " and " are converted to " and ". Accented characters like á and ä may lose their accents, while characters which occur in non-Roman writing systems may be rendered as gobbledegook or lost completely. Corpus analysis packages which take into account letters and symbols which occur above the standard ASCII or ANSII character sets are being developed. For example, both Mike Scott's WordSmith version 4.0 and Oxford University's XAIRA allow Unicode handling of text (Unicode being a character set which contains all or nearly all of the world's writing systems).

One problem with saving the entire page from a website address is that we may end up with unwanted text such as menus, titles or links to other pages (see Figure 2.1). It may be easier to strip (or 'clean') this from individual files once they have been saved as text. Or it could be quicker to simply copy and paste the relevant parts of the website directly into an empty Notepad or Word document, saving afterwards. Some corpus builders who collect data websites have tended to use this technique, particularly when copying and pasting text from multiple web pages into a single file. This saves time, as a different file does not have to be saved for each web page that is copied. However, it also means that the resulting corpus is treated as a single 'text', and it therefore becomes difficult to make comparisons between different parts of it.

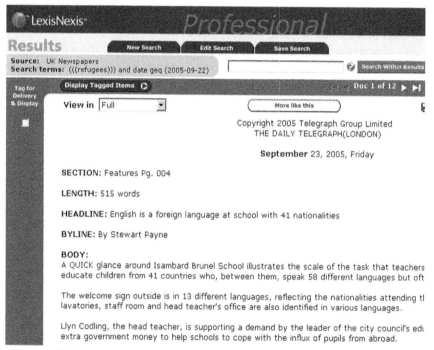

Figure 2.1 *Screenshot from LexisNexis. Text gathered from this webpage would need to be 'cleaned' before inclusion in a corpus*

If there are a lot of pages to collect from a website archive, and the site itself is structured in a relatively accessible format, then it may save time to utilize a website copier, such as HTTrack.[11] This software allows the user to download a website or part of a site from the internet to the user's PC, building recursively all directories, getting html, images, and other files. Once the site has been copied, it may still be necessary to strip the files of unwanted text in any case, and some websites are constructed in order to prevent copiers from taking their content in this way, which brings us to another issue, that of copyright and permission (see below).

Scanning and keying in

If texts cannot be obtained from the internet, then in some cases there may be other ways that they can be collected electronically. For example, British newspapers like *The Guardian* or *The Independent* publish CD-ROM archives of texts. It may also be the case that personal contacts will give or sell data from their own PCs. For example, learner corpora (which usually consist of essays of student writing) are generally collected by language teachers who inveigle students to submit their essays electronically. Placing a request for particular text types at a relevant internet bulletin board or newsgroup may result in access to private collections of data that are not available anywhere else.

If existing electronic sources are unavailable, then two other (more time consuming) options present themselves. The first involves converting paper documents by running them through a scanner with Optical Character Recognition (OCR) software. For most people this is probably quicker than keying in the document by hand, although it is generally not a 100 per cent accurate process (see Renouf 1987). The print quality of the document is likely have an impact on the accuracy of the output, and the data will probably need to be hand-checked, spell-checked and corrected for errors (which, in the worst cases can be an even lengthier process than typing the data oneself). In general, the best types of texts that respond to OCRing are those which are published in a straightforward format (e.g. do not contain different types of fonts or multiple columns). Newspaper print, which is often very small, can get blurred and smudgy and may contain several articles over a range of different sized columns on the same page, does not always respond well to scanning. Kennedy (1998: 80) reports that current scanners have problems with hyphens, apostrophes and certain letters or groups of letters such as a (car is rendered as cor), cl (clear becomes dear), in (innate becomes mnate) and the number 1 vs. the letter l.

The final, and usually last resort of the corpus builder is to key in the text by hand (or pay someone to do it professionally). Kennedy (1998: 79) estimates that an experienced touch typist can achieve about 10,000 words a day, working full-time. There are numerous companies which offer keying in services, and this is one form of service industry which is increasingly going global, for example, with companies based in India providing relatively inexpensive keying in services (in numerous languages) to the West.

Spoken texts

Certain types of texts will present their own unique problems to the corpus builder. For example, written data is generally much easier to obtain than spoken data. Conversations and monologues (whether occurring on the television or radio, at home or the workplace) will need to be transcribed by hand – a task which tends to take much longer than keying in written texts for a number of reasons: parts of spoken texts are sometimes unclear, there can be overlapping dialogue and the tape recorder or audio file needs to be continually stopped and rewound as people normally talk faster than the average typist can keep up with. There is also a range of additional information that may or may not be required: who is speaking at any given point and how they speak; e.g. prosodic information such as volume, speed and stress as well as paralinguistic information (laughter, coughing, etc.) and non-linguistic data (dogs barking, cars passing). Pauses and overlap may need to be transcribed too. There may also be problems involved in accurately rendering different types of accents or other phonetic variation, which can add to the complexity of spoken data.

Sometimes archives containing transcripts of spoken data are already in existence, either on the internet (as with many government debates) or as pre-built spoken corpora. However, it should be noted that in cases where studying linguistic phenomena is not the main goal of archiving this data, these transcripts may have been 'cleaned' or glossed in order to remove or limit the effect of interruptions, false starts, hesitations, etc. (see Slembrouck 1992). It is also sometimes possible to obtain scripts from films, plays or television programmes, which contain spoken data. However, again it should be noted that these forms of scripted data do not always reflect how people really speak. For example, in the spoken section of the British National Corpus, the frequencies per million words for the words *yes* and *yeah* are 3,840 and 7,891 respectively. Compare this to the frequencies of the same words in a 400,000 word corpus of scripts from sitcoms. Here, *yes* only occurs 1,080 times per million words and *yeah* occurs 3,266 times per million words. Such discourse markers therefore tend to be less frequent in scripted written-to-be-spoken data.

Online texts

Different types of problems need to be overcome when collecting data from the internet, particularly when this data is not in the form of archived written texts that were originally published elsewhere. One growing area of interest, for example, is in the analysis of computer-mediated-communication (CMC) itself, consisting of the language which occurs in text messages, emails, chat rooms, bulletin boards and newsgroups. One advantage of including this sort of data in a corpus for analysis, is that it is already in electronic format, so retrieval issues should be at a minimum. However, sometimes formatting styles like colour, font, size, etc. are used, as well as images (particularly in terms of identity creation, e.g. the use of 'avatars'), so these may need to be taken into account when saving data as plain text.

Another issue concerns the relatively reflexive nature of internet texts as hyper-text and how to take account of this within a corpus. For example, in email exchanges, people may include part of the sender's original email to them within the email they send, choosing to respond directly to various parts. This is sometimes indicated by the use of a > symbol at the start of a line, with responses to responses requiring >> or >>>, in order to refer to even earlier emails (Figure 2.2).

When collecting a corpus of email exchanges, this may result in repetitions, where a sentence or paragraph from an initial email is reproduced in all of the emails which follow on from it. Such repetitions are likely to skew a corpus analysis by affording higher frequencies to certain words or phrases. A solution could be to strip any text from an email which originates from an earlier source. However, it may also be quite important to know which parts of an email are specifically in response to earlier emails, particularly if some sort of Conversation Analysis or other qualitative approach is going to be taken with the data. Therefore, it may be a good idea to save different versions of the corpus, one which retains everything in the format it originally occurred in, the other which only contains unique 'first time' entries. Alternatively, an annotation scheme (see below) could be developed, in order to highlight such cross-references within the corpus, without the need to repeat older extracts of text.

The situation is made more complex when moving beyond simple two-person email exchanges to study postings made to bulletin boards or newsgroups. Here the nature of hyper-text means that text structure goes beyond a simple A to Z linearity. For example, different parts of a single posting to a bulletin board may be responded to by many people at different times, who all may receive their own responses. Posters may refer back to part of someone else's communication in their own responses, sometimes including pastings of text written by earlier respondents in their own postings. Again, including multiple 'versions' of the corpus, or using an annotation scheme may help to maintain the overall structure of the interaction, without resulting in repetitions that will skew frequency data.

```
From Baker, Paul
Sent Fri 25/02/2005 10:56
To McEnery, Tony
Re: response

Yes I'll do it
>Perfecto, are you going to write back to them (or email)
>> What do you think?
>> <<file response_to_reviewer.doc.>>
>>> Are you going to handle this one or shall I?
```

Figure 2.2 Email exchange containing references to earlier emails

In addition, many newsgroups or bulletin boards contain instances of 'spam' or unwanted advertising, which may skew a corpus-based analysis of a CMC discussion. On the other hand, it may be argued that spam is just another part of internet language and needs to be taken into account, rather than simply deleted as if it never existed. For example, in some cases, bona fide users of newsgroups may respond to spam emails in humorous or angry ways, which may result in extended exchanges between users. And finally, emails may contain embedded files as attachments within them (see Figure 2.2). Should the contents of such attachments be included in email corpora or not? There are no set ways of responding to these issues, rather, corpus builders must reach decisions themselves, based on their own research goals. The most important aspect, however, is to be clear about the decisions made during the corpus building stage of research and provide ample justifications for them.

Permissions

Kennedy (1998: 76) notes that 'before texts are copied into a corpus database, compilers must seek and gain the permission of the authors and publishers who hold copyright for the work, or the informed consent of individuals whose rights to privacy must be recognized'. This is certainly the case when creating corpora that are intended to be commercially available or shared among a research community. Often in such cases, obtaining signed permissions can be a slow and complex task, as individual permission must be gained for each text that is placed in the corpus. The permissions process can be made all the more lengthy by the fact that commercial corpora are often large and contain representative texts from many sources.

When creating a smaller corpus for sole use, it is often the case that obtaining permission is an easier matter, particularly if the texts are from a single source or a few sources. Making it known that you are the only person who intends to analyse the corpus, you do not intend to sell or give it to anyone else and if required, you will destroy the corpus after you have finished using it, should make the permissions process a less arduous task.

One ethical issue, however, is in obtaining permission to carry out corpus-based (critical) discourse analysis on texts, which may result in findings which show the texts or even the text producers in an unfavourable light, for example, by revealing the construction of racist or sexist discourses. For this reason, it seems unlikely that everyone who carries out corpus analysis (or any form of CDA via other methods) always obtains permission from authors or copyright holders before collecting and analysing texts that are already available in the public domain. Otherwise, it is unlikely that a great deal of research in existence would have ever been published. Having spoken to several academics on the issue of gaining permission to carry out sole-authored, non-commercial research, there still appears to be a degree of inconsistency and confusion over whether permission in writing is *always* required. There sometimes appear to be gaps between the creation of rules and their application in practice. Additionally, different publishers and funding bodies may vary in regard to their attitude towards the necessity of permissions. So it is perhaps useful to couch permissions in terms of 'best practice', but also be aware that there are some cases where permission cannot be obtained. In such cases, including a statement in published work like 'every possible effort has been made to obtain permission ...' may help to safeguard the researcher.

Annotation

It is usually recommended that corpus builders employ some form of annotation scheme to their text files, however brief, in order to aid analysis and keep track of the structure of the corpus. Because the conventions for representing typographical features in electronic texts (aspects like line breaks, formatting of headings, paragraphs, pound signs, quotes, etc.) can vary depending on the software used to edit or view the text, it is often sensible to mark up such features using a standardized coding system.

One such system is the Standard Generalized Markup Language (SGML) which was created in the 1980s as a standard way of encoding electronic texts by using codes (also informally called 'tags' and more formally called 'elements') to define typeface, page layout, etc. In general, the codes are enclosed between less than and greater than symbols: < >. So for example the element <p> is used to indicate the start of a new paragraph. However, many codes also have a corresponding closing or end tag, which is demonstrated by the use of a forward slash / sign after the less than symbol. So the end of a paragraph would be encoded as </p>.

Elements may also contain attributes and values. For example, the element <pause dur=4> could be used in a spoken transcription to indicate the occurrence of a pause during speech, the duration being 4 seconds. Here, the attribute is *dur* (duration) and its value is 4 (seconds).

Different forms of SGML have been employed for a range of purposes. So web pages are encoded in HTML (Hyper Text Markup Language) which uses a predefined set of codes that are based on the general SGML rules. For example, bold print is specified in HTML with the code pair <b> and </b>. See Bryan (1988) and Goldfarb (1990) for more information about SGML.

The Text Encoding Initiative (TEI) is a related system, developed in the mid-1990s, which specifies a set of SGML codes which are to be specifically used for different types of text mark up (including written and spoken varieties).[12] In addition, XML (eXtensible Mark-up Language) allows users to develop their own codes for different types of data. XML is Unicode-compliant, and in ensuring that its users strictly adhere to its rules and syntax, it is rather less forgiving of inconsistencies than HTML.

There is no reason why corpus builders must adopt some form of SGML if they encode their corpora, but it is worth knowing about the existence of such codes and what they look like in case they are encountered in other corpora. Also, if an annotation scheme is required, then it seems a shame to have to reinvent the wheel, when a perfectly good set of standards already exists. Finally, corpus analysis packages like WordSmith tend to be capable of handling SGML codes, but they may be less equipped to deal with an *ad hoc* coding system created by a researcher working alone.

So in what contexts would annotation be useful for corpus-based discourse analysis? One aspect is in the creation of headers (see Figure 2.3). A header, marked with <head> ... </head> normally appears at the beginning of a file in a corpus (or exists as a separate file) and gives reference information about that particular text, perhaps in terms of the title, who created it and when and where it was published. The following <body> ... </body> part of the file contains the actual text itself. Headers can be a useful form of record keeping, particularly if a corpus consists of many files from different sources, created at different times. Alternatively, you might want to include this sort of meta-information within file names or sort different types of files into folders that are named accordingly.

The header may also contain information about the author or genre of the file, which can be useful at a later analytical stage, if you want to make comparisons between different genres, or say, only look at a sub-section of your corpus which was authored by women. It would then be a matter of instructing your analysis software to only consider files that contain a tag like <sex="female">.

```
<head>
<title>Pride and Prejudice Chapter One - excerpt</title>
<author>
<name="Jane Austen">
<sex="female">
</author>
</head>
<body>
Chapter One. It is a truth universally acknowledged....
</body>
```

Figure 2.3 A short sample header from a written text

Other meta-linguistic information that could appear in headers for written files includes the publication date (sometimes using categories such as 1960s, 1970s, 1980s, etc. can be useful when making comparisons over time), medium of text (book, magazine, letter), genre (science, fiction, religious, news), level of difficulty, audience size, age and sex of author and target audience. For spoken corpora, we may be interested in encoding information about the different speakers in each text (their age, sex, socio-economic status, first language or geographic region), whether the text is a monologue or dialogue, public or private, scripted or spontaneous. At the end of Chapter 3, I look in more detail at some of the different speaker classifications in corpora.

Leaving the header, the actual body of the text can also be given different types of annotation, some of which are discussed in more detail later in this book (especially Chapters 6 and 7). Grammatical annotation is one procedure that is commonly assigned to corpora at some stage towards the end of the building process. This usually involves attaching codes to each word (or in some cases groups of words) which denote a grammatical class such as noun, verb or adjective. Some encoding systems can be quite complex, encoding different tenses of verbs (past, present, future) or numbers of nouns (singular vs. plural). Grammatical annotation can be useful in that it enables corpus users to make more specific analyses. For some words, their meaning and usage can change radically depending on their grammatical class. For example, *text, horse, field* and *hits* can all be nouns or verbs. Having an indication of part-of-speech information, and being able to specify this within corpus searches can save a lot of time. We may also find it useful to split words and tag different parts of them separately – so with a word like *don't*, we could tag the first morpheme as a verb, and the second as a negator. This would allow more flexibility when looking at just verbs or just negators or combinations of both. Figure 2.4 shows a grammatically tagged sentence from the British National Corpus, which was annotated using an encoding scheme called the C5 tagset.[13] Each word is preceded by an SGML element <w> (word) which also contains a value, the three character code which represents the grammatical class. So NN1 indicates a singular common noun while NN2 is a plural common noun.

```
<w  CJC>And  <w  ATO>a  <w  AJO>trained  <w  NN1>singing  <w
NN1>voice <w VBZ>is <w AVO>undoubtedly <w ATO>a <w AJO>valued
<w NN1>asset <c PUN> -- <w EXO>there <w VMO>may <w AVO>well
<w VBI>be <w DTO>some <w NN1>competition <w PRP>for <w ATO>a
<w NN1>place <w PRP>on <w VVG>singing <w NN2>tutorials <c
PUN>.
```

Figure 2.4 A grammatically tagged sentence from the British National Corpus

However, grammatical information does not always provide the fullest picture of differences in word usage. We may also want to distinguish between semantic differences, e.g. the difference between 'a *hits* album' or '*hits* to the body'. In this case, semantic tags can be applied to words in order to draw out crucial differences in word meaning. And other types of tags can be assigned where necessary, for example, in spoken files, to indicate different speakers or types of non-linguistic or prosodic information. When I was building a corpus of personal adverts, I used tags to distinguish between the information which described the advertiser and the text which was related to the sort of person being sought (Baker 2005).

However, one problem with annotation is that carrying it out by hand can be a painfully slow (and often error-prone) process. For this reason, computer programs have been developed which accomplish certain forms of tagging automatically. For example, both the Universities of Birmingham and Lancaster have developed grammatical taggers and offered free trial services in the past.[14] It should be noted though, that the accuracy rates of automatic taggers rarely reach 100 per cent (although are generally around 97 per cent). The more predictable a text is in terms of following grammatical rules and having a low proportion of rare words, the greater the likelihood that the tagger will have a high accuracy rate. Grammatically unpredictable texts (such as conversations which contain repetitions and false starts) or texts with a lot of recent jargon or slang (which tend not to be recognized by the tagger's internal lexicon) may result in errors. Some taggers attempt to circumvent this problem by incorporating 'portmanteau tags', basically a combination of the two (or more) most likely tags in ambiguous cases. And for large corpus building projects, it is usual for at least part of the corpus annotation to be hand-corrected. But even with an unchecked corpus, grammatical tagging can still be very useful.

A final stage of corpus annotation usually involves some form of validation, by running the corpus through a piece of software which checks the encoding and alerts the researcher to any syntax errors or problems found such as missing < symbols, or incorrectly nested tags.

Annotation may sound like a great deal of work, and it is not necessary to carry out tagging for the sake of it. Instead, corpus builders need to think about what sort of research questions they intend to ask of their corpus, and then decide whether or not particular forms of tagging will be required. It is always possible to go back to the building stage at a later point in order to carry out new forms of annotation, once the need has been established. The important point to take away from this section is that different forms of annotation are often carried out on corpora and can result in more sophisticated analyses of data, but that this is not compulsory.

Using a reference corpus

I discussed reference corpora at the beginning of this chapter (and described the British National Corpus, The Bank of English and The Brown family of corpora as some examples of reference corpora). Obtaining access to a reference corpus can be helpful for two reasons. First, reference corpora are large and representative enough of a particular genre of language, that they can themselves be used to uncover evidence of particular discourses. For example, in Chapter 5 I use the British National Corpus to examine discourses surrounding never-married people by looking at words which commonly occur near or next to the words *bachelor* and *spinster*. In this case, I did not need to engage in any form of preliminary corpus building. Instead, the issue became gaining access to the corpus (something which I address below).

Secondly, a reference corpus acts as a good benchmark of what is 'normal' in language, by which your own data can be compared to. So in other chapters in the book I have built smaller specialized corpora, such as a corpus of holiday leaflets in Chapter 3, and have then used a reference corpus to explore hypotheses about language that I formed, when looking at how words are used in the specialized corpus. For example, we can compare a large reference corpus to a smaller corpus (or even a single file), in order to examine which words occur in the smaller text more frequently than we would normally expect them to occur by chance alone. Obtaining such a list of *keywords* from a file is a useful technique in the examination of the discourses evoked within it (see Chapter 6).

Additionally, reference corpora may help us to test out theories. For example, I may hypothesize that a certain word occurs in a text in order to achieve a certain stylistic effect, e.g. by sounding scientific or informal or masculine, which may be contributing towards the discursive construction of the reader or writer's identity in some way. By looking at the frequency of such a term in a reference corpus, investigating exactly what genres it is likely to occur in, what sort of people use it, etc. what its associations are, I can start to provide evidence for this hypothesis.

So clearly, access to a reference corpus is potentially useful for carrying out discourse analysis, even if the corpus itself is not the main focus of the analysis. Therefore, a pertinent question to ask at this stage is, which reference corpus is applicable to use? Again, there are no simple answers, but as a usual rule of thumb, we should at least try to obtain reference corpora which reflect some aspect of the smaller corpus or text sample we are studying. For example, if we have obtained a text that was created in the 1960s by British authors, then we would preferably want the reference corpus to also have been created around the same time and contain mainly (or all) British English – in which case, the one million word LOB Corpus would probably suffice. If such a corpus is not forthcoming, then trying to find as close a match as possible is preferable. It is, of course, possible to use a completely different reference corpus, but any interesting aspects of difference that are shored up from comparisons between a smaller text or corpus and a reference corpus may be due to differences in language variety rather than telling us anything of note about the smaller text. So for example, using LOB as a reference corpus to examine aspects of a British text created in 2005 is likely to reveal diachronic linguistic differences between the early 1960s and 2005. So we may find that modal verb use occurs less often in the recent text, when compared to LOB. However, this is more likely due to the fact that modal verb use has decreased over time in British English (Leech 2003) rather than telling us something interesting about our particular text under analysis. So care should be taken when comparing texts with reference corpora, to ensure that findings are not due to diachronic or synchronic differences between the two.

But at times, a perfectly matching reference corpus may not be forthcoming, and in cases like this, a 'best fit' will have to suffice, although this needs to be made clear when reporting findings. Another, perhaps more problematic issue, is to do with gaining access to corpora. While such corpora are in existence, they can be expensive to obtain (although much less expensive than building them). Researchers who have funding or are aligned to university departments with spare funds (and a positive attitude towards corpus-based research) will be at an advantage. Some corpus builders allow users limited access for a trial period before buying, or will offer a smaller 'sample' portion of their corpus free of charge. And because large reference corpora can require a great deal of computer memory, they are increasingly being offered via internet-based platforms, whereby users can access a website which allows searches, concordances, collocations, etc. to be carried out. The advantage of such stand-alone platforms is that only a password is purchased and no permanent hard drive memory is taken up. However, at the same time, the user is limited to what the creators of the analysis program thought were necessary, so for example, the corpus may not be grammatically annotated. Also, such web-accessible corpora cannot normally be used in conjunction with stand-alone analysis packages such as WordSmith Tools or MicroConcord (see Chapter 4) and this may limit the types of questions that can be asked of them.

44

Conclusion

This chapter has raised a number of issues, both theoretical and practical, concerned with building or obtaining corpus. While there are certain procedures that do need to be followed (e.g. taking into account representativeness or gaining permissions), the researcher ultimately does have freedom in choosing what type of corpus to build or use, how to encode the data into an electronic format and how to annotate the text (if at all).

Having come this far, it is now time to turn to the remaining part of the book, which is more concerned with analysis, rather than building corpora or justifying their use at all. The following five chapters each consider different methodological procedures of using corpora to analyse discourses, covering a range of different types of data, as well as providing a more critical account of the possible problems that could be encountered. Each chapter gradually builds on the information covered in the others. So with that in mind, I begin with what is usually considered to be the least complex corpus-based process, analysing frequency data.

Notes

1. There are some types of corpora that will not be discussed in this book as they are not essentially relevant for discourse analysis: e.g. parallel/aligned corpora, learner corpora, dialect corpora – instead I refer the reader to McEnery and Wilson (1996), Kennedy (1998) and Hunston (2002) for fuller descriptions.
2. As Burnard (2002: 64) points out, the BNC for example, which was built in the 1990s, only contains two references to the World Wide Web: 'the BNC is definitely no longer an accurate reflection of the English language.'
3. http://infoweb.newsbank.com/.
4. http://web.lexis-nexis.com/professional/.
5. www.parliament.uk/hansard/hansard2.cfm.
6. http://groups.google.com.
7. www.google.com. An interesting aspect of Google relates to the issue of different texts having different amounts of 'influence' on discourses. When a search for a word or phrase is carried out on Google, the results are given in order of relevance, based on popularity: the web links which were selected most frequently by others in previous searches for the same term are presented first. If a concordance is created from such a list, then the user would be able to take into account this notion of prior selectivity, which suggests that the first few concordance lines may have had more power to influence discourses (by light of being encountered more often)

than others. However, care should be taken – a page may be popular in its own right but simply not score highly in terms of appearing relevant to a particular Google search.

8. www.bibliomania.com/.
9. http://ota.ahds.ac.uk/.
10. http://etext.lib.virginia.edu/uvaonline.html.
11. www.httrack.com/.
12. www.tei-c.org/Guidelines2/.
13. See www.comp.lancs.ac.uk/ucrel/bnc2/bnc2guide.htm#tagset for the list of grammatical codes used.
14. See www.comp.lancs.ac.uk/ucrel/claws/trial.html for a free trial service.

3 Frequency and Dispersion

Introduction

Frequency is one of the most central concepts underpinning the analysis of corpora. However, its importance to this field of research has resulted in one of the most oft-heard misconceptions of corpus linguistics – that it is 'only' a quantitative methodology, leading to a list of objections: frequencies can be reductive and generalizing, they can oversimplify and their focus on comparing differences can obscure more interesting interpretations of data. It is the intention of this chapter to introduce the reader to the uses (and potential dangers) of frequency lists – as one of the most basic tools of the corpus linguist, they are a good starting point for the analysis of any type of corpus. Used sensitively, they can illuminate a variety of interesting phenomena. This chapter examines how frequency lists can be employed to direct the researcher to investigate various parts of a corpus, how measures of dispersion can reveal trends across texts and how, with the right corpus, frequency data can help to give the user a sociological profile of a given word or phrase enabling greater understanding of its use in particular contexts. None of these processes are without problems, however, so the potential shortcomings of frequency data, and possible ways to overcome them, are also discussed here. This chapter also provides a good grounding for the later methodological chapters – without discussing frequency it is more difficult to understand the concepts of collocation and key words.

Why is frequency of interest to discourse analysis? It is important because language is not a random affair. As we will see in Chapter 5, words tend to occur in relationship to other words, with a remarkable degree of predictability. Languages are rule-based – they consist of thousands of patterns governing what can and can not be said or written at any given point. However, despite these rules, people usually have some sort of choice about the sort of language that they can use. This argument is summed up by Stubbs (1996: 107), who writes 'No terms are neutral. Choice of words expresses an ideological position.'

It is the tension between these two states – language as a set of rules vs. language as free choice – that makes the concept of frequency so important. If people speak or write in an unexpected way, or make one linguistic choice over another, more obvious one, then that reveals something about their intentions, whether conscious or not.

For example, as Zwicky (1997: 22) points out, one contested choice is between the use of *gay* as opposed to *homosexual*. Other choices could include the use of euphemisms (*that way inclined, confirmed bachelor*, etc.), derogatory terms (*faggot, sissy*) or reclaimings of such terms (*queer, dyke*). Danet (1980) describes a case where a doctor who carried out a late abortion was tried for manslaughter. The language used in the courtroom was an explicit concern of the trial, with lawyers negotiating the different connotations of terms such as *products of conception, fetus, male human being, male child* and *baby boy*. The choice of such terms assume different frames of reference, e.g. *baby boy* suggests helplessness, whereas *fetus* expresses a medical position. However, choice need not be lexical. Another type of choice relates to grammatical uses of words: the use of *gay* as a noun or *gay* as an adjective. Most people would (hopefully) argue that 'he is gay' is somewhat less negatively biased than 'he is a gay'. Here the adjectival usage suggests a person is described as possessing one trait among many possible attributes, whereas the noun usage implies that a person is merely the sum total of their sexuality and no more. More specifically, we could consider *gay* as an attributive adjective (occurring before a noun), e.g. 'the gay man' or *gay* as a predicative adjective (occurring after a link verb), e.g. 'he is gay'.

In describing the analysis of texts using critical discourse analysis, Fairclough (1989: 110–11) lists ten sets of questions relating to formal linguistic features, each one indicating that a choice has been made by the author – e.g. pronoun use, modality, metaphors, agency, passivization, nominalization, etc. (see Chapter 7 for further exploration of some of these features). While Fairclough frames his questions in terms of appearing within 'a specific text', there is no reason why such an analysis of linguistic choices cannot be carried out on a corpus in order to uncover evidence for preference which occurs across a genre or language variety. However, as Sherrard (1991) argues, such a view of choice presupposes that language users feel that they actually *have* a choice or are aware that one exists. She points out that speakers will always be restricted in their ways of using language – for example, people in the 1950s would not have used a term like *Ms* because such a choice was not available to them. It is therefore important that as researchers we are aware of the range of possible choices open to language users and interpret their decisions accordingly.

48

Related to the concept of frequency is that of dispersion. As well as knowing that something is (or isn't) frequent in a text or corpus, being able to determine *where* it occurs can also be extremely important. Again, language is not random: texts have beginnings, middles and ends. Narrative structures are usually imposed on them.[1] It may be relevant to know that a particular word form is more frequent at the start of a text than at the end. It may be useful to ascertain whether its occurrences are all clumped together in one small section of the corpus, or whether the word is a constant feature, cropping up every now and again with regularity. Dispersion analyses are one way that we can take into account the fact that texts are discrete entities within themselves, and they also allow us to begin to consider context, albeit in a rather impressionistic way, although the relevance of context is something which will be developed in further chapters as we proceed.

Join the club

In order to demonstrate some possible uses of frequency and dispersion I am going to describe how they can be employed on a small corpus of data which consists of 12 leaflets advertising holidays. These leaflets were produced by the British tour operator Club 18–30, which was established in the 1960s and describes itself in its website as being 'all about having a positive attitude. It's about the clothes that you wear, the music you listen to and the places you go but more importantly it's about you.'[2]

The holiday leaflets were all published in 2005 and my goal in collecting them was to investigate discourses of tourism within them. As well as considering the leaflets as a single corpus, I was also interested in whether there was any variation between them – so were there different discourses to be found or was this a relatively homogenous corpus with a great deal of lexical and discursive repetition?

Morgan and Pritchard (2001: 165) report how in 1995 (ten years prior to my study) Club 18–30 used a campaign of

> sun fun and sex ... Posters were launched carrying slogans such as "Discover your erogenous zone", "Summer of 69" and "Girls, can we interest you in a package holiday?" with a picture of a man, described by *The Times* as wearing "a well-padded pair of boxer shorts". In addition to this high profile poster campaign (which was later extended to cinemas), the company continued the sexual theme in the pages of their brochures.

However, Club 18–30 holidays have more recently been criticized in the media. For example, in August 2005, in the UK, Channel 5 broadcast a television programme called 'The Curse of Club 18–30' which featured interviews by people who had not enjoyed their holiday, including a man who had been temporarily blinded at a foam party and a girl who had had her head shaved by a gang of drunken men. *The Telegraph* reported a story in 2003 about a Club 18–30 resort in Faliraki that had been reviewed by holiday goers as being a place to avoid if you are over 30, teetotal or not promiscuous.

Perhaps as a response to these and other criticisms, at the Club 18–30 website is a section on 'myths' about the holiday operator.[3] One such myth reads: 'All Club 18–30 holidays are about being forced to drink too much and having sex. I've heard that the reps shove drink down your throat and make sexual innuendos all the time!' The Club 18–30 response is: 'We are not moral guardians – what you do on your holiday is 100 per cent down to you. If you want to drink on holiday, you drink, if you don't, you don't – simple as that! Young people drinking abroad is not exclusive to Club 18–30.' It would therefore be interesting to see the extent to which Club 18–30 holiday brochures currently refute or support the 'myths' of alcohol consumption and promiscuity.

Holiday brochures are an interesting text type to analyse because they are an inherently persuasive form of discourse. Their main aim is to ensure that potential customers will be sufficiently impressed to book a holiday: 'The drive to create impactful *and* effective advertising still remains a major advertising challenge, despite the development of sophisticated advertising tracking and evaluation techniques' (Morgan and Pritchard 2001: 17).

However, as with most advertising texts, writers must take care to engage with what can be a diverse audience in an appropriate way. For example, by deciding what aspects of the holiday are foregrounded (or backgrounded) and what assumptions are made about the interests and lifestyles of the target audience. Language, therefore is one of the most salient aspects of persuasive discourses. The message must be sufficiently attractive for the potential audience to want to engage in something that will essentially result in a financial exchange.

With that in mind, Table 3.1 shows the filenames and word counts of the 12 leaflets used in the holiday corpus. It should be noted from the filenames of the leaflets (which are derived from their titles), that the leaflets mainly advertise holidays on Spanish and Greek islands.

Table 3.1 Holiday leaflets

Filename	Words
cancun.txt	756
corfu.txt	1258
crete.txt	1995
cyprus.txt	1146
gran.txt	1089
ibiza.txt	2273
intro.txt	3639
kos.txt	1126
mallorca.txt	1764
rhodes.txt	1206
tenerife.txt	918
zante.txt	695

While the analysis of this corpus focuses on the language used in the leaflets, it should be noted that there is a visual aspect to the holiday leaflets which also plays an important role in how the leaflets are understood and the discourses contained in them. As Hunston (2002: 23) points out, a corpus cannot show that a text does not consist of words alone but is encountered by audiences within its visual and social context (see Kress 1994; Kress and van Leeuwen 1996). As well as drawings, diagrams and photographs the text itself is not 'plain'. The font, colour, size and positions of text also play a role in how tourist discourses are likely to be interpreted. Therefore, although this chapter focuses on the analysis of the electronically encoded text in the corpus of leaflets, visuals are also an important part of these leaflets and ought to be examined in conjunction with the corpus-based findings (something I return to at the end of this chapter).

Frequency counts

Using the corpus analysis software WordSmith, a word list of the 12 text files was obtained. A word list is simply a list of all of the words in a corpus along with their frequencies and the percentage contribution that each word makes towards the corpus. Considering frequencies in terms of standardized percentages is often a more sensible way of making sense of data, particularly when comparisons between two or more data sets of different sizes are made. Figure 3.1 shows how the word list is represented by WordSmith. The output consists of three windows (F), (A) and (S), only the top window (F) is shown in Figure 3.1. The (F) window shows frequencies in terms of the highest first, whereas the (A) window re-orders the word list alphabetically. The (S) window gives statistical information about the corpus, including the total number of words (tokens), in this case 17,865 (this is only a very small corpus), the number of *original* words (types) and the type/token ratio, which is simply the number of types divided by the number of tokens expressed as a percentage. For example, the word *you* occurs 348 times in the corpus, although it only consists of one *type* of word. We could also refer to the type/token ratio as 'the average number of tokens per type'. A corpus or file with a low type/token ratio will contain a great deal of repetition – the same words occurring again and again, whereas a high type/token ratio suggests that a more diverse form of language is being employed. Type/token ratios tend to be useful when looking at relatively small text files (say under 5,000 words). However, as the size of a corpus grows, the type/token ratio will almost always shrink, because high frequency grammatical words like *the* and *to* tend to be repeated no matter what the size of the corpus is. Because of this, large corpora almost always have very low type/token ratios and comparisons between them become difficult. Therefore WordSmith also calculates a standardized type/token ratio which is based on taking the type/token ratio of the first 2,000 words in the corpus, then the type/token ratio of the next 2,000 words and the next 2,000 words after that, and so on, and then working out the mean of all of these individual type/token ratios. This standardized type/token ratio is almost invariably higher as a result and a better measure of comparison between corpora. For example, the type/token ratio of our corpus is 12.16, whereas the standardized type/token ratio is 40.03.

Why is the type/token ratio useful? It can give an indication of the linguistic complexity or specificity of a file or corpus. A low type/token ratio is likely to indicate that a relatively narrow range of subjects are being discussed, which can sometimes (but not always) suggest that the language being used is relatively simplistic. For example, the standardized type/token ratio in the FLOB corpus of British English (which contains a range of written texts from different genres) is 45.53, where the same figure in a sample of transcribed informal spoken conversations from the British National Corpus is 32.96, reflecting the fact that written language tends to contain a higher proportion of unique words, whereas informal spoken language is more lexically repetitive. Comparing this to the standarized type/token ratio of the holiday leaflets (40.03), we find that it falls somewhere in between spoken and written language, a fact we may want to keep in mind for later. Clearly, however, the type/token ratio merely gives only the briefest indication of lexical complexity or specificity and further investigations are necessary.

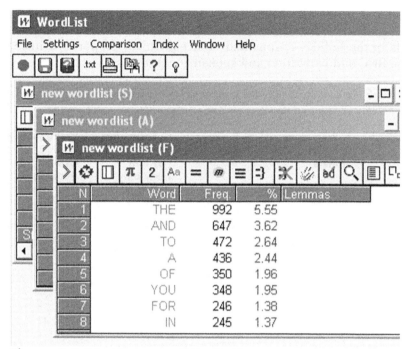

Figure 3.1 Word list output of WordSmith

Looking at Figure 3.1 again, there are two columns of numbers. The 'Freq.' column gives raw frequencies, whereas the per cent column gives the overall proportion that a particular word contributes towards the whole corpus. So the word *you* occurs 348 times and occurrences of this word contribute to 1.95 per cent of the corpus overall. When comparing multiple corpora of different sizes it is useful to refer to the per cent column as this presents a standardized value. However, for the purposes of this chapter, where we are only using one corpus, we will simply use raw frequencies.

From Figure 3.1 it becomes apparent that the most frequent words in the corpus are grammatical words (also known as function words). Such words belong to a closed grammatical class each consisting of a small number of high frequency words (pronouns, determiners, conjunctions, prepositions), these categories tend not to be subject to linguistic innovation – we don't normally invent new conjunctions or pronouns as a matter of course.

With few exceptions, almost all forms of language have a high proportion of grammatical words. However, in order to determine whether any of these words occur more often than we would expect,

53

it can be useful to compare our holiday corpus to a corpus of general language like the British National Corpus. Table 3.2 shows the top ten words in the holiday corpus and their equivalent proportions in the whole BNC and its written and spoken components.

Table 3.2 *Percentage frequencies of the ten most frequently occurring words in the holiday corpus and their equivalencies in the BNC*

	Word	% Frequency in holiday leaflets	% Frequency in BNC	% Frequency in BNC (written texts only)	% Frequency in BNC (spoken texts only)
1	the	5.55	6.20	6.46	3.97
2	and	3.62	2.68	2.70	2.53
3	to	2.64	2.66	2.70	2.26
4	a	2.44	2.21	2.24	1.99
5	of	1.96	3.12	3.29	1.69
6	you	1.95	0.68	0.45	2.59
7	for	1.38	0.90	0.93	0.64
8	in	1.37	1.97	2.05	1.37
9	on	1.15	0.74	0.74	0.78
10	all	1.04	0.28	0.26	0.42

Comparing the frequencies in the holiday corpus with their equivalencies in the BNC reveals some interesting findings. Some words in the holiday corpus have similar rates of occurrence in the spoken section of the BNC (*to, of, in*), other words have higher rates compared to the BNC, including those which generally occur more in the written section (*and, for*) or the spoken section (*on, all*). The use of *you* in the holiday corpus is closer to the figure for the spoken section of the BNC than it is for the written. This suggests that although the texts consist of written documents, there are at least some aspects of the language within them that are similar to spoken language. The high use of *you* (the only pronoun to appear in the top ten) also suggests a personal style of writing, where the writer is directly addressing the reader.

Comparing frequencies of function words can be useful in terms of discerning the register of a text. For example, Biber, Conrad and Reppen (1998) show how frequencies of different function words (among other things) can be used to categorize texts across a range of five stylistic dimensions (for example dimension 1 is 'involved vs. information production'). However, perhaps we can get a better idea of *discourses* within the corpus if we put the grammatical words to one side for the moment, and only consider the most frequent lexical words and terms (e.g. the nouns, verbs, adjectives and lexical adverbs). Table 3.3 shows what the top ten looks like if we do this.

Table 3.3 *The most frequent ten lexical words in the holiday corpus*

	Word	Frequency
1	beach	124
2	pool	122
3	studios	116
4	sleep	107
5	club	99
6	facilities	96
7	bar	94
8	private	87
9	bars	79
10	apartments	78

This table gives us a much better idea of what the corpus is *about*. There are words describing holiday residences (*studios, facilities, apartments*) and other attractions (*beach, pool, club, bar*). One aspect of the table worth noting is that *bar* and *bars* both appear in the top ten list. Added together, their total frequency is 173, meaning that the noun lemma BAR would potentially be the most common lexical term in the corpus. A lemma is the canonical form of a word. Francis and Kučera (1982: 1) define it as a 'set of lexical forms having the same stem and belonging to the same major word class, differing only in inflection and/or spelling'. Lemmatized forms are sometimes written as small capitals, e.g. the verb lemma WALK consists of the lexemes *walk, walked, walking* and *walks*.

Considering that the lemma BAR is so frequent, it is possible that other lemmas may have important roles to play in the corpus. Therefore, Table 3.4 shows the top ten recalculated to take into account the most frequent lexical lemmas.

Table 3.4 *The most frequent lexical lemmas in the holiday corpus*

Rank	Lemma	Frequency
1	BAR	173
2	CLUB	144
3	BEACH	136
4	POOL	128
5	STUDIO	116
6	FACILITY	96
7	APARTMENT	80
8=	BALCONY	78
8=	DAY	78
10	NIGHT	70

The ordering of the lexical lemmas list is rather different to the simple frequency list. Now the two most frequent items are BAR and CLUB which give us an idea about the focus of the holiday brochure. The other words in Table 3.4 are similar to those in Table 3.3, although we now also find DAY and NIGHT appearing as frequent lexical lemmas. Obviously, at this stage, while we can make educated guesses as to why and in what contexts these terms appear (for example, we would expect BAR to usually, if not always, refer to contexts of consuming alcohol, rather than say, an iron bar), it is always useful to verify these guesses, using other techniques. In Chapters 4 and 5 I look at two ways to do this (by using concordances and collocates), but in this chapter I'm going to focus on frequent clusters (see below).

So now that we have a list of frequent terms, what can we do with them, and how can this information be used to tell us anything about discourses within the corpus? Let us examine the most frequent term, BAR, in more detail.

Considering clusters

How are bars described in the corpus? In order to do this we need to consider frequencies beyond single words. Using WordSmith it is possible to derive frequency lists for *clusters* of words. For example, by specifying the cluster size as 3, the word list in Figure 3.2 is found.

N	Word	Freq.	%	Lemmas
1	ALL HAVE PRIVATE	135	0.76	
2	HAVE PRIVATE FACILITIES	62	0.35	
3	PRIVATE FACILITIES AND	34	0.19	
4	MINUTES FROM THE	27	0.15	
5	COM OR TEXT	26	0.15	
6	AND APARTMENTS SLEEP	24	0.13	
7	MINUTE STROLL FROM	22	0.12	
8	BARS AND CLUBS	21	0.12	
9	AND ALL HAVE	20	0.11	
10	METRES FROM THE	20	0.11	

Figure 3.2 Wordlist of three word clusters

56

Using this word list, it is possible to search for clusters which contain the term *bar* or *bars* in order to uncover the ways that they are used. An examination of three word clusters reveals some of the most common patterns: *bars and clubs* (21 occurrences), *loads of bars* (6), *the best bars* (6), *bar serving snacks* (6), *pool and bar* (4). There are a number of other clusters which emphasize the amount of bars: *heaps of bars, plenty of bars, never-ending stream of bars, tons of bars, variety of bars.* How else are bars described? Some two-word clusters include *well-stocked bar* (4), *vibrant bars* (2), *lively bars* (3), *24-hour bar* (3), *excellent bars* (4) and *great bars* (3).

What about the second most popular lexical lemma, CLUB? The most common two word cluster is *Club 18–30* (53 occurrences or about 37 per cent of cases of the word *club*). Other frequent clusters include *bars and clubs* (21), *club tickets* (10), *club nights* (3) and *club scene* (3). Two word clusters that involve evaluation include: *great club* (3), *best clubs* (2), *lively club* (1), *hottest club* (1) and *greatest clubs* (1).

At this stage, we can say with certainty that places where alcohol can be consumed are the most frequent concept in the Club 18–30 brochures (taking priority to other places such as the beach or the apartment where people will be staying). We also know that bars are repeatedly evaluated positively (great, excellent, vibrant, lively) as well as being plentiful (heaps, plenty, never-ending, tons). The frequency of such terms coupled with the use of evaluations suggests a process of normalization: readers of the brochures will be encouraged to believe that bars are an important part of their holiday.

However, we need to be careful about jumping to conclusions too early in our analysis. While BAR and CLUB are the most frequent lexical lemmas in the holiday corpus, they are also the *only* lemmas in the top ten that relate to alcohol. We would perhaps expect other alcohol-related words to be reasonably frequent. And sometimes what is not present in a frequency list can be as revealing as what is frequent. With this in mind, I scanned the remainder of the frequency list to see where (if at all) other alcohol-related words appeared: *cocktail* (3 occurrences), *cocktails* (3), *daiquiri* (1), *margaritas* (1), *hungover* (1). The single use of *hungover* was interesting, and I examined its occurrence in the corpus: 'If you're too lazy (or hungover!) to cross the road to the beach you can chill out and lounge on a sunbed round the pool area.' However, despite this statement, which carries an assumption on the behalf of the reader (that they might be hungover), the list of other alcohol-related terms is very small, while words like *beer, lager, wine* and *alcohol* do not appear at all. Perhaps then, it is the case that encouragement to consume alcohol is a Club 18–30 myth and the high frequency of BAR is due to other reasons, concerned with say, the social function of bars.

So while the findings so far are somewhat suggestive, we can not say at this stage that the brochures actively advocate consumption of alcohol (or if they do, to what degree). In order to begin to answer this question, we need to consider another class of words: verbs. Verbs play a particularly interesting role in tourist discourses as they can often be instructional, giving advice on the sort of activities and behaviours that tourists should and should not engage in while on holiday. Omoniyi (1998: 6) refers to imperative verb phrases as invitational imperatives, the reader is invited to partake of an activity, but under no obligation to do so. However, invitational imperatives are another way that norms are imposed in tourist discourses.

What verbs, then, are the most frequently occurring in the holiday corpus? Here it is helpful to have carried out a prior part-of-speech annotation (see Chapter 2) of the corpus, so that it is possible to distinguish words which can belong to multiple grammatical categories (e.g. *hits* can be a noun or a verb). Table 3.5 shows the most frequent lexical verb forms in the corpus.

Table 3.5 The most frequent lexical verbs in the holiday corpus

Rank	Verb	Frequency
1	sleep	107
2	book	34
3	want	30
4	cost	29
5	work	26
6	miss	24
7	make	23
8	chill	29
9	find	18
10	relax	17

Here, overwhelmingly, it looks as if the most frequent verb is concerned with sleeping, a curious and unexpected finding. However, an examination of clusters reveals that all cases of *sleep* involve the phrase *studios/rooms sleep 2–3/3–4* which are used to detail how many people can book an apartment or room. Similarly, the verbs *book* and *cost* are also concerned with aspects of booking a holiday or flight, rather than activities to do on the holiday. The remaining seven verbs in Table 3.5 are more interesting to examine. Frequent imperative verb clusters include *don't miss out* (16), *chill out* (15) and *make sure* (12). A closer examination of *chill* and *relax* may be useful here. There are seven references in the corpus to 'chilling out during the day'. The following sentences taken from the corpus illustrate the main pattern of 'chilling' as an invitational imperative:

'The hotel pool is a great place to chill-out during the day before starting your night with a drink in Bar Vistanova.'

'The swimming pool is a great place to chill-out during the hot sunny days and the hotel bar is the ideal choice for your first drink before heading into the vibrant bars of Rhodes Town.'

'The Partit Apartments are right on the doorstep of Club base Casita Blanca where you can have a swim in the pool, chill out with a cold drink and grab some snacks at the bar or just lounge around in the sun and re-charge your batteries!'

'The 24 hour bar, Petrino's, is usually rammed at 5am as everyone gets together to chill out after a heavy night partying!'

The verb *relax* also follows a similar pattern:

'The Green Ocean has all the qualities of a great Club 18–30 property, with the added bonus of being the ideal place to relax and catch up on some well-earned snoozing!'

'The pool area is the perfect place to hang out whether you want to be active or simply relax and recover.'

'There is also a fantastic Vital Wellness Centre where you can relax and recharge in the spa or sauna before heading into the vibrant nightlife of Playa Del Ingles.'

Chilling/relaxing is therefore suggested as a precursor before 'starting the night' or after a 'heavy night partying'. It is also used to catch up on sleep, recover or recharge batteries. Therefore, the frequent use of the verbs *chill* and *relax* are attached to the presupposition that such activities will be required, due to the fact that holidaymakers are expected to be out all night partying. Despite the fact that we do not find frequent imperative phrases to the reader to party or get drunk, the relatively high number of 'recovery' imperatives suggests a more subtle way that alcohol consumption is normalized to the reader.

Dispersion plots

One word in Table 3.5 is somewhat unexpected: the verb *work* which occurs 26 times in the corpus. We would perhaps not expect work to feature too often in a corpus about holidays. So it is interesting to explore this word further.

Interestingly, not all of the citations of work actually refer to paid work. The phrase *work on your tan* occurs three times, for example, while *work out cheaper* occurs twice (referring to different holiday

59

packages). However, the phrase *work 2 live* occurs 14 times in the corpus. So far we have considered the term *work* simply in terms of the clusters which it tends to be most (and least) often embedded in. However, another way of looking at the word is to think about where it occurs within individual texts and within the corpus as a whole. Does it generally occur at the beginning of each pamphlet, towards the end or is it evenly spread out throughout each pamphlet? Also, does it occur more often in certain pamphlets than others?

In order to answer these questions it is useful to carry out a dispersion plot of the phrase *work 2 live* across the whole corpus. A dispersion plot gives a visual representation of where a search term occurs (see Figure 3.3).

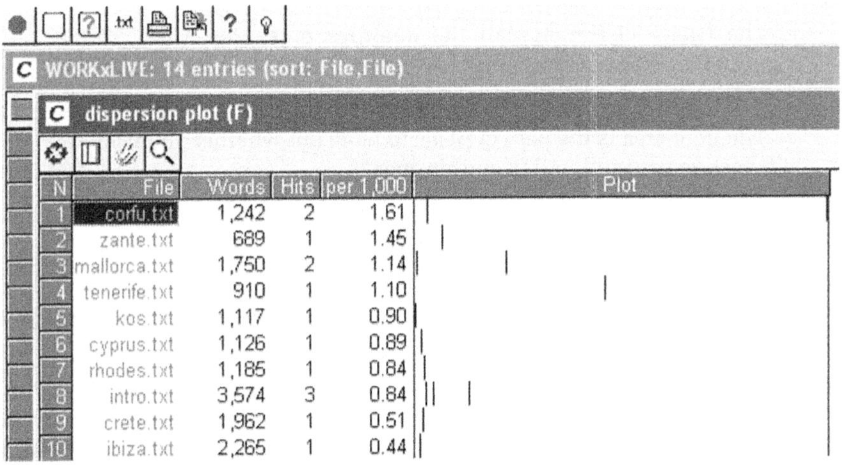

N	File	Words	Hits	per 1,000	Plot
1	corfu.txt	1,242	2	1.61	
2	zante.txt	689	1	1.45	
3	mallorca.txt	1,750	2	1.14	
4	tenerife.txt	910	1	1.10	
5	kos.txt	1,117	1	0.90	
6	cyprus.txt	1,126	1	0.89	
7	rhodes.txt	1,185	1	0.84	
8	intro.txt	3,574	3	0.84	
9	crete.txt	1,962	1	0.51	
10	ibiza.txt	2,265	1	0.44	

Figure 3.3 *Dispersion plot of the phrase* work 2 live *in the holiday corpus*

The dispersion plot shows ten of the files in the corpus, each represented by a single row. Two of the files, cancun.txt and gran.txt did not contain any references to *work 2 live*, so do not appear on the dispersion plot. As well as giving the file name, we are also told the total number of words in each file, the number of 'hits' (occurrences of the phrase *work 2 live*) and the number of occurrences per 1,000 words in the corpus. Then we are given a visual representation of where each occurrence of the phrase *work 2 live* occurs in the corpus. Each vertical black line represents one occurrence. The plot has also been standardized, so that each file in the corpus appears to be of the same length. This is useful, in that it allows us to compare where occurrences of the search term appears, across multiple files.

Looking at the plot, we can see then that for nine of the files, the term *work 2 live* occurs very close to the beginning of each individual text. Why is this the case? An investigation of the texts themselves is required. By taking a closer look at the beginnings of the pamphlets it becomes apparent that the majority of them begin with a short description of a (possibly fictional) holidaymaker:

> Clare, Bank Clerk: just worked the last 3 Saturdays – this Saturday she's having a laugh on the beach ... don't miss out, work 2 live

> Thea, Waitress: fed-up with serving food and drink to everyone else. Up for being the customer herself ... don't miss out, work 2 live

> Matt, Chef: the pressure of 80 covers a night has done his swede in, now he's letting off steam ... don't miss out, work 2 live

Therefore, the beginning of each brochure follows the same pattern:

> [Name of person] [Occupation] [Description of undesirable working conditions] [Description of preferable holiday] don't miss out, work 2 live.

The importance of this pattern, occurring as it does at the beginning of most of the brochures, and having the same structure, illustrates the over-arching ideology of Club 18–30, as a holiday destination that offers escapism from the mundanity and grind of everyday working life. The pattern ends with two imperatives: *don't miss out* and *work 2 live*. The phrase *work 2 live* therefore implies that working is somehow not living, but a means to living – and that a Club 18–30 holiday constitutes living.

So that gives us an idea about discourses of tourism in the Club 18–30 holiday leaflets. However, a further aspect of discourses is that they help to construct the identity of both the producer and consumer of a text. For example, the descriptions of characters employed in unfulfilling jobs, escaping to a holiday, sets up a process of identification for the reader, constructing expectations about why readers may want to go on holiday and what activities they will engage in on arrival. Identity construction and identitification are important processes in advertising discourses. Readers may be encouraged to identify with aspirational ideals or with identity constructions who are more realistic, e.g. less aspirational but similar to themselves. In what other ways can reader identity be constructed? Blommaert (2005: 15) suggests:

> Language users have repertoires containing different sets of varieties ... People, consequently are not entirely free when they communicate, they are restrained by the range and structure of their repertoires, and the distribution of elements of the repertoires in

> any society is unequal… What people actually produce as discourse
> will be conditioned by their sociolinguistic background.

Therefore, we could argue that lexical choices here are related in some way to identity.

On reading this chapter, you may have noticed a number of informal terms and phrases which have appeared in the holiday corpus: *heaps of bars* or *chill out* for example. At this stage we may want to inquire why such terms are so popular in the corpus, and what contribution they make towards identity construction.

In order to determine how and why this is the case, it is useful to carry out an exploration of these informal lexis, both in the holiday corpus and in a general corpus of spoken English in more detail.

Comparing demographic frequencies

By examining the frequency list again, the most frequent informal terms in the corpus were collected and are presented in Table 3.6.

Table 3.6 *The most frequent informal terms in the holiday corpus*

Rank	Verb	Frequency in holiday corpus	Frequency in written BNC	Frequency in spoken BNC
1	action	30	239.78	87.9
2	chill	29	8.73	2.22
3	loads	25	9.15	64.21
4	mates	15	7.42	9.67
5	cool	12	41.69	17.7
6	chilled	11	3.9	0.58
7	massive	11	45.48	32.49
8	fab	10	1.29	0.58
9	info	10	2.26	0.97
10	tons	10	12.33	7.06

Clearly, in compiling this table it was necessary to explore the contexts of some of these words in detail, in order to remove occurrences that were not used in a colloquial or informal way. In addition, the categorization of a word as being 'informal' is somewhat subjective. For example, the most frequent informal word *action* occurred in phrases like 'There's always plenty of action here during the day' rather than in phrases like 'The government took action to establish her whereabouts.' So in the holiday corpus, *action* refers to general excitement, activity and fun.

The table also shows the frequencies per million words of the terms in the written and spoken sections of the British National Corpus.

Perhaps surprisingly, most of the terms occurred proportionally more often in written, rather than spoken British English (the exceptions being *loads* and *mates*). However, this is due to the fact that most of the colloquial terms in the list are derived from non-colloquial words, so would be expected to occur more often in formal, written English. For example, *tons of steel* (formal) vs. *tons of fun* (informal). The spoken texts tend to contain many of the more informal meanings of the words in Table 3.6. And when the words occurred as informal in the written texts in the BNC, a high proportion of these cases referred to reported speech in novels. So why do we find a reasonably high proportion of informal lexis in the holiday corpus? One line of enquiry I want to explore is to consider which sorts of people are more likely to use informal language in their speech, by referring to a reference corpus.

Using the spoken section of the BNC, I explored the demographic frequencies of the words *loads, mates, cool, massive, fab, info* and *tons*. I did not look at *chill, chilled* and *action* as these words did not occur very often in their colloquial form in the BNC, even in spoken British English. Therefore the data would need a great deal of combing through and editing before any conclusions could be made. Table 3.7 shows the combined frequencies per million words for these three words in terms of sex, age and social class.[4]

Table 3.7 Combined frequencies per million words of loads, mates, cool, massive, fab, info and tons in the BNC for age, sex and social class

Demographic	Group	Frequency per million
Age	0–14	538.85
	15–24	615.88
	25–34	304.19
	35–44	371.6
	45–59	235.02
	60+	225.32
Sex	Male	376.75
	Female	334.65
Social Class	AB	268.63
	C1	369.39
	C2	311.74
	DE	347.8

From this table it can be seen that in terms of age, the 15–24 group use these terms most often, males use these terms slightly more than females, and social class C1 use the terms more than other social class grouping. The strongest influence on usage seems to be age, whereas the weakest appears to be gender. However, it is important at this stage not to conclude that the most typical speaker of these sorts of words is a composite of these three demographics, e.g. a male aged 15–24 from social class C1. Different demographic factors can cause interaction effects – for example, hypothetically the high proportion of C1 speakers in the table could be due to the fact the these words are very commonly used by C1 females rather than C1 males, whereas the combined occurrences of these words from social groupings AB, C2 and DE could all consist of males only. It is therefore useful to cross tabulate the demographics in order to get a clearer picture of how they interact together (see Table 3.8).

Table 3.8 Combined frequencies per million words of loads, mates, cool, massive, fab, info and tons in the BNC, cross-tabulated for sex, age and social class

	Males				Females			
	AB	**C1**	**C2**	**DE**	**AB**	**C1**	**C2**	**DE**
0–14	187.72	559.69	367.95	417.01	216	56.64	319.71	0
15–24	702.76	263.44	313.17	680.59	422.42	417.81	587.9	406.91
25–34	0	214.4	171.8	178.52	218.48	155.38	201.11	365.21
35–44	125.37	106.52	177.61	0	128.21	119.68	122.73	125.39
45–49	182.07	127.22	45.77	63.75	77.77	138.92	130.3	118.9
60+	43.67	0	54.35	143.82	107.24	68.47	74.4	218.73

Table 3.8 gives a much more sophisticated and complex picture of the frequencies of these informal words in society. While males aged 15–24 from social class C1 use these words quite often (263.44 occurrences per million words) they are by no means the most frequent users. This distinction goes to males aged 15–24 from social class AB (702.76 occurrences per million words). Other high users are males aged 0–14 from social class C1 and females aged 15–24 from social class C2.

How can we then link these findings to the presence of these sorts of terms in the holiday corpus? There are a number of possible answers. First, perhaps the texts were written by males aged between 15–24. This is possible, but unlikely.

More likely then, is that the leaflets were written with certain social groups in mind, emulating the typical language that those groups would use themselves and therefore be familiar with. Unsurprisingly, Club 18–30 specifically target their age demographic in their own name, so it makes sense for them to aim the language in their brochures at a young age group – this is confirmed by the high use of colloquial terms found in the 15–24 group in the BNC and in the holiday corpus.

Although AB speakers, on the whole, tend to use fewer colloquial words than other groups, the exception to this are AB males aged 15–24, who, interestingly, use more colloquial terms than anyone else. Perhaps this is an attempt to over-compensate, with young middle-class men desirous to appear more streetwise.

It perhaps should also be noted that some of the cells in Table 3.8 contained frequencies of zero. This shows up one of the potential limitations of this sort of analysis. We should not conclude that males from social group AB instantly stop using colloquialisms once they reach the age of 25, but rather, the refined data sets of different sorts of speakers are perhaps too small to draw accurate conclusions.

So when looking at demographic frequency data it is important to take care before drawing strong conclusions as there are many possible factors at play. When considering different types of demographic data (e.g. age *and* sex *and* social class) it should be borne in mind that individual categories may become quite small or in some cases non-existent, meaning that results may be due to the eccentricities of a small range of speakers. It may also be necessary to take into account context such as the location of the speech (at home vs. outside) or the audience (are young people more likely to use informal language around other young people? Will the presence of older people inhibit their informal language?) Additionally, it may be necessary to take into account issues such as reported speech. One example from a young woman in the BNC illustrates this: 'she said there are loads of them on the cycle path without lights on!' Should this use of *loads* count in the same way as non-reported speech?

Finally, just because words like *loads* occur with a higher frequency in certain social groups than others, that doesn't mean that all people from that social group use words like that all the time, or that people from other groups don't use those words. Instead, high or low frequencies simply tell us about the typical (even stereotypical) language of a particular group. They do not tell us *why* a particular group uses language often (or not) in that way. It may not always be necessary for us to fully explore reasons for that and some socio-linguists do not go beyond descriptions of incidences. If we do try to offer explanations (and as discourse analysts it is generally important to answer the *why* question) we should also try to avoid tautologies: 'young people say *loads* because they are young'. A better (although still somewhat circular) explanation would be 'young people say *loads* because by using informal language they are constructing/performing their identity as distinct to people who do not use this word'. However, in order for such a hypothesis to make sense, we need to assume that people somehow know (consciously or not) what sort of language is

65

typical of different types of identities. And as discussed in Chapter 1, people's intuitions about actual language can be quite poor, e.g. generally people think that more words in English start with 'k', than have 'k' as their third letter (Tversky and Kahneman 1973). However, estimating frequencies of different types of words may be different from estimating stereotypical usage between different social demographics, and people may be more attuned to do the latter.

In any case, for the authors of the holiday leaflets to use informal language in order to index youthful identities we need to assume that they believed that such language was typical of this identity and that the target audience would also 'read' the leaflets in the same way. We may have to find other examples to support our case (for example – does this type of informal language occur very frequently in magazines or television programmes aimed at young people?), and also use our judgement of the author's own linguistic competence (will a highly literate L1 speaker be a better judge of the social nuances and stereo-typical demographic distributions of language than an L2 speaker?)

So I do not therefore advocate over-reliance on demographic frequency data, nor would I recommend using it to make bald statements about absolute 'differences' in language use between social groups. What is more useful, however, is by investigating how a particular word or phrase may be used in order to index a stereotypical social identity based on age, sex or class or a combination of all three, or other factors (bearing in mind that writers/speakers and audiences may or may not all have access to the same sort of stereotypical notions of language and social identity).

What we should be able to glean from the BNC spoken data though, is that the colloquialisms which co-occur in the holiday corpus are most strongly associated with young adults and have clearly been used as a means of creating identification and making the message attractive to its target audience. By using a form of language which is strongly associated with youthful identities, the audience may feel that they are been spoken to in a narrative voice that they would find desirable (the voice of a potential friend or partner) or at least are comfortable with. Here it is perhaps useful to bring in additional non-corpus-based evidence, by looking at the visual aspects of the leaflets.

An examination of the images used in many of the leaflets seems to support this hypothesis – many of them depict young, attractive men and women having fun, either in swimming pools or the sea, or at nightclubs or bars. Several of the pictures show young people enjoying a drink together, while one of the brochures contains a full page advertisement for the vodka-based drink WKD. Another advertisement advises holidaymakers to 'pack some condoms and always choose to use one', while there is also a full page 'Model search' contest, looking for '3 gorgeous girls and 3 fit fellas to be our models of the year ... All you have to do is send a full-length picture in swimwear'. The images of happy holidaymakers in the leaflets are perhaps somewhat idealized, everyone is happy, healthy and attractive; the women are all slender, the men muscular; there are no people who are overweight or wearing glasses. So while these images may not reflect the physical appearances of many of the potential readers of the leaflets, they do show desirable identities, suggesting to readers that these will be the types of people they will meet while on holiday, or even the types of people that they could *become* if they take the holiday.

In addition, the use of colloquialisms also contributes to normalization of certain types of youthful identities. It suggests a shared way of speaking for young people, which may not even be noticed by those who it aims to target. However, young people who do not use informal language may be alerted to a discrepancy between their linguistic identities and those of the people featured in the brochure (and the narrative voice). In a similar way, young people reading the Club 18–30 brochure will be made aware of the expectations placed on them, if they are to take a holiday with the tour operator. They may decide not to go, but if they do, they may face pressure to conform to the over-arching ideology of clubbing, chilling and more clubbing that the brochures put forward, particularly as this ideology is represented as both attractive (through the use of positive evaluation) and hegemonic (due to its repetition and high frequency in the brochures).

Conclusion

To summarize, what has the corpus analysis of the Club 18–30 leaflets revealed about discourses of tourism? The analysis of frequent lexical lemmas revealed some of the most important concepts in the corpus (*bar, club*, etc.) and a more detailed analysis of clusters and individual incidences containing these terms revealed some of the ways that holidaymakers were constructed, for example, as being interested in information about the variety and number of places to drink which are near their holiday accommodation, and likely to need periods of 'chilling' to recover from the excesses of the previous evening. The analysis of the dispersion plot for *work 2 live* revealed how this term constituted a salient part of the overall discourse in the leaflets, being used at the start of each brochure in a repetitive structure which emphasized how working is a means to living which can be achieved by being on holiday.

Interestingly, the leaflets did not explicitly advise holidaymakers to get drunk (and elsewhere in the Club 18–30 website, accusations that tourists are encouraged to drink are dismissed as a myth). However, the frequency analysis does suggest that there are more subtle messages at work. References to sex (another 'myth' according to the Club 18–30 website) also do not appear to be frequent in the leaflets, however, an analysis of the visual content suggests that the leaflets are somewhat sexualized, again with implicit messages. As Morgan and Pritchard (2001: 165) note 'The sheer dominance of these images – many of them taking up a whole page – creates the brochures' atmosphere of sexuality.' Perhaps, in reacting to criticism, Club 18–30 have changed the tone of their leaflets, but at the same time used more oblique references to ensure that certain types of tourist discourses remain intact.

Finally, by investigating how high frequency informal language occurred in a reference corpus of spoken British English, we were able to gain evidence in order to create hypotheses about how the readership of the holiday leaflets were constructed.

Frequency counts can be useful, but as we have seen, their functionality is limited. Their main use is in directing the reader towards aspects of a corpus or text which occur often and therefore may or may not show evidence of the author making a specific lexical choice over others, which could relate to the presentation of a particular discourse or attempts to construct identity in some way. Comparing the relative frequencies in a text or smaller corpus to a reference corpus is one good way of denoting whether a word occurs more or less often than expected (we will look at a more thorough way of doing this in Chapter 6). Examining frequent clusters of words or their dispersions across a text (or set of texts) may be more revealing than just looking at words in isolation, and as the course of this chapter developed it became clear that context plays an important role in the analysis of particular words, something which is difficult to achieve from looking at frequencies alone. For this reason, the following chapters expand on the notion of simple frequency to consider corpus-based analyses which take into account context. In the following chapter we consider the investigation of concordances in detail.

Notes

1. Exceptions could include extremely restricted forms of language which do not adhere to usual grammatical rules, such as shopping lists.
2. www.club18–30.biz/attitude.asp.
3. www.club18–30.com/ab_myths.php.

4. The social classifications in the BNC are based on occupation and are as follows AB: higher and intermediate managerial, administrative and professional. C1: Supervisory, clerical and junior management, administrative and professional. C2: Skilled manual. DE: Semi-skilled and unskilled manual, casual labourers, state pensioners and the unemployed.

4 Concordances

Introduction

So far we have seen some of the ways that frequencies can be used in order to uncover the existence of discourses in text. We have considered word counts (and comparisons across different texts or between different types of speakers) and the use of dispersion data which shows the spread and position of particular terms in a text. We have also expanded on the notion of simple lexical frequencies to examine multi-word units or clusters. The notion of clusters is important because it begins to take into account the context that a single word is placed in.

Frequency lists can be helpful in determining the focus of a text, but care must be taken not to make presuppositions about the ways that words are actually used within it. This is where taking an approach which combines quantitative and qualitative analysis will be more productive than simply relying on quantitative methods alone. A *concordance analysis* is one of the most effective techniques which allows researchers to carry out this sort of close examination.

A concordance is simply a list of all of the occurrences of a particular search term in a corpus, presented within the context that they occur in; usually a few words to the left and right of the search term. A concordance is also sometimes referred to as key word in context or a KWIC, although it should be noted that 'key word in context' has a different meaning to the concept of key words which is discussed in Chapter 6. Here *key word* simply means the word that is currently under examination – and that can be any word that takes the interest of the researcher. In Chapter 6 I outline a way of determining the most salient words in a text or corpus by more statistical, precise means.

In order to demonstrate how concordances can be of use to discourse analysis, I want to use this chapter to carry out an examination of a new set of data – a corpus of newspaper articles. Newspaper articles are one of the easiest text types to collect; thanks to the existence of numerous searchable internet archives the data already exists in electronic form (see Chapter 2 for a discussion of this and some of the issues involved in collecting internet data). Indeed, the relative ease in which newspaper data can be appropriated for corpus use suggests that it should be employed with care rather than overused (see also Cameron 1998: 41–3). However, newspaper data is clearly a very useful area of producing and reproducing discourses. As Fairclough (1989: 54) observes:

> The hidden power of media discourse and the capacity of ... power-holders to exercise this power depend on systematic tendencies in news reporting and other media activities. A single text on its own is quite insignificant: the effects of media power are cumulative, working through the repetition of particular ways of handling causality and agency, particular ways of positioning the reader, and so forth.

Journalists are able to influence their readers by producing their own discourses or helping to reshape existing ones. Such discourses are often shaped by citing the opinions of those in powerful and privileged positions. Becker (1972: xx) calls this the 'hierarchy of credibility' whereby powerful people will come to have their opinions accepted because they are understood to have access to more accurate information on particular topics than everyone else. Hall *et al* (1978: 58) say 'The result of this structured preference given in the media to the opinions of the powerful is that these "spokesmen" become what we call the primary definers of topics.'

However, audiences are not passive: as McIlvenny (1996) suggests, meaning is created from interaction between a text and its readers. Texts can only take on meaning when consumers interact with them. For example, Hermes (1995) shows how readers of traditional women's magazines viewed them as a marker of low-status, e.g. 'You forget as soon as you've read it' but used them as an activity that filled time and did not require much attention. The readership of a newspaper also has the opportunity to respond, via its letters page, although only a proportion of letters are published, and the newspaper has the capacity to veto, edit or prioritize those which it decides to print. Readers may also refuse to buy a newspaper if they disagree strongly enough with the discourses it regularly employs. For example, the *Daily Mirror's* circulation fell to below two million for the first time in 70 years during its coverage of the 2003 war on Iraq, which was linked to its anti-war stance (Gibson 2003).

Discourses within newspapers are usually the result of collaboration between multiple contributors. For example, while each newspaper generally has an overarching political stance, within a single edition of a newspaper, different articles may express a variety of views on the same subject (particularly among newspapers which aim to represent 'balanced' coverage of an event). So some writers might be employed specifically because they hold unpopular or controversial views. In addition, a single story is unlikely to have been 'written' by just one person. Articles may be cropped or changed by numerous copywriters, sub-editors and editors before they are published. Also, newspapers can alter their stance on different subjects over time, so we would expect discourses within newspapers to be conflicting and shifting over any given period. Therefore when using a corpus of newspaper articles it is important to bear in mind that the processes of production and reception of any particular article are complex and multiple. Newspaper discourses, where they exist, should not therefore be taken out of context or always viewed as mainstream or hegemonic just because they have occurred within a newspaper.

Investigating discourses of refugees

Bearing this in mind, the topic I wish to examine in newspaper discourse is that of refugees. Refugees are a particularly interesting subject to analyse in terms of discourse because they consist of one of the most relatively powerless groups in society. One aspect of this conceptualization of discourse relating to 'ways of looking at the world' is that it enables or encourages a critical perspective of language and society. The Foucaultian view of discourse has been used in connection with *critical social research*, a form of academic enquiry which aims to achieve a better understanding of how societies work. Fairclough (2003: 202) defines a number of starting questions for critical social research such as 'how do existing societies provide people with the possibilities and resources for rich and fulfilling lives, how on the other hand do they deny people these possibilities and resources?' Consequently, critical discourse analysis (CDA) is a form of critical social research that can be applied to a range of texts in order to address these and other questions. Wodak and Meyer (2001: 96) refer to CDA as 'discourse analysis with an attitude', although the lines between DA and CDA are sometimes rather blurred. Van Dijk (2001: 353) notes that CDA does not have a unitary theoretical framework although there are conceptual and theoretical frameworks (e.g. Marxism) which are closely linked to CDA. Two basic questions of CDA are 'How do (more) powerful groups control public discourse' and 'How does such discourse control the mind and action of (less)

73

powerful groups, and what are the social consequences of such control, such as social inequality?' (van Dijk *ibid.* 355).

Van Dijk (1996: 91–4) also points out that minority groups are frequent topics of political talk and text, but have very little control over their representations in political discourse. Lack of access to journalists means that minority speakers tend to be less quoted than majority speakers (van Dijk 1991), and those who are quoted tend to either be chosen because they represent the views of the majority, or because they are extremists who are quoted in order to facilitate attack (Downing 1980). In the media, refugees are rarely able to construct their own identities and discourses surrounding themselves, but instead have such identities and discourses constructed for them, by more powerful spokespeople.

In order to construct the corpus of newspaper articles an internet-based archive called Newsbank[1] was used. Newsbank contains articles from a large variety of British broadsheet and tabloid newspapers including the *Daily Mail*, the *Daily Mirror*, *The Guardian*, *The Times*, *The Observer* and *The Independent*. In order to make the corpus manageable, only articles which were published in the year 2003 were considered. However, it should be noted that in creating a corpus containing newspaper articles from a broad range of political and ideological positions it will not be possible to say anything about discourses from say, a right-wing or a tabloid perspective without further restricting the corpus data or examining different parts of it separately – instead, we can only talk about *newspaper discourses* in the broadest sense of the term.

Newsbank allows users to carry out searches for articles containing a particular word or phrase, so this enabled the creation of a corpus containing all of the articles from the year 2003 which included the words *refugee* or *refugees*. In itself this restricts the analysis of discourse further – there may be articles that do not refer to refugees explicitly but still contain discourses of refugees by using say, euphemistic or more racist terminology, e.g. *illegals*, *aliens*, *detainees*. Examining the relative frequencies of such words and how they are used would certainly be a worthwhile component of a corpus-based study into refugees but is beyond the scope of this chapter.

The total size of the corpus of newspaper articles was 76,205 words, which contained 53 occurrences of the word *refugee* and 87 cases of the word *refugees* – a total of 140 examples to examine. So how would a researcher set about analysing a concordance of these two words?

In the first instance, it is necessary to create a concordance. This can be achieved by loading the corpus into a concordancing program.

A number of concordancers are available (see Table 4.1 which was accurate at the time of writing – costs and website addresses are subject to change however).

Table 4.1 *Some concordance software available from the internet at the time of writing*

Concordancer	Platform	Cost	Website
Conc	Mac	freeware	www.sil.org/computing/conc/conc.html
MicroConcord	PC	freeware	www.liv.ac.uk/~ms2928/software/
WordSmith Tools	PC	£50 UK	www.lexically.net/wordsmith/index.html
Concordance	PC	£55 UK	www.concordancesoftware.co.uk/
Mono Conc	PC	$85 US	www.athel.com/mono.html
Simple Concordance Program	PC	freeware	www.textworld.com/scp

Note that this is only a small sample of available concordancers, there are many older concordancers which are now more difficult to obtain, e.g. the Longman Mini Concordancer and WordCruncher, and there are still others in development. Potential corpus users are encouraged to carry out their own internet-based searches for concordancers and decide for themselves which would be the most appropriate for them to use, taking into consideration price, platform, features, output, search options and relative ease of use. In addition, there are other concordancers in existence which can only be used in conjunction with a particular corpus: BNCweb and Cobuild Direct for example.

For the purposes of this corpus, as with the previous chapter I will be using WordSmith Tools as it has a high level of functionality and is a concordancer that I am already familiar with. However, other types of concordance software are likely to be equally as useful for this task. Figure 4.1 shows a screenshot from WordSmith's Concord tool which is used in order to carry out concordances. Note that within WordSmith it is possible to carry out searches on more than one word at a time by using the forward slash symbol /. More complex searches may be carried out by using the asterisk symbol * which acts as a 'wildcard'. For example, if we specify a search for the term *refug**, we will actually be searching for all of the words that begin with *refug*: *refuge*, *refuges*, *refugee* and *refugees*. Different concordance programs offer their own distinct search syntax, some more sophisticated than others.

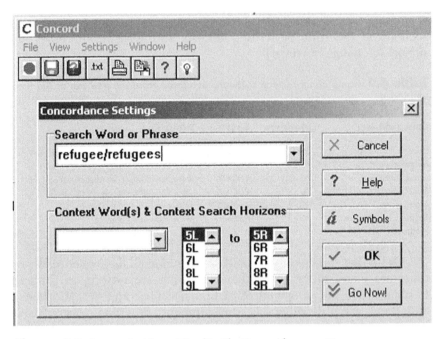

Figure 4.1 Screenshot from WordSmith: Concordance settings

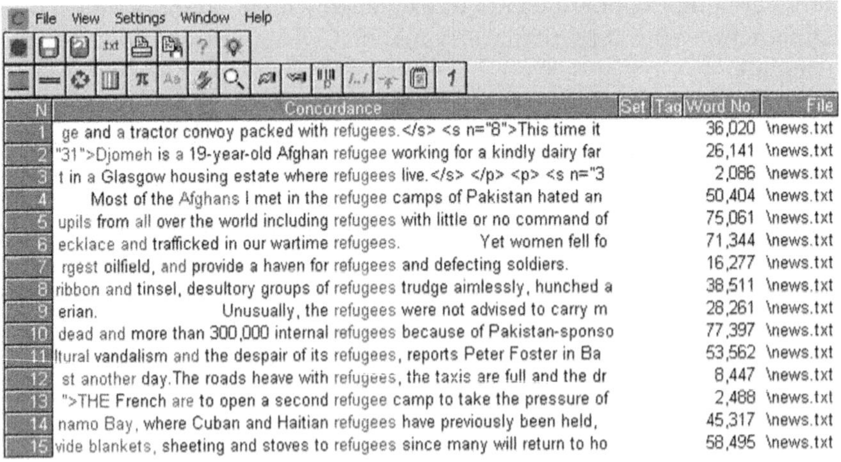

Figure 4.2 Concordance of refugee/refugees

Having specified the search terms, Figure 4.2 shows the first 15 lines of the concordance for *refugee/refugees*. We are going to consider the terms *refugee* and *refugees* at the same time, although it may also be useful to examine them separately as well. For example, Partington (2003: 14) notes that absent quantifiers (occurring when using plural nouns) may result in information being obscured, allowing text producers to be imprecise and thereby creating over-generalizations (e.g. *men are rapists*).

Each concordance line shows an occurrence of the search term, with a few words of context either side of it. In all, this concordance contains 140 lines of data, so lines 16–140 are not shown in Figure 4.2. So now we have a concordance, what can we do with it and how can it tell us something about discourses of refugees in newspapers? The object of creating concordances is to look for patterns of language use, based on repetitions. Identifying such patterns may help us to note discourses, particularly if the patterns are relatively common. So we first need to scan the concordance lines, trying to pick out similarities in language use, by looking at the words and phrases which occur to the left and right hand sides of the terms *refugee* and *refugees*. We can see then, that this is a much more qualitative form of analysis than simply looking at frequency lists.

What (if anything) is interesting about this concordance? Looking at lines 1–15, there are a couple of small patterns which might warrant further examination. The phrase *refugee camp* and *refugee camps* occur. There are also several cases where a proper noun indicating nationality or location occurs before the search term: *Haitian, Afghan*. Some of the verbs: *trafficked, trudge, heave, packed* are also quite suggestive. However, in terms of discourses, this is not particularly illuminating so far.

Sorting concordances

Perhaps the problem is that the patterns are difficult to spot because the concordance lines are presented to us in order in which they occur in the corpus. While this may make sense in one way – e.g. to start at the beginning and work towards the end, it doesn't help us to spot language patterns so easily. Because of this, most concordancers give the researcher the option to sort the concordance in various ways. For example, we could sort the list alphabetically one or more places to the left or right of the search term. WordSmith allows multiple sorts (up to three at once) to be carried out at the same time. So for example, we could sort the concordance one place alphabetically to the left, then two places to the left, then one place to the right. Figure 4.3 shows the beginning of the concordance for *refugee/refugees* which has been alphabetically sorted first one place to the left and secondly two places to the left. What does this sorted concordance tell us? Lines 1–6 all contain numbers – which in terms of sorting are placed before the letters a–z. After that, lines 7–12 contain the phrase *a refugee* – because the word *a* occurs first in the alphabet. After that, we have *Afghan refugee*. Looking at lines 7–12 though, we have evidence of our second sort occurring here – this is on the word which occurs two places to the left of *refugee*. So *as a refugee* (lines 7 and 8) occurs before *in a refugee* line 9), because *as* occurs alphabetically before *in*.

N	Concordance
1	nd TV and video equipment to help Sighthill's 1,200 refugees learn English.</s> </p> </text> </doc
2	injuries after being pelted with stones by up to 100 refugees.　　　　Last night Fisk was rec
3	fghanistan have called for an end to US bombing 11 Refugees return Tens of thousands of Afghan ref
4	ral months before the bulk of the Shomali's 200,000 refugees return: "The major obstacle is the prese
5	> </p> <p> <s n="8">"And the tragedy of 22million refugees is another deep wound in our world - a w
6	ed people could follow.　　Pakistan hosts 3m refugees and Iran 2.5m, while a further 1.5m are c
7	ed mullah had fled across the Pakistan border as a refugee in the company of his senior men, and c
8	table, the Holy Family was forced to take Him as a refugee to Egypt.</s> <s n="20">Herod was blin
9	Africa.　　He was filming for Comic Relief in a refugee camp.　　"There was a boy there \
10	mething to savour.　　Owen may look like a refugee from a Hovis ad, but as Sven-Goran Eriks
11	0 wounded early today as Israeli tanks moved on a refugee camp in the Gaza Strip.</s> </p> <p> <
12	<p> <s n="1">A RED CROSS boss kept secret a refugee plot to storm the Channel Tunnel on Chris
13	to the canal in Peshawar, home to 300,000 Afghan refugees.　　On the ground floor two gyna
14	Daily Mail: Newsman Fisk stoned by Afghan refugees　　NULL　　NULL
15	iting.</s> </p> <p> <s n="9">Children like Afghan refugee Roya Mosleni, ten, who is spearheading
16	sk was attacked and beaten up by a mob of Afghan refugees in Pakistan yesterday.　　F

Figure 4.3 Concordance of refugee/refugees sorted alphabetically 1 place to the left, then 2 places to the left

A concordance, when sorted in this way, starts to reveal some of its patterns of language. And even this small sample (remember that the full concordance consists of 140 entries) is interesting. For example, the fact that six of these entries contain numbers when sorted one place to the left suggests that quantification is one way that refugees are characterized. However, it is not only in lines 1–6 where numbers occur. Line 13 refers to *300,000 Afghan refugees*. Therefore some form of quantification occurs in almost half of the first 16 lines of the concordance. Our sorted concordance gave us evidence for one pattern by alerting us to its existence, but it is then useful to look through the remaining concordance lines to see if numbers occur elsewhere.

And our further investigation bears fruit. Table 4.2 shows cases taken from the whole concordance where quantification of some kind occurs in conjunction with the search term. Note that these quantification terms don't always occur one place to the left, nor are they restricted to a single word, or have to contain an exact reference to a number. Phrases like 'more and more' and 'swelling the number of' are ways of quantifying without giving precise numbers.

Table 4.2 *Quantification of refugees*

1	Pakistan hosts **3m**	refugees	and Iran **2.5m**, while a further **1.5m** a
2	s concerned for the **thousands of** Afghan	refugees	and she wanted to spotlight their terr
3	**Tens of thousands of** Afghan	refugees	are streaming home in the vanguard o
4	000 dead **and more than 300,000** internal	refugees	because of Pakistan-sponsored te
5	a fascinating documentary has traced **five**	refugee	children who were rescued from p
6	anistan, which is **swelling the number of**	refugees	daily, and tightened security by ferry
7	more grieving widows and children, **more**	refugees	fleeing in terror and dying in agony.
8	Our coverage of the deaths of **eight**	refugees	found in a container near Wexford
9	**Four million**	refugees	have fled in a quarter of a century of
10	terror network rages, **two** Afghan	refugees	in northern Iran seek solace in the scr
11	tacked and beaten up by **a mob of** Afghan	refugees	in Pakistan yesterday.
12	**EIGHT**	refugees	, including two children, were found
13	"And the tragedy of **22 million**	refugees	is another deep wound in our world -
14	fter being pelted with stones by **up to 100**	refugees	. Last night Fisk was recovering in hi
15	video equipment to help Sighthill's **1,200**	refugees	learn English.
16	shawar, home to **300,000** Afghan	refugees	. On the ground floor two gynaeco
17	before the bulk of the Shomali's **200,000**	refugees	return: "The major obstacle is the pre
18	**Eight**	Refugee	Stowaways Die In Lorry
19	in March after **19** Kurdish	refugees	were found in the back of his lorry.
20	the problem is in sight as **more and more**	refugees	are delivered to northern France by t

In some cases, these types of quantification suggest that the amount of refugees is troublesome. In the example below (an expansion of line 11 in Table 4.2), the reference to the large number (*a mob, up to 100*) of refugees in the article serves to enhance their danger.

> BRITISH journalist Robert Fisk was attacked and beaten up by a mob of Afghan refugees in Pakistan yesterday ... He suffered head, face and hand injuries after being pelted with stones by up to 100 refugees.

Some of the attempts to quantify refugees suggest an underlying discourse concerning alarm over their growing numbers.

> The camp ... is currently filled far beyond capacity. Because of the upheaval in Afghanistan, which is swelling the number of refugees daily ...

Interestingly, this example (taken from line 6 in Table 4.2) uses a liquid metaphor – refugees are described as filled beyond capacity and their numbers are swelling.

As well as the pattern of quantification connected to refugees,

Table 4.2 shows evidence of another pattern. In line 3 refugees are described as 'streaming home', in line 7 they are 'fleeing', in line 9 they 'have fled', in line 17 they 'return' and in line 20 they are 'delivered'. This pattern suggests that refugees are often described in terms of their movement. An examination of the other concordance lines reveals more instances like this (see Table 4.3).

Table 4.3 Movement of refugees

1	and the Holy Family **fleeing** as	refugees	to Egypt. Jesus relives exodus and e
2	les of 1950, Shaw was engaged in **carrying**	refugees	from East Pakistan to Calcutta and t
3	They can also help to **attract**	refugees	**back** to their homes and thousands of
4	oilfield, **and provide a haven for**	refugees	and defecting soldiers.
5	ght the Taliban bombed Talin Chee, **forcing**	refugees	**into another village** and finally the
6	d and broke down close to a village **housing**	refugees	who had **fled** across the border fro
7	which is **swelling** the number of	refugees	daily, and tightened security by ferry
8	and tinsel, desultory groups of	refugees	**trudge aimlessly**, hunched against a
9	alert to deal with the **flood of**	refugees	. Border residents also left their hom
10	e brightly painted trucks bearing **returning**	refugees	sitting on tottering piles of their pos
11	kish gangsters who have been **transporting**	refugees	from Ankara and Istanbul via Zeebru
12	a bridge and a tractor convoy **packed with**	refugees	. This time it is thought the Americ
13	nother day. The roads **heave with**	refugees	, the taxis are full and the drivers stil
14	e Holy Family was forced to **take** Him as a	refugee	to Egypt.
15	llah had **fled** across the Pakistan border as a	refugee	in the company of his sen
16	N Pushtuns who were **stranded** in nearby	refugee	camps when the Taliban fled may be
17	starvation or disease in the **overflowing**	refugee	camps, then clearly the number of d
18	e problem is in sight as more and more	refugees	**are delivered to** northern France by
19	Tens of thousands of Afghan	refugees	**are streaming back** to their homes a
20	Tens of thousands of Afghan	refugees	**are streaming home** in the vanguar
21	tal hit, or children crippled by landmines, or	refugees	**driven** from their homes by military
22	e more grieving widows and children, more	refugees	**fleeing** in terror and dying in agony.
23	Four million	refugees	have **fled** in a quarter of a century of
24	Guantanamo Bay, where Cuban and Haitian	refugees	have previously **been held**, and is
25		Refugees	... **have returned** to rubble
26	d Kabul risked straining under the weight of	refugees	**in transit**.
27	mercy mission to **bring** the young European	refugees	into homes all over the country.
28		Refugees	**Return**. Tens of thousands of Afgh
20	ths before the bulk of the Shomali's 200,000	refugees	**return**: "The major obstacle is the
30	, and those shots of	refugees	**smuggling themselves** on to Eurost

This pattern often uses verb phrases which suggest a range of evaluative responses which construct refugees as victims or a collective group undergoing suffering: e.g. *fleeing refugees, refugees_trudge aimlessly, hunched against a biting wind, roads heave with refugees*. As with the *filled to capacity* example noted earlier, a number of movement metaphors liken refugees to liquid (usually water) in some way: *swelling the numbers of refugees, the flood of refugees, refugees are streaming home, refugees are streaming back to their homes, overflowing refugee camps.*

In a sense then, refugees are constructed as a 'natural disaster' like a flood, which is difficult to control as it has no sense of its own agency. Phrases such as 'trudge aimlessly' help to construct refugees as having no real understanding of their situation or what motivates them. Consider also the phrase 'desultory groups of refugees' (Table 4.3, line 8).

The movement of refugees is constructed as an elemental force which is difficult to predict and has no sense of control. If refugees are likened to the movement of water, then they are dehumanized and something that requires control in order to prevent disaster to others (e.g. non-refugees).

As well as describing the movement of refugees as being uncontrolled, a number of phrases focus on movement in terms of large quantities: e.g. *roads heave with refugees, packed with refugees.*

Closely related to the notion of packed refugees are another set of movement descriptors connected to refugees being associated with the transportation of objects and goods. Other concordance lines show that refugees are *in transit, delivered, transported, carried* and *smuggled.*

> For the locals, no end to the problem is in sight as more and more refugees are delivered to northern France by traffickers.

Therefore, as well as being described as an elemental force (water), refugees are also constructed in terms of metaphors which construct them as transported goods or packages – again, as a token of their dehumanization.

We have uncovered a great deal from where we started from – just by looking at the first few lines of a sorted concordance and extrapolating from an obvious pattern involving the quantification of refugees. However, going back to that original sorted concordance, it becomes clear that there are other patterns within it. For example, in Figure 4.4, which shows lines 49–63 of the sorted concordance, there is a different sort of pattern – the phrase *for refugees.*

A closer look at this pattern reveals that it always occurs as [noun phrase] *for refugees* and that in each case the noun phrase describes something positive: *assistance, reception centre, UN high commissioner, haven, school.* Therefore this pattern suggests that refugees are the subject of help in some way. A closer look at the remainder of the concordance reveals additional cases which do not follow the pattern [noun phrase] *for refugees* but do entail official attempts to help them (see Table 4.4). This involves the use of words such as *help, agency, action, concerned, mercy, shelters* and *rescued.*

N	Concordance
49	rived just before 3am. There ensued refugee-like scenes where pregnant women, elde
50	ating a mercy mission to bring the young European refugees into homes all over the country.</s> </ɽ
51	piritual home to the reclusive one-eyed cleric', every refugee's bundle being 'pathetic', every enclave be
52	"2">Now a fascinating documentary has traced five refugee children who were rescued from poverty-s
53	for children in India and humanitarian assistance for refugees in Afghanistan. A sad s
54	at Citywest will be turned into a reception centre for refugees and the homeless. President I
55	ty chief of mission of the UN high commissioner for refugees. Agencies are racing to
56	de agreements with the UN High Commissioner for Refugees on the role of the peacekeeping forces;
57	, seize Iraq's largest oilfield, and provide a haven for refugees and defecting soldiers. This w
58	s a day. On the first floor is the school for refugees and orphans. His home
59	e next night the Taliban bombed Talin Chee, forcing refugees into another village and finally the haven
60	ISRAELI helicopters hit a Gaza refugee camp with missiles twice, killing three Pa
61	ere still clashes between the two groups at a Gaza refugee site.</s> </p> <p> <s n="16">Two peop
62	gun at Guantanamo Bay, where Cuban and Haitian refugees have previously been held, and is expec
63	antanamo housed thousands of Cuban and Haitian refugees in the mid-1990s and offers huge securi

Figure 4.4 Concordance lines 49–63

Phrases such as *refugee action*, *refugee service* and *refugee agency*, describe official bodies involved in running organizations, and discuss attempts to enable refugees to 'integrate into society', particularly by learning the language of their host country or by going to school. Therefore this suggests a particular discourse of refugees – as a group who are the passive recipients of help.

Looking down the rest of our sorted concordance I wasn't able to find any other patterns which stood out as particularly interesting. Rather than ending the analysis here, I decided to carry out the same

Table 4.4 Official attempts to help refugees

1	**helped** the UNHCR return	refugees	in East Timor;
2	Margaret Curran welcomes new funding to **help**	refugees	integrate into society.
3	Last week we looked at	Refugee	**Action**. Here, Belinda Beresfor
4	id expansion was straining resources, said the UN	refugee	**agency**.
5	Now a fascinating documentary has traced five	refugee	children who were **rescued** fro
6	, who is chief executive of the Northern England	Refugee	**Service**, said: "If she went into
7	Bob Dylan and Eric Clapton performed **in aid of**	refugees	of Bangladesh in 1971.
8	"She was **concerned for** the thousands of Afghan	refugees	and she wanted
9	ing a **mercy mission** to bring the young European	refugees	into homes all over the
10	On the first floor is the **school for**	refugees	and orphans.
11	tywest will be turned into a **reception centre for**	refugees	and the homeless.
12	hildren in India and **humanitarian assistance for**	refugees	in Afghanistan.
13	hief of mission of the **UN high commissioner for**	Refugees	. Agencies are racing to provide
14	agreements with the **UN High Commissioner for**	Refugees	on the role of the peacekeeping
15	He was filming for **Comic Relief** in a	refugee	camp.
16	the French close the **Red Cross**	refugee	camp at Sangatte. However, th
17	into the love which feeds the hungry, **shelters** the	refugee	, and confronts violence and p

exercise again, but this time by using a different sort. Often a different perspective reveals fresh information. This time I sorted two places to the left and then three places to the left. An examination of this newly sorted concordance revealed other patterns – including a relatively high occurrence of the phrase *of X refugee(s)* (see Figure 4.5). So why does this pattern occur? At a first glance the most obvious pattern is the phrase *thousands of Afghan refugees,* which occurs in lines 88–91. There are also other concordance lines containing quantification here: lines 79, 81, 83 and 92. So is this simply evidence of something we have already found?

Taking a closer look at Figure 4.5 reveals another pattern. Lines 86 and 87 both feature the phrase *the plight of X refugee(s).* Are there any other concordance lines which express similar sentiments? Line 82 mentions *the despair of its refugees,* whereas line 92 refers to *the tragedy of 22 million refugees.* So here we have four cases which tell a similar story – the words *plight, tragedy* and *despair* all have similar meanings, and they all occur as part of a similar grammatical pattern containing the term *refugees.* Line 81 refers to *deaths of eight refugees,* which although this phrase doesn't fit as neatly into the pattern as the other cases, is still describing a tragic incident. I therefore looked through the other concordance lines, making notes of all of the cases where refugees were described in a way that connected them to tragic circumstances.

N	Concordance
77	, who is chief executive of the Northern England Refugee Service, said: "If she went into Af
78	NULL EIGHT refugees, including two children, were foun
79	l in Afghanistan, which is swelling the number of refugees daily, and tightened security by f
80	b Dylan and Eric Clapton performed in aid of the refugees of Bangladesh in 1971.
81	<s n="14">Our coverage of the deaths of eight refugees found in a container near Wexforc
82	s with ; cultural vandalism and the despair of its refugees, reports Peter Foster in Bamiyan
83	the BBC said its story was accurate Four of the refugees who led the Chunnel charge were
84	as attacked and beaten up by a mob of Afghan refugees in Pakistan yesterday.
85	they're too rotten to save. None of the refugees has enough calcium. II
86	<p> <s n="93">After seeing the plight of these refugee children, I could not do anything of
87	king undercover to report on the plight of Afghan refugees.</s> </p> <p> <s n="5">But her
88	Tens of thousands of Afghan refugees are streaming home in the vangu;
89	She was concerned for the thousands of Afghan refugees and she wanted to spotlight their
90	She was concerned for the thousands of Afghan refugees and she wanted to spotlight their
91	11 Refugees return Tens of thousands of Afghan refugees are streaming back to their home
92	/p> <p> <s n="8">"And the tragedy of 22million refugees is another deep wound in our wor
93	<p> <s n="31">Djomeh is a 19-year-old Afghan refugee working for a kindly dairy farmer in

Figure 4.5 Concordance showing pattern of X refugee(s)

There were quite a large number of concordance lines where this happened (see Table 4.5). Other words which suggest tragedy in connection with the refugee corpus are, *beg, tottering, solace* and *stricken*. Refugees are reported as starving, dying while locked in containers, seeking solace in religion, queuing for food and attacked by soldiers.

Table 4.5 Tragic circumstances of refugees

1	After seeing the **plight of** these	refugee	children, I could not do any
2	ver to report on the **plight of** Afghan	refugees	. But her f
3	"And the **tragedy of** 22million	refugees	is another deep wound in our world -
4	ltural vandalism and the **despair of** its	refugees	, reports Peter Foster in Bamiyan
5	**wounded** as Israeli tanks moved on a	refugee	camp in the Gaza Strip.
6	Israel **fires** on	refugee	camp
7	Israelis **attacked** the Rafah	refugee	camp – thought to be a stronghold of
8	e **poverty-stricken** Palestinian	refugee	camps of Lebanon, giving your life t
9	s, the ones who haven't made it to the	refugee	camps and **have no relatives** in
10	Cambodian refugees	refugees	continue to **starve**.
11	widows and children, more	refugees	fleeing in terror and **dying** in agony.
12	Our coverage of the **deaths** of eight	refugees	found in a container near Wexford
13	None of the	refugees	**has enough calcium**.
14	two Afghan	refugees	in northern Iran **seek solace** in the sc
15	EIGHT	refugees	.. . were found **dead**
16	ightly painted trucks bearing returning	refugees	on **tottering piles** of their possession
17	t is closing on the gang that sent eight	refugees	to their **deaths** in a lorry container, it
18	Unusually, the	refugees	were **not advised** to carry mobile tele
19	Eight	Refugee	Stowaways **Die** In Lorry
20	It's here you find	refugee	camps that have turned into **shabby** c

Analysing the remainder

Carrying out further sorts on the concordance (for example, by sorting one place to the right) didn't reveal any more interesting patterns or clues about discourses. Is it sensible to end the analysis at this point, assuming that the concordance has yielded everything it has to offer?

One possible avenue of research at this point is simply to consider all of the concordance lines that have *not* already been used to demonstrate the discourses of refugees described above. By removing what we already know about, we are left with what we haven't considered – the remainder, and it might be easier to spot patterns that are less based on words or phrases appearing in repetitive positions, but more due to meaning.

Table 4.6 shows one finding of this exercise. It should be noted that some of the concordance lines are longer than usual, meaning that more context needed to be taken into account before patterns of meaning could be derived from the concordance.

Table 4.6 Refugees as criminals and a nuisance

1	Newsman Fisk **stoned by** Afghan	refugees	
2	**manufactured the explosive** in laboratories hidden in	refugee	camps. Mr Reid is said to have
3	known number of Somali and Djibouti	refugees	have been **arrested** in the past week.
4	There have been **complaints** the	refugees	have caused a steep rise in **petty crime and pushed down house prices**
5	Four of the	refugees	who led the Chunnel charge were **jailed for four months**
6	Palestinians in the Gaza and West Bank	refugee	camps **resent their lavish lives**.
7	Israelis attacked the Rafah	refugee	camp – thought to be a **stronghold of militants**
8	ushtuns who were stranded in nearby	refugee	camps when the Taliban fled may be **hiding arms and plotting revenge**.
9	A RED CROSS boss kept secret a	refugee	**plot to storm the Channel Tunnel**

In Table 4.6 refugees are characterized somewhat negatively – as being involved in plots, as resenting the lavish lives of others, as being violent or as causing a rise in crime and pushing down house prices. Such fears invoke a more general discourse of capitalism, whereby refugees are seen as a threat to the capitalist way of life by reducing the value of property.

Refugee camps are also reported as hiding grounds for extremists or militants and refugees are also involved in plans to enter countries illegally – e.g. 'to storm the channel tunnel'.

A final, quite rare use of *refugee* in the corpus is more metaphorical, being used to describe people who look like someone or something else. As these occur in long sentences, the examples below are quoted in full, rather than as concordance lines:

> Coming on **like some refugee from the Ricky Lake Show**, burly Fred spent much of the programme successfully convincing Sandra that he thought the first marriage had been annulled, and moaning to the camera that he "shouldn't be put in jail for falling in love".
>
> Extracted from News Corpus of Refugee Articles

85

Owen may **look like a refugee from a Hovis ad**, but as Sven-Goran Eriksson said: 'He's very cold when he gets a chance and he's very quick.'

Extracted from News Corpus of Refugee Articles

Last week I watched some do-it-yourself programme where **a couple of refugee presenters from the makeover toolbox** showed you how to have a kitsch Christmas.

Extracted from News Corpus of Refugee Articles

These cases are not from newspaper articles which are concerned with actual refugees. Instead, in the first two cases the phrase (*like*) [determiner] *refugee from* ... is used to allude to a person's similarity to something else. In the third case, two people are simply described as refugees. It is interesting that all three cases refer to television programmes. However, this is a construction which contains an implicitly negative evaluation – the fact that such people are described as refugees at all accesses an existing negative discourse of actual refugees, but it also implies that they are not viewed as possessing the identity they are supposed to have, possibly because they weren't competent at it, or because they look as if they should be something else. So Michael Owen (in the second example) is viewed not so much as a footballer, but a 'refugee from a Hovis ad(vert)'. Finally, the identity they are supposed to resemble is constructed negatively – so the phrase implies that the person isn't even competent to perform a stigmatized identity properly and instead is a refugee from it.

Semantic preference and discourse prosody

Our concordance-based analysis of the terms *refugee* and *refugees* in the small corpus of newspaper articles has been useful in revealing a range of discourses: refugees as victims, as the recipients of official attempts to help, as a natural disaster and as a criminal nuisance.

A concordance analysis therefore elucidates *semantic preference*. Semantic preference is, according to Stubbs (2001b: 65) 'the relation, not between individual words, but between a lemma or word-form and a set of semantically related words'. For example, in the British National Corpus the word *rising* co-occurs with words to do with work and money: e.g. *incomes, prices, wages, earnings, unemployment,* etc. Semantic preference also occurs with multi-word units. For example *glass of* co-occurs with a lexical set of words 'drinks': e.g. *sherry, lemonade, water, champagne, milk,* etc. Semantic preference is therefore related to the concept of collocation (see Chapter 5) but focuses on a lexical set of semantic categories rather than a single word or a related set of grammatical words. Table 4.2 showed that refugees had a semantic preference for quantification. One of the pieces of information that is often given about refugees involves how many of them there are.

However, semantic preference is also related to the concept of *discourse prosody* where patterns in discourse can be found between a word, phrase or lemma and a set of related words that suggest a discourse. The difference between semantic preference and discourse prosody is not always clear-cut. Stubbs (2001b: 65) says it is partly a question of how open-ended the list of collocates is. So it may be possible to list all of the words for 'drinks', indicating a semantic preference, but a more open-ended category such as 'unpleasant things' might be seen as a discourse prosody. Stubbs (2001b: 88) later notes that even a category of semantic preference will be open-ended, but will contain frequent and typical members.

In addition, semantic preference denotes aspects of meaning which are independent of speakers, whereas discourse prosody focuses on the relationship of a word to speakers and hearers, and is more concerned with attitudes. Tables 4.5 and 4.6 could be seen as examples of discourse prosodies, where refugees are described in terms of victims and criminals/nuisances respectively. Semantic preference is therefore more likely to occur in cases where attitudes are not expressed. However, even the absence of an attitude can be significant, for example, by showing a speaker's desire to remain 'on the fence'. And the case of writers giving refugees a semantic preference for quantification could involve a discourse prosody – why are writers so concerned with how many refugees there are? When we look at the discourse prosody which associates refugees with growing numbers that are described as swelling, filled beyond capacity, overflowing, etc. it is possible that at least in some cases of quantification there is anxiety about a situation that is viewed as spiralling out of control – large numbers of refugees are not a good thing!

It is apparent though, that there is some inconsistency between the exact meanings of semantic preference and discourse prosody. Louw (1993) and Sinclair (1991) refer to yet another term called *semantic prosody*, which has been used by other researchers in a way which makes it akin to discourse prosodies. For example, Cotterill (2001) uses the term *semantic prosody* when analysing the language used in the high-profile trial of O.J. Simpson for marital violence. However, her analysis of phrases like *to control* and *cycle of* indicates that they contain patterns of evaluation, which suggests they could be classed as discourse prosodies. Therefore, I refer to discourse prosody in this chapter, although with an awareness that others may class this as semantic prosody (or semantic preference!)

Many of the linguistic strategies used to refer to refugees – such as referring to them as an indistinguishable mass or vague quantity, using water or package metaphors, referring to them as a pest or a threat, etc. are linked to the more overarching concept of racist discourse. As van Dijk (1987: 58) describes, there are four topic classes for racist discourses: they are different, they do not adapt, they are involved in negative acts and they threaten our socio-economic interests. Hardt-Mautner (1995b: 179) points out, 'National identity emerges very much as a relational concept, the construction of "self" being heavily dependent on the construction of "other"'. The racist constructions of refugees therefore not only construct a threat to the status quo and national identity (which may help to sell newspapers), they also help to construct national identity by articulating what it is not.

However, more encouraging aspects of the corpus data suggest a less prejudiced picture than earlier researchers have found when looking at newspaper data. Stereotypes of refugees as criminal nuisances were present in the corpus, yet they were relatively rare. Discourses which focused on the problems encountered by refugees and/or attempts to help them were relatively more frequent, suggesting that in the year 2003 at least, there was a growing awareness of the need for sensitivity when discussing issues connected to immigration in the UK. As Law *et al* (1997: 18) found, about three quarters of news articles concerned with race contained media frames 'which seek to expose and criticise racist attitudes, statements, actions and policies, which address the concerns of immigrant and minority ethnic groups and show their contribution to British society, and which embrace an inclusive view of multi-cultural British identity'. A study by Jessika ter Wal concludes that 'the British tabloid press no longer seem to merit the overly racist tag that they were given by studies in the early 1980s' (2002: 407).

A corpus-based approach is therefore useful, in that it helps to give a wider view of the range of possible ways of discussing refugees. A more qualitative, small-scale approach to analysis may mean that saliency is perceived as more important than frequency – whereby texts which present shocking or extreme positions are focused on more than those which are more frequent, yet neutral. While it is important to examine extreme cases, it is also useful to put them into perspective alongside a wide range of other cases. In addition, corpus data can help us to establish which sorts of language strategies are most frequent or popular. For example, the refugees as water metaphor was found to be much more frequent than other metaphors, such as refugees as illegal packages or as invaders. Rather than simply listing the metaphors which appear in the data then, we are able to get a more accurate sense of which ones are naturalized, and which ones may be particularly salient *because* they are so infrequent (in Chapter 7 I look more closely at obtaining metaphors from corpora).

Points of concern

A concordance analysis is one of the more qualititative forms of analysis associated with corpus linguistics. While concordance programs allow researchers to sort and therefore view the data in a variety of different ways, it is still the responsibility of the analyst to recognize linguistic patterns and also to explain why they exist. A concordance analysis is therefore only as good as its analyst.

First, it should be noted that words aren't always used in a straightforward way. As with the cases of italicized words in this chapter, authors sometimes refer to words meta-linguistically in order to examine, discuss or critique the word's usage or meaning. For example, Kaye (1998) carried out an analysis of the words *bogus* and *phoney* in British broadsheet newspaper articles about asylum seekers. He found that in 35 per cent of cases of these words, they occurred in the context of writers criticizing others for using them. He also found that liberal newspapers used such terms more often, but were also more critical of them, when compared to more conservative newspapers. Additionally, the majority of these words appeared in the context of writers reporting or quoting someone else, usually a politician or government official, suggesting that the newspapers were not taking the lead in setting the agenda, but were largely accepting the agenda as defined by others. Therefore the context of a word is important in how it contributes towards particular discourses. This issue is dealt with in more detail in the section on resistant discourses in Chapter 5.

One aspect of the concordance analysis that I haven't considered so far is that when carrying out searches on a particular subject (particularly a noun), as well as euphemisms and similes for that subject, it might also be the case that it is referred to numerous times with determiners (*this, that, these, those*) or pronouns (*it, them, they, she*).

For example, the terms *they* and *them* were sometimes used to refer to refugees in the newspaper corpus,: e.g.:

> There have been complaints the refugees have caused a steep rise in petty crime and pushed down house prices. "**They** are a pest,"

89

> says a woman in the brightly-decorated village boulangerie. "We don't really speak to **them**."

It is important that these cases of anaphora – referring back to an expression – are taken into consideration. Referrals can also be cataphoric – referring to a subject that is to follow it, e.g. '*I don't know them personally, but there seem to be refugees everywhere*'. Expanding a corpus search to include pronouns and determiners may yield further evidence of patterns or even completely different discourses. However, concordances of pronouns and determiners are likely to include many irrelevant examples – not all cases of *they* in the newspaper corpus referred to refugees, some referred to journalists, members of the United Nations or teachers. There were also more cases of the word *they* in the corpus than the terms *refugee/refugees* (339 vs. 140). Therefore taking anaphora and cataphora into account is likely to make the process of analysis more time-consuming, although it is likely to result in interesting findings. A related issue concerns cases where specific refugees are referred to in a corpus, by name. Here it may be worthwhile carrying out additional searches on the names of individual refugees, although it may be less easy to generalize any discourses found to the wider class of 'refugees'. However, it should be borne in mind that individuals can be used as prototype examples for a whole class of people, making discourses more subtle, yet still apparent. For example, Morrish (2002) reports how newspapers constructed homophobic discourses around a gay government minister, Peter Mandelson, even though the words *gay* and *homosexual* were not used in articles about him.

The corpus I collected was relatively manageable – having only 140 concordance lines meant that patterns were apparent, yet I was not overwhelmed by thousands of lines of data. What about cases where we are dealing with corpora of millions of words? For example, rather than building a small corpus myself, I could have used something like the 100 million word British National Corpus. Carrying out a concordance of *refugee/refugees* on the BNC results in 2,730 lines of data – more than I would like to analyse. In cases like this, Sinclair (1999) recommends selecting 30 lines at random, noting their patterns, then moving on to another 30 lines, then another and another until nothing new is found. Hunston (2002: 52) adapts this procedure by describing a method called hypothesis testing – once a pattern has been spotted, further searches are carried out in order to determine whether the pattern occurs on a wider scale. With a large amount of data, it may also be useful to consider a term's strongest or most frequent collocates (see the following chapter) first by using mutual information or a collocation table.

90

What about exceptional or rare instances in the corpus? The pattern *like a/some refugee* occurred only twice in the news corpus. Again, consulting a larger reference corpus like the BNC is useful in seeing whether or not a more widely recognized discourse is being accessed here. The BNC contains nine cases of phrases involving *refugee* or *refugees* being used as similes (see Table 4.7). These also generally contain a negative discourse prosody: *like a refugee from a bad horror film, like a refugee prop from a Boris Karloff Frankenstein film*, etc. So while this use of language is relatively rare, there is evidence to suggest that its appearance in the news corpus draws on and contributes to an existing discourse of refugees being bad things that are out of place.

Table 4.7 Metaphorical references to refugees in the British National Corpus

1	ruined my gold stilettos. I look like a	refugee	from a Verdi opera, stranded in the d
2	I did – and that he too looks like a	refugee	from a Verdi opera. The Nigerian wh
3	with them. One boy, dressed like a	refugee	from Woodstock, was spinning arou
4	You're starting to sound like a	refugee	from a bad horror film. The role of m
5	s. Mr Hunter was what he resembled: a	refugee	from the sixties. His fat hand squeeze
6	covering all her hair. She looked like a	refugee	from one of those films that at the
7	, shoulders down, face averted, like a	refugee	."You couldn't lend me some money,
8	nderful for its purpose but looks like a	refugee	prop from a Boris Karloff Frankenst
9	n outdoor clothing, stood huddled like	refugees	from a foreign land waiting to be told

What about instances which don't occur at all? Here the analyst's own intuitions, initial hypotheses and expectations will play some sort of role. For example, I had expected to see evidence of discourses that labelled refugees as being real or fake – possibly linked to phrases such as *genuine refugee* or *bogus refugee*. Such a discourse would imply that some people claim refugee status when they are not entitled to do so. It also implies that refugees undergo a decision making process where they will either be found genuine or bogus – there are no shades of grey. However, in the newspaper corpus I didn't find any evidence of this discourse. No refugees had their status as refugees questioned. In order to see if this discourse existed elsewhere, I carried out a concordance of *refugee/refugees* in the British National Corpus. Interestingly, both *genuine* and *bogus* appeared numerous times in this concordance. However, the data in the BNC was gathered in the early 1990s, whereas the newspaper data I collected was from the year 2003. Perhaps this discourse has shifted somewhat since then. A concordance search of *bogus* in the BNC reveals that it often occurs with the term *asylum seekers*. Perhaps then, it is the case that in 2003, terms like *bogus* are still used to refer to asylum seekers, but not refugees any more. However, more data would need to be collected to explore this hypothesis.

Finally, it should be borne in mind that a concordance-informed discourse analysis is still a matter of interpretation. The patterns of language which are found (or overlooked) may be subject to the researcher's own ideological stance. And the way that they are interpreted may also be filtered through the researcher's subject position. This is true of many other, if not all, forms of discourse analysis. However, the corpus-based approach at least helps to counter some of this bias, by providing quantitative evidence of patterns that may be more difficult to ignore. Additionally though, an analyst identification of a discourse may not mean that the same discourse is viewed in the same way, if at all by other readers. Taking account of the issues surrounding text production and reception, as well as the historical context of the subject under discussion are paramount in supporting the more linguistic-informed analysis of a corpus.

Step-by-step guide to concordance analysis

1. Build or obtain access to a corpus.
2. Decide on the search term (e.g. *refugee*) – bearing in mind that search terms can be expanded to include plurals (*refugees*), euphemisms (*aliens*), anaphora (*them, they*) and proper nouns of relevant individuals. In order to do this it might be useful to initially carry out a pilot study, looking closely at a small sample of the corpus, or consulting other sources.
3 Obtain a concordance of the search term(s).
4. Clean the concordance – e.g. by removing repetitions or other lines which are not relevant – for example, references that refer to aliens from space rather than aliens as refugees.
5. Sort the concordance repeatedly on different words to the left and right while looking for evidence of grammatical, semantic or discourse patterns.
6. Look for further evidence of such patterns in the corpus.
7. Investigate the presence of particular terms more closely – e.g. by exploring their collocates or distribution in reference corpora of general language.
8. When no more patterns can be found, carry out a close analysis of the remaining concordance lines, looking for similarities or patterns in terms of meaning or discourse.
9. Note rare or non-existent cases of discourses based on your

own intuitions. See if such discourses occur in other more general corpora.

10. Attempt to hypothesize why the patterns appear and relate this to issues of text production and reception.

Notes

1. http://infoweb.newsbank.com.

5 Collocates

Introduction

In the last chapter we saw how carrying out a close analysis of search terms via a concordance can be helpful in revealing traces of discourses within texts. However, concordances can be disconcerting to researchers who are unfamiliar with the analytical techniques required to make sense of the patterns within them. In some cases a concordance can consist of hundreds or even thousands of lines. Given that situation, researchers can rely on sampling methods, which are helpful in reducing the length of time spent on analysis, but may also fail to reveal salient aspects of the concordance.

Another problem with concordances is that patterns are not always as clear-cut in a concordance as we would like them to be. Consider the relationship between the words *forgive* and *sins*. A concordance of *sins* in the British National Corpus, sorted one place to the right reveals the pattern *forgive sins*, which occurs 13 times. This isn't a particularly large number. However, further sorts, two, three, four and five places to the right reveal that *forgive* and *sins* occur near each other in other ways, e.g. *forgive our sins, forgive us our sins, forgive me all my sins*. In all, *sins* occurs near or next to *forgive* a total of 29 times, and if we take into account related forms of these words (e.g. by looking at *forgiving* and *sin*, etc. as well), the relationship between the two concepts is much higher. However, in order to get an idea of the strength of the relationship between *forgive* and *sins*, we have had to carry out analyses of the same concordance, sorted in lots of different ways, which is time consuming and reliant on the researcher's attention not wandering. It would be more convenient, at least at the beginning, to be simply given a list of words which tend to occur near or next to *forgive* relatively often – we can worry about where they actually appear and what their relationship means later.

All words co-occur with each other to some degree. However, when a word regularly appears near another word, and the relationship is statistically significant in some way, then such co-occurrences are referred to as collocates and the phenomena of certain words frequently occurring next to or near each other is *collocation*. As Firth (1957) famously wrote: 'You shall know a lot about a word from the company it keeps'. Collocation is therefore a way of understanding meanings and associations between words which are otherwise difficult to ascertain from a small-scale analysis of a single text. Words (or *signifers* to use Saussure's term (1974)) can only take on meaning (that which is *signified*) by the context that they occur in. So in order to understand the meanings of words, we have to compare them in relation to other words.

> Suppose you want to know the meaning of a signifier, you can look it up in a dictionary; but all you will find will be yet more signifiers, whose signifieds you can in turn look up, and so on. The process is not only infinite but somehow circular: signfiers keep transforming into signifieds, and vice versa, and you never arrive at a final signified which is not a signifier in itself.
>
> (Sarup 1986: 35)

While we must accept that there is no final signified, it should be seen that one way at arriving at some form of meaning is to examine how words are used in context (as opposed to dictionary definitions), and also which contexts they do *not* occur in. As Stubbs (1996: 172) points out, '... words occur in characteristic collocations, which show the associations and connotations they have, and therefore the assumptions which they embody.'

In order to explore how discourse analysis can be carried out by focusing primarily on collocation, I want to consider the subject of people who have never been married. A central facet of critical discourse analysis involves examining the ways that institutions are created, maintained and afforded power in societies. *Marriage*, in its various forms, has often been characterized as an *institution*[1] (e.g. Westermarck 1921) supporting and being supported by religious and economic structures whilst enabling traditional conceptualizations of gender and sexuality. For example, in most societies heterosexual marriages are sanctioned while homosexual ones are (currently) not, while women are 'given away' by their fathers: see also Rich (1980).

So bearing in mind that marriage is one way in which a range of hegemonic social discourses converge, how are people who do not enter this 'institution' discursively constructed? Are there any clues in language use which can suggest discourse traces of the never-married? And are there any discursive differences based around gender? In British English we can refer to never-married male adults as *bachelors* and unmarried female adults as *spinsters*.[2] These two terms could be viewed as semantic equivalents of each other. However, along with other pairs of male/female terms, it is not always the case that discourses surrounding these concepts are the same.

In order to carry out a linguistic analysis of bachelors and spinsters, it is therefore useful to examine their usage in a corpus. However, rather than build a corpus from scratch, as we have done in earlier chapters, in this case, we are going to use an existing large corpus – the British National Corpus (BNC) – viewing it as being more or less representative of general British English. Because the BNC is so large (about 100 million words), we can expect to find a good number of occurrences of even quite rare words. I used BNCweb (see Figures 5.1 and 5.2), an online concordance program for use with the BNC to carry out concordances and collocations.

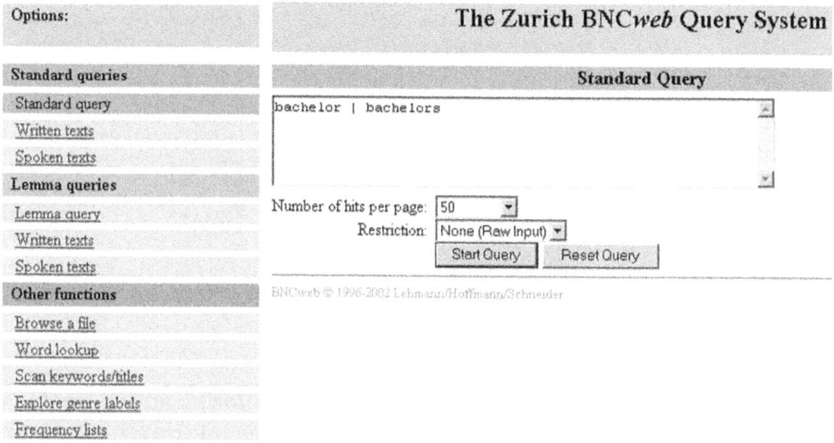

Figure 5.1 *Screenshot of BNCweb: Standard Query*

In the British National Corpus *bachelor* occurs 424 times and *spinster* 140. Their respective plural forms occur 82 and 36 times respectively. In this case my analysis will treat *bachelor/bachelors* as one term, with the same applying for *spinster/spinsters*. However, it should be noted that it is not always wise to combine variants of a lemma together into one search as some collocates are dependent on particular word forms. For example, the plural noun *stitches* collocates with the preposition *in*, due to phrases like 'I was in stitches', but the singular noun *stitch* does not collocate so strongly with *in* – we do not use phrases like 'I was in stitch'. Despite this, I have decided to treat *bachelor/bachelors* as a single term due to the relatively low frequency of these words in the BNC. However, where a collocate is limited to a set pattern of language and only ever occurs with *bachelor* or *bachelors*, then this needs to be noted accordingly. It is hoped that by deriving and then comparing lists of the strongest collocates of *bachelor/bachelors* and *spinster/spinsters*, we can obtain a better idea of some of the main discourses surrounding unmarried people and the ways that such discourses are gendered.

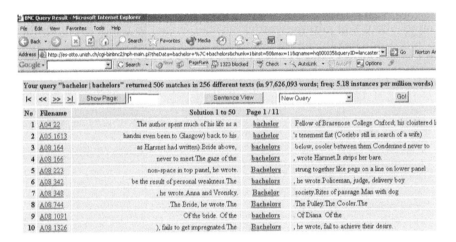

Figure 5.2 *Screenshot of BNCweb. The first few lines of a concordance search on bachelor/bachelors*

   Before looking at the collocates of *bachelor(s)* and *spinster(s)* there is an important point concerning issues of production and reception to make about using general corpora (consisting of texts from a wide range of sources) in order to examine discourses. As noted in Chapter 1, not every text in a general reference corpus will have had the same size and type of audience. Therefore, individual instances of a word like *bachelor* may have had different values in terms of their power to influence discourse. For example, a citation in a popular newspaper text or speech by a religious leader may be more influential than a citation in a personal letter. These issues of production and reception are worth taking into account when considering the discourses elicited from texts – when carrying out small-scale analyses on a few texts or even a corpus analysis on a specialized corpus, they can be more straightforward to investigate. However, despite its name, it can sometimes be difficult to make generalizations about a general corpus.

Fortunately, as discussed in Chapter 3 when we looked at spoken conversation, the texts in the BNC are categorized in a range of ways. We could take advantage of this categorization in order to obtain a better idea about the way that *bachelor(s)* and *spinster(s)* are distributed across language in general. Table 5.1 shows the distributions of these words across the different categories of text in the BNC. Again, in order to reduce the complexity of this table I have considered *bachelor* and *spinster* along with their respective plurals at the same time. After the totals for spoken and written texts are given, the remaining nine rows give a more detailed breakdown of the different written genres in the corpus (imaginative, arts, etc.).

Table 5.1 Distributions of bachelor(s) and spinster(s) across the BNC

	bachelor(s)		spinster(s)	
	Total occurrences	Frequency per million words	Total occurrences	Frequency per million words
Spoken texts	12	1.16	3	0.29
Written texts	494	5.66	173	1.98
Imaginative	149	9.09	47	2.87
Arts	56	8.59	27	4.14
Leisure	80	6.57	20	1.64
World affairs	96	5.6	49	2.86
Belief and thought	14	4.66	5	1.66
Social science	58	4.17	20	1.44
Natural and pure sciences	12	3.17	0	0
Applied science	15	2.11	1	0.14
Commerce and finance	14	1.93	4	0.55

What can be concluded from the table? It is perhaps more useful to look at the 'Frequency per million words' columns when comparing rows. Here we can see that the terms under investigation tend to occur more in written texts than spoken conversations. *Bachelor(s)* occurs more often in the imaginative and arts domains, whereas *spinster(s)* is most common in the arts domain. Carrying out more detailed concordances of the words, based on the different written domains, reveals more information: when *bachelor(s)* occurs in the three science domains it tends to refer to an academic degree (Bachelor of Arts), a usage we will discuss in more detail later. It is in the imaginative (fiction) and world affairs (news) domains that we find *bachelor(s)* occurring more in its sense of an unmarried man. Discourses of unmarried people, then, are perhaps more likely to be perpetuated within non-scientific text domains – they are certainly not equally distributed across all types of language, and appear particularly salient in fiction and news media. Bearing this in mind, it is time to return to the subject of collocation.

Deriving collocates

So how are collocations calculated? There are a number of different procedures. The simplest is to count the number of times a given word appears within, say a 5-word window to the left or right of a search term. We may or may not decide to count cases which cut across sentence boundaries here. If we use this procedure on *bachelor/bachelors* (not counting across sentence boundaries) we get a list of words which appear in the column marked 'Rank by frequency' in Table 5.2. For the sake of saving space, only the top ten words are included here.

Table 5.2 Collocates of bachelor/bachelors *using ranked frequencies. The numbers in brackets alongside each word indicate how many times that word occurs within 5 spaces to the left and right of the search term*

	Rank by frequency (all words)	Rank by frequency (lexical words only)
1	a (225)	degree (27)
2	the (222)	education (18)
3	of (185)	eligible (18)
4	and (122)	life (15)
5	to (74)	button (14)
6	in (74)	said (14)
7	was (67)	old (11)
8	his (61)	arts (10)
9	he (50)	bachelor (10)
10	with (40)	degrees (9)

As can be seen from the first column of words, the most common collocates are grammatical or function words: articles, prepositions, conjunctions and pronouns. One of the problems with using a frequency-based technique to calculate collocates is that these high frequency words generally tend to be function words – which does not always reveal much of interest, particularly in terms of discourse. One way of resolving this is to simply look further down the list until we come to the lexical words as we did in Chapter 3 when we looked at frequency lists derived from holiday leaflets. If we do this (see the final column in Table 5.2) we find words like *old, said, eligible* and *education*. So far so good? Unfortunately though, there is another problem. Just because *said* occurs often within five places of *bachelor* we cannot be certain that frequency is the same as saliency. It is fairly likely that *said* occurs with a great number of other words as well and also that it occurs lots of times in the corpus when the word *bachelor* is not nearby. Other than using our intuition, we need a way of taking into account when a relationship between two words is fairly exclusive and not just due to one or both words being common.

Therefore a number of statistical tests have been devised, which take into account the frequency of words in a corpus and their relative number of occurrences both next to and away from each other. One such test is called Mutual Information or MI. Put simply, mutual information is calculated by examining all of the places where two potential collocates occur in a text or corpus. An algorithm then computes what the expected probability of these two words occurring near to each other would be, based on their relative frequencies and the overall size of the corpus. It then compares this expected figure to the observed figure – what has actually happened, and converts the difference between the two into a number which indicates the strength of the collocation – the higher the number, the stronger the collocation. Some measures of MI divide the score by log base 2 (such as BNCWeb, which automatically does this – see Figure 5.3, and WordSmith Tools which gives this calculation as an option). For the log base 2 calculation, any score higher than three is usually deemed to be indicative of a strong collocation.

Collocation parameters:					
Information:	collocations ▾		Statistics:		Mutual information ▾
Window span:	-5 ▾ - 5 ▾		Basis:		whole BNC ▾
F(n,c) at least:	5 ▾		F(c) at least:		5 ▾
Filter results by:	Specific collocate:		and/or tag: no restrictions ▾		Submit changed parameters ▾

There are 1281 different types in your collocation database for "bachelor | bachelors". (Your query "bachelor | bachelors" returned 506 mat 256 different texts)

No.	Word	Total No. in the whole BNC	As collocate	In No. of texts	Mutual information value
1	spinster	140	5	5	9.61691268
2	gilbey	172	6	5	9.58296543
3	bachelor	424	10	5	9.01827529
4	eligible	1330	18	13	8.21698179
5	button	1629	14	2	7.56185191

Figure 5.3 Screenshot of BNCweb. Some collocates of bachelor/bachelors using MI at a −5 to +5 span

Table 5.3 Collocates of bachelor/bachelors *using different statistical techniques (shown in order of collocation strength). The numbers in brackets alongside each word indicate how many times that word occurs within 5 spaces to the left and right of the search term*

	Mutual Information	MI3	Z-score	Log-likelihood	Log-log	Observed/expected
1	spinster (5)	a (225)	eligible (18)	a (225)	eligible (18)	spinster (5)
2	gilbey (6)	eligible (18)	bachelor (10)	of (185)	bachelor (10)	gilbey (6)
3	bachelor (10)	bachelor (10)	gilbey (6)	the (222)	button (14)	bachelor (10)
4	eligible (18)	of (185)	spinster (5)	and (122)	degree (27)	eligible (18)
5	button (14)	degree (27)	button (14)	his (61)	gilbey (6)	button (14)
6	middle-aged (5)	the (222)	degree (27)	degree (27)	spinster (5)	middle-aged (5)
7	bride (6)	button (14)	males (9)	was (67)	males (9)	bridge (6)
8	males (9)	gilbey (6)	middle-aged (5)	eligible (18)	degrees (9)	males (9)
9	lonely (6)	spinster (5)	bride (6)	he (50)	bride (6)	lonely (6)
10	habits (5)	and (122)	degrees (9)	in (74)	arts (10)	habits (5)

However, one problem with MI is that it can tend to give high scores to relatively low frequency words. Looking at the column labelled Mutual Information in Table 5.3 we have a list of the strongest collocates calculated using MI: *spinster, gilbey, bachelor, eligible*, etc. However, these words tend not to occur very often. For example, *Gilbey* only occurs six times next to *bachelor*, due to references to James Gilbey, a friend of Princess Diana. Therefore other calculations have been suggested in order to take the frequency of collocates into account. For example, the z-score (Berry-Rogghe 1973), MI3 (Oakes 1998: 171–2), log-log (Kilgarriff and Tugwell 2001) or log-likelihood (Dunning 1993) scores. As can be seen from the columns in the rest of Table 5.3, different algorithms tend to favour different types of words. Log-likelihood and MI3 place more emphasis on grammatical words. I tend to favour log-log as it focuses on lexical words rather than grammatical words, yet it doesn't give as much importance to very low-frequency words as the MI score. However, it should be noted that some of the calculations tend to give quite similar results – many of the words in the top ten for the log-log column are also in the MI column. The best technique to use, then, should be dependent on the sorts of words that the researcher is interested in obtaining – high frequency function words (Rank by frequency), low frequency content words (MI, Z-score, log-log, observed/expected), or a mixture of both (MI3, log-likelihood). Each technique gives some sort of trade-off between frequency and saliency, so another option could be to consider the results from more than one algorithm. It should also be borne in mind that some corpus-based tools do not allow for the full range of collocational techniques to be carried out so you may have to settle with what is on offer.

What if we change the span – the number of words left and right of the search word? How does that affect the sorts of collocates that are derived? Table 5.4 shows the top ten collocates of *bachelor(s)* (via log-log) using a range of different spans.

Table 5.4 Collocates of bachelor(s), with span changed

−10 to +10	−5 to +5	−3 to +3	−1 to +1	−5 to +1	+1 to +5
bachelor	eligible	eligible	eligible	eligible	button
eligible	bachelor	button	elderly	bachelor	degree
degree	button	degree	brother	middle-aged	gilbey
button	degree	gilbey	a	elderly	bachelor
degrees	gilbey	males	status	lonely	education
males	spinster	education	confirmed	males	arts
gilbey	males	degrees	days	a	habits
spinster	degrees	elderly	old	degrees	brother
bride	bride	lonely	his	confirmed	science
education	arts	arts	life	degree	status

Bearing in mind that the collocates differ depending on the span that is used, which span is the best one to focus on? First, we should note that while the columns contain different words, there are also a number of similarities between them. For example, the −10 to +10 span contains seven of the ten words in the −3 to +3 span. With that said, the −10 to +10 span is probably too large for us to be certain that the words in it are true collocates of *bachelor(s)*. And the −1 to +1 span is perhaps too small. The −5 to −1 and the +1 to +5 spans only concentrate on words to the left and right of the node word respectively and therefore disregard a good deal of potentially useful context. I decided to use the −3 to +3 span because this was most likely to include words which were included in noun phrases containing the word *bachelor(s)*. However, it should be noted that the choice of span length, as with the choice of statistical measure of collocation, is likely to yield slightly different results depending on how it is set.[3]

There is a danger here that we may try experimenting with a range of different spans and ways of calculating collocation until we arrive at the most 'interesting' results – or results which confirm our initial hypotheses. For example, I was interested in the fact that the word *habits* strongly collocated with *bachelor(s)* but this only occurred when the span was set at +1 to +5. The collocation occurred in phrases like 'a bachelor of fixed habits' and 'a bachelor of somewhat eccentric habits' – which suggested a discourse of bachelors as rigid and strange. However, the word *habits* didn't occur in any of the other spans I looked at, and to have selected the span +1 to +5 would have meant missing out on other potentially significant words such as *elderly* and *lonely*. I surmised that if *habits* was such an important collocate of *bachelor(s)* then it would have occurred in some of the other columns in Table 5.4. It may be worth referring again to *habits* if it supports or strongly contradicts a discourse found later, but for the present, I decided not to investigate it in any more detail.

Identifying discourses from collocates

So using the log-log algorithm and only considering the lexical words, what are the collocates of *bachelor(s)* and *spinster(s)*? Table 5.5 shows this information (only words which have a log-log value of over 5 are considered – a span of three sides either side of the search term was used).

Table 5.5 Collocates (log-log) of bachelor(s) and spinster(s)

bachelor(s)	eligible, button, degree, gilbey, males, education, elderly, lonely, arts, brother, science, confirmed, status, son, flat, life, living, james, old, days, party
spinster(s)	elderly, widows, sisters, three

It can immediately be seen from the table that *bachelor* has more collocates than *spinster*. This is partly due to the fact that *bachelor* occurs more frequently in the corpus. One reason why *bachelor* occurs more than *spinster* can be seen by a quick look at some of the collocates: *degree*, education, *science*, *arts* (this was something we also discovered via our text domain distribution analysis at the beginning of the chapter). Examining concordances which contain *bachelor* along with these collocates, it is clear that they all relate to having a degree, e.g. *bachelor of arts*. Here the meaning of *bachelor* (a type of degree) is different to the meaning we are concerned with (a man who has not married). Should we therefore discount these collocates because *bachelor* is a homonym and clearly a bachelor of arts does not imply an unmarried man? It might be best to do this. However, Löbner (2002: 44) states that actual homonyms are a rare and accidental phenomenon. Polysemy, where two words with the same spelling have interrelated meanings are much more common. This is therefore a point where it is actually useful to step outside the corpus for a moment and consider other types of historical information.

The term *bachelors degree* can be traced back to the thirteenth century at the University of Paris using a system established under Pope Gregory IX. Historically, *bachelor* has also meant a young monk, someone belonging to the lowest stage of knighthood or the younger members of a trade guild. The term has therefore variously referred to young men at the beginning of their careers. Although *bachelor* now means 'unmarried man', it is not difficult to see how this meaning is related to the early meaning of a young person (in the past almost certainly male) studying for a preliminary degree. So while the collocates of *bachelor* which suggest a meaning of university education no longer have the same association with bachelor as unmarried man, the two meanings are perhaps due to historical polysemy rather than being accidental homonyms. It is notable that there are no collocates of *spinster* which suggest having a university education; historically it is a male term.

What about the collocates that do not refer to university education? The collocate *button* refers to a name of a horse: Bachelor's Button, which only occurs in sports reporting. Again, we need to look outside the corpus to find the origin of this term. A bachelor's button is a type of plant – possibly named because it was traditionally used in (unmarried) men's buttonholes at weddings. The collocates *brother* and *son* tend to occur in cases involving inheritance or descriptions of family trees, e.g.: 'On the grandfather's death, the farm was taken over by a bachelor son'; 'Edward Cheyney inherited the Badger Hall estate in December 1866 on the death of his bachelor brother Henry'. With some of the other words, the collocates are more useful in suggesting discourses of bachelorhood. *Eligible* almost always occurs in the phrase *eligible bachelor*, meaning a man who is worth marrying. *Party* occurs in the phrase *bachelor party* – a celebratory and sometimes raucous event which occurs for a man and his (usually male) friends the day or night before his wedding. *Flat* occurs in the phrase *bachelor flat* – accommodation for an unmarried man. What about the collocates *days*, *life* and *living*? Here it is useful to present a concordance.

Table 5.6 Concordance of bachelor *when it collocates with* days, life *and* living

1	ipes that my husband attempted in his	bachelor	**days**
2	d been Charles's girlfriend during his	bachelor	**days** and in Diana's mind his contin
3	n and Queen Mother. Certainly in his	bachelor	**days** Johnnie Spencer was the catch
4	new life, and keep in memory of his	bachelor	**days** and the friends he has left beh
5	his party for me. May he enjoy happy	bachelor	**days**, but not too many, before he re
6	her future, in memory of our happy	bachelor	**days** together.
7	nted), perhaps with a memento of her	bachelor	**days**, such as a cassette by her favo
8	The author spent much of his **life** as a	bachelor	Fellow of Brasenose College Oxfor
9	armingly primitive today) but also of	bachelor	**life** in upstate New York in the 195
10	rje believed that Phillip was living a	bachelor	**life** at a London hotel between trys
11	No. Things to do first. My	bachelor	's **life** is catching up on me."
12	wer nearby. Ackroyd enjoyed a quiet	bachelor	**life** and lived in a small house by th
13	ourse because he was happy with his	bachelor	**life**. If he had his fishing tackle rea
14	eldest son, who lived out his **life** as a	bachelor	of somewhat eccentric habits, bec
15	to him on the telephone." A	bachelor	's **life** suits you far better. You never
16	ed to Edinburgh to live an agreeable	bachelor	**life** among his family and friends.
17	to Japan you intend to go on living a	bachelor	**life**, almost as if I don't exist."
18	a contrast with the experience of the	bachelor	**living** solitary amid echoing halls. I
19	52. The narrator Michael, an elderly	bachelor	**living** in genteel poverty, describes
20	arje believed that Phillip was **living** a	bachelor	life at a London hotel between trys
21	ast gloomy kitchen and the clutter of	bachelor	**living**. Alexandra looked at her clo
22	to Japan you intend to go on **living** a	bachelor	life, almost as if I don't exist."
23	the decision that Harold Newstead, a	bachelor	hairdresser **living** in Camberwell, w

What patterns can be seen from Table 5.6? Bachelor days are described as *happy* in lines 5 and 6. In line 12 someone *enjoyed* a quiet bachelor life, in line 13 someone is *happy* with their bachelor life while in line 16 there is an *agreeable* bachelor life. Line 6 also talks about the *memory* of happy bachelor days, and the theme of memory is also found in lines 4 and 7. *Bachelor days*, then, tend to have a positive discourse prosody, connected to nostalgia. We can, however, look for more evidence to support this point, by examining the word *days* in the corpus, in order to get a better idea of what its other collocations are. Table 5.7 shows some of the strongest immediate left hand collocates of *days*, grouped in terms of their similarity:

Table 5.7 Main collocation groupings of days

Semantic group	Collocates
Good weather	palmy, balmy, sunny, hazy, windless, glorious
Bad weather	foggy, rainy, overcast, darkest, cloudy, windy
Pleasure	halcyon, heady, carefree, happiest, lazy, glory, leisurely
The past	olden, bygone, far-off, old, pioneering
Youth	salad, boyhood, courting
Quantities	twenty-eight, few, 365, 91, 90, 14, 28, 21, 360

It appears that *days* has several semantic or discourse prosodies associated with it. It is often used in phrases which describe weather or lengths of time, e.g. *foggy days, few days*. We may want to identify these as semantic prosodies as they don't appear to express speaker attitude. However, a closer look at concordances of the weather correlates suggests that descriptions of weather are sometimes linked to speaker emotions or attitudes: e.g. 'I was happy to let the pleasant sunny days go by'. However, because *days* correlates about equally with the semantic categories of good and bad weather, it is unlikely that when we see the word *days*, we are going to be primed to think of a particular type of weather or emotion associated with it. On the other hand, there are a number of other (non-weather) immediate left-hand collocates of *days* which suggest a much more positive discourse prosody: *halcyon, carefree, glory*, etc. It is therefore possible, that when encountering a phrase like *bachelor days* for the first time, we are likely to attribute a more positive meaning to the word *bachelor*, because of the existence of a positive discourse prosody of *days* (although it's very unlikely that this would be a conscious association, unless we had previously examined this in a corpus!) The fact that other words such as *happy* (in lines 5 and 6 of Table 5.6), which has a much more transparent meaning than *days* is also a collocate, will only help to reinforce the positive association of *bachelor*. Note here, that this is one case where examining related forms of *days*, e.g. *day* would not be particularly helpful. The word *day* has a very different set of collocates, for example, it holds a somewhat negative discourse prosody for being tired: *gruelling, hectic, busy, exhausting, tiring*, which *days* does not seem to have.

The pairing of *bachelor* and *life* is rather more varied – while there are a couple of positive descriptions of bachelor life, there are also others which suggest different experiences: line 14 – 'life as a bachelor of somewhat eccentric habits' – perhaps there is a cause/effect relationship here – someone's eccentric habits meaning they don't want to marry or they are unmarriable. In line 12 a bachelor life is described as *quiet*, whereas in line 11 someone says 'My bachelor's life is catching up with me'. In lines 9 and 10, we have connections with a bachelor's life and large cities: New York and London – describing an urban lifestyle.

The discourse prosody of bachelor *living* is less positive – in line 18 there is the phrase 'experience of the bachelor living solitary', in line 19 a bachelor lives in 'genteel poverty', line 21 describes a gloomy kitchen and clutter, whereas line 23 refers to a *bachelor hairdresser*. This could be referred to as a euphemism for homosexuality – particularly as the person in question has been inaccurately libelled as a bigamist.

What about the collocates *elderly*, *lonely* and *old*? Table 5.8 shows concordances for these terms with *bachelor*.

Table 5.8 Concordance of bachelor(s) *when it collocates with* elderly, lonely *and* old

1	Strange, because he, an **elderly**	bachelor	, dry and very conventional, seem
2	years, it was occupied by an **elderly**	bachelor	who was one of the several mill o
3	52.The narrator Michael, an **elderly**	bachelor	living in genteel poverty, describes
4	's only the oddities who make **elderly**	bachelors	."
5	take her to supper. He was an **elderly**	bachelor	("I shall never marry, my dear,"
6	domestic arrangements of an **elderly**	bachelor	like myself cannot be of much inter
7	ood ADC – something of the **elderly**	bachelor	's habits. Ordering a staff car, he dr
8	today, he wrote. All those **lonely**	bachelors	. The Grinder grinds but no chocola
9	A **LONELY**	bachelor	who died in his bath has been found
10	tmouth, Devon is linking **lonely** local	bachelors	with Russian girls.
11	cajoling. "Take pity on a **lonely**	bachelor	I'd love to take you out. I
12	A **LONELY**	bachelor	, who was the victim of a vicious ha
13	of taste – "It is time that **old**	bachelor	on the Tiber got married", – "
14	elor's Button. Now seven years **old**,	bachelor	's Button was to take Pretty Polly on
15	ickering to set up together as two **old**	bachelors	. ROBERT BOAS Brixworth, Nort
16	ghtly more likely to reach **old** age as	bachelors	.
17	Remember the **old**	bachelors	button? When we wore braces, you
18	mid power. She says the 38-year **old**	bachelor	hangs a three-foot brass and crystal
19	ew intends to move back into his **old**	bachelor	pad at Windsor Castle when his Ba
20	ng tea with one of my tutors, an **old**	bachelor	don at Magdalen; and the same en
21	I'd like to bet on it. An **old**	bachelor	like him must be lonely. There's onl
22	's face. The seventy five year **old**	bachelor	had finally got his girl at the second

Here most of the collocates suggest a more negative discourse prosody of *bachelor* – particularly for *elderly* and *lonely*. In line 1 the bachelor is also *dry* and *conventional*. In line 4 is the phrase 'only the oddities who make elderly bachelor'. Line 7 refers to an elderly bachelor's *habits*. The combination of the word *lonely* with *bachelor* suggests a negative discourse prosody in itself, although when we look at the concordance, we can see that some of the situations describe even more unpleasant circumstances. In line 9, a lonely bachelor has died in his bath. In line 12 another lonely bachelor is the victim of a vicious hate campaign. In line 11 there is the word *pity* while line 10 reports a news item where lonely bachelors are being linked with Russian girls – one implication being that they have been unsuccessful at forming relationships with local women. However, the collocate *old* does not tend to be as negative. Three of the cases of *old* occur in phrases which state someone's age (lines 14, 18 and 22). However, in line 21 we have the phrase 'An old bachelor like him must be lonely'. There is a description of an old bachelor don at Magdalen – someone who is perhaps 'married' to their work and in line 13 the phrase 'It is time that old bachelor ... got married' suggests that bachelorhood is not a preferable state of affairs for someone.

What about the other collocates of *bachelor* in Table 5.5? It may be tempting to discount *James* and *Gilbey* as they refer to a single person. However, we may also want to ask, why is this person referred to as a bachelor six times in the BNC? As noted earlier, references to James Gilbey always occur in connection to a news story involving Princess Diana, who was allegedly taped saying 'I love you' to him over the telephone (Table 5.9). As Princess Diana was married at the time, this news story was treated as a scandal. The marital status of Gilbey is made explicit, perhaps because of the connotations of *bachelor* with a somewhat glamorous or racy lifestyle – as collocations like *eligible*, *days*, *life*, *flat* and *party* suggest.

Table 5.9 Concordance of bachelor *when it collocates with* James *and* Gilbey

1	itted her daughter had been out with	bachelor	**Gilbey** – named as the man on the in
2	gy" call between Princess Diana and	bachelor	**James Gilbey**, says consultant Jane
3	i was taped speaking on the phone to	bachelor	**James Gilbey**, who told her "I love y
4	The new threat came as	bachelor	**James Gilbey** – said to be the man r
5	pes, a man believed most likely to be	bachelor	**James Gilbey** is heard calling Di "Sq
6	Diana was said to have used	bachelor	friend James **Gilbey** and other pals to

What about the collocate *males*? In this case, six of the eight cases of collocation between *bachelor* and *males* occur in the Applied Science category of the British National Corpus. The concordance shows that in this case, *bachelor* is used in a more scientific 'neutral' context, relating to the sexual behaviour of animals and birds (Table 5.10).

Table 5.10 Concordance of bachelor *when it collocates with* males

1	ual harems move separately and the "	bachelor	" **males** are found in their own discre
2	ly rejected. However, **males** from the	bachelor	section of the band harass owners unt
3	of issues need to be resolved.These	bachelor	**males** may not be more deprived of s
4	(8)The **males** in the	bachelor	groups of gelada may show homose
5	paired males to be more vigilant than	bachelor	**males**.In a study of mallard and tufte
6	ignificantly higher peeking rates than	bachelor	**males** (Figure 3).So it looks as thoug
7	their youngsters. Surplus **males** form	bachelor	groups. A solitary horse is a rarity, a
8	st of the mating; and many **males** die	bachelor	. Polygyny, often combined with a d

The word *status* collocates six times with *bachelor*. Again, this seems to be used in a descriptive sense. A close look at the concordance (Table 5.11) reveals that lines 1 and 5 are taken from official documents, whereas the others are from romantic novels. The use of *bachelor status* in the romantic novels is linked to the concept of the 'eligible bachelor' – the unmarried state of a man is seen as something worth commenting on. The final concordance line also implies that being a bachelor means that home comforts will be denied, which ties in with the view of bachelors as lonely.

Table 5.11 Concordance of bachelor *when it collocates with* status

1	I contract is for two years, married or	bachelor	**status**, renewable annually by mutual
2	e had last broached the subject of his	bachelor	**status**.
3	been surprised that the subject of his	bachelor	**status** had not been pursued with gre
4	g, considering that you appear to find	bachelor	**status** the answer."
5	in more remote locations may be on a	bachelor	**status** with more frequent air ticket
6	upply a few of the home comforts my	bachelor	**status** denies me, perhaps?" He was

An examination of other immediate left hand collocates of *status* in the BNC produced a set of words which were linked to notoriety, finance and work (Table 5.12). However, the fact that *status* seems to collocate with a range of both positive and negative terms suggests that there is no single obvious discourse prosody. This is perhaps an important point to make – not all words contain hidden discourse prosodies waiting to be discovered, or in some cases, discourse prosodies may simply cancel each other out!

Table 5.12 Main collocational groupings of status

Semantic group	Collocates
Inferior	servile, lowly, second-class, inferior
Superior	celebrity, cult, superstar, legendary, privileged, sovereign
Economic/work	grant-maintained, fundholding, charitable, trust, socio-economic, self-employed, occupational

The final collocate of *bachelor* I want to consider is *confirmed*. I had expected that the phrase *confirmed bachelor* would be a euphemism for homosexuality. However, in the five cases of its uses, it tends to refer to heterosexual men who had appeared to be bachelors but had surprised their friends and family by getting married late in life. What else does *confirmed* collocate with in the BNC? Restricting collocations to just nouns which occur immediately after confirmed, we find the following list: *sightings, hypotheses, diagnosis, fears, reports, cases* and *plans*. A further examination of these collocates in context reveals that they tend to relate to scientific, medical or news texts. In particularly, things that get confirmed are generally classified as bad news, e.g. an unpleasant medical diagnosis, an arrest or a crime. The phrase *confirmed bachelor* therefore could hold a discourse prosody for bad news or a scientific frame of reference – in general then, not a particularly positive construction.

What we see then with the strongest collocates of *bachelor* is a somewhat dualistic picture of discourse. A young bachelor receives a positive discourse prosody – connected to living a happy, possibly urban existence. This is supported by an analysis of the collocates *days*, *life*, *eligible* and *party*. However, the positive discourse prosody is tied to the fact that a bachelor life is expected to be a short-term situation. When bachelorhood becomes a long-term state, then it is viewed as more problematic: repeatedly characterized in the corpus by poverty, eccentricity, old age and loneliness. There is an implication that there is something wrong or unfortunate about a man who goes through his whole life without marrying.

What about the collocates of *spinster*? Here we only have four collocates to analyse: *elderly*, *widows*, *sisters* and *three*. Table 5.13 shows concordances for these words with *spinster*.

Table 5.13 Concordance of spinster when it collocates with elderly, widows, sisters and three

1	ler knocked on the door of an **elderly**	spinster	's Knightsbridge flat and talked her
2	esign. I outlined an **elderly** atrocious	spinster	and established her in Lamb House.
3	. 52 lived Mr. Maton with his **elderly**	spinster	sister, a very quiet couple whose fa
4	AN **ELDERLY**	spinster	froze to death on Christmas Day, an
5	I was given was to bathe an **elderly**	spinster	I infuriated the officer in charge by
6	men and the stereotype of the **elderly**	spinster	, in part reflect cohort effects; future
7	istory and Geography, was an **elderly**	spinster	who, under a kindly face, was very t
8	AN **ELDERLY**	spinster	with "a heart of gold" was battered
9	the field; so suddenly that an **elderly**	spinster	had to furnish him with stars unsew
10	husbands [Hill, 229 – 30].	spinster	and **widows** enjoyed the legal status
11	many women died too, in a sense, as	spinster	and **widows** of the lost generation
12	men associated with my mother, all	spinsters	or **widows**, never smiled and were c
13	as a preoccupation with the cause of	spinsters	and **widows**. The League emphasise
14	shopkeepers and also from **widows**,	spinsters	and clergymen, whose concern was
15	"We're **sisters** and	spinsters	," they told me with a laugh; but,
16	by three bachelor brothers and three	spinster	**sisters**. Senior brother, John Isbister
17	, known as Tammy, who with his two	spinster	**sisters** ran "Moulds Dining Rooms"
18	invented.) Irene had three much older	spinster	**sisters** who adored her, and her one
19	women, pairs of widowed **sisters** or	spinster	daughters with ageing mothers, and
20	by three bachelor brothers and **three**	spinster	sisters. Senior brother, John Isbister
21	like the Misses Cardings, the **three**	spinster	ladies who kept the hat shop beyond
22	nvented.) Irene had **three** much older	spinster	sisters who adored her, and her one
23	If deeply in church affairs. His **three**	Spinster	daughters, whom he had not registe
24	rd: three died young, one remained a	Spinster	, **three** were Edwardian brides, two
25	gure prominently. In one house **three**	spinsters	, all younger than fifty, earned only
26	The **three**	spinsters	of the English school have had full-t

Here we see a more limited range of discourse prosodies. First there is the characterization of spinsters as victims. This occurs in line 1 (expanding this concordance line reveals that it is from a news story about a man who swindles a spinster out of her fortune). In line 4 a spinster freezes to death, while in line 8 a spinster is battered to death. Spinsters are described as having a heart of gold or a kindly face in line 7 and 8. However, in line 2 a spinster is described as *atrocious*, whereas an expansion of concordance line 7 reveals that this spinster 'under a kindly face, was very tough'. The concordance lines connected to *widows* (lines 10–14) are interesting because they all use a co-ordinating conjunction. Spinsters are described as a similar category to widows. Lines 15–19 describe a type of spinster – generally sisters who live together. This continues with the concordance of *three* (lines 20–26). Spinsters are described variously as running a hat shop (line 21), running 'Moulds Dining Rooms' (line 17) or teaching (lines 7 and 26). As with looking at the historical antecedents of the word *bachelor*, it is useful to consider the etymology of spinster as well. The term *spinster* derives from the word *spin* and refers to the spinning of wool. From about the thirteenth century, any woman who spun wool for a living was known as a spinster. Eventually the word was added to a woman's name to refer to her occupation and by the seventeenth century it was used in legal documents to refer to unmarried women. It is possible that it refers to older women, because the longer a woman remained unmarried, the longer she would be known as a spinster. The strong collocation of *elderly* and *spinster* here is therefore explained more clearly when we consider the historical context of the term.

The appearance of *three* as a collocate of *spinster* is particularly interesting: this number does not collocate with *bachelor(s)*, nor do any other numbers collocate with *spinster(s)*. What other words collocate with *three* in the BNC? *Three*, being a very frequent word, has many collocates. Restricting collocates to only types of females, we find: *daughters, girlfriends, sisters, queens* (due to games of cards) and *witches* (due to Macbeth). It is perhaps the latter collocation which is the most culturally salient – the link between three spinsters and Macbeth's three witches is not made explicit in the corpus, but it is perhaps subconsciously there (the witches are also referred to in the Shakespeare play as weird *sisters* – another collocate of *spinster(s)*). This linking of *spinsters – three – witches* is therefore worth mentioning, suggesting a subtle connection of spinsters to witches via the word *three*. The notion of such 'second-order' collocates is discussed in more detail later in this chapter.

It is also interesting how the theme of death seems to occur in the concordance (lines 4, 8, 10–14, 19 and 24). Therefore the strongest collocates of *spinster* tend to be more closely linked to the 'elderly bachelor' discourse, with some similarities. However, spinsters aren't described as particularly lonely, perhaps because they are living with their sisters or other relatives. Therefore spinsters tend to be constructed as more dependent on others than bachelors.

Resistant discourses

A collocational analysis has shown us some of the most salient discourses and different ways of referring to bachelors and spinsters. However, a collocational analysis will not always reveal the full picture. For example, the four collocates of *spinster(s)* only yielded 26 concordance lines. There were another 150 occurrences of *spinster* in the BNC which we did not examine. While these other concordance lines did not contain collocates, they may also contain patterns. For example, we find terms like *frustrated, love-starved, sex-starved, repressed* and *lonely* which all refer to the sexuality of spinsters, but do not occur often enough to be collocates (Table 5.14).

Table 5.14 Concordance of spinster *showing a discourse prosody of repression*

1	Miss Symes, a seemingly **frustrated**	spinster	if ever there was one, have it to ex
2	as the good hearted and **love-starved**	spinster	.Peter's Friends (15) opens in
3	It was one of the rituals of this **lonely**	spinster	's life that every day she would take
4	shipboard romance with a **repressed**	spinster	, Bette Davis, who has been prescr
5	ly cruel stereotype of the **sex-starved**	spinster	fantasising about rape. At the clima
6	h, then hand one to the **sex-starved**	spinster	, sometimes even going to the leng

There are also another set of terms: *atrocious, dried-up, over-made-up, plain-Jane, whey-faced* and *waspish* which characterize spinsters as unattractive (Table 5.15).

Table 5.15 Concordance of spinster *showing a discourse prosody of unattractiveness*

1	sign.I outlined an elderly **atrocious**	spinster	and established her in Lamb House
2	wise elder, set against the **dried-up**	spinster	, the interfering granny, the miser, t
3	but not the standard **over-made-up**	spinster	secretary. She looked very positive
4	, in which her repressed, **plain-Jane**	spinster	blossoms overnight into chic, radian
5	Miss Weeton was a **waspish**	spinster	, but the picture is not wholly unkin
6	in all my life," sighs the **whey-faced**	spinster	, and Williams is wryly sympathetic

It is therefore still worth considering all of the concordance lines, as more subtle discourse prosodies are likely to exist which may support or counter what has already been found. For example, the discourse prosody which characterizes spinsters as unattractive forms part of the overall negative discourse associated with the term – the idea that they are unmarried not through choice, but because they are unable to attract a man. Within this assumption is the implicit notion that to be married is better than not being married, particularly when we consider the related discourse which frames spinsters as sex-starved and bachelors as lonely and eccentric, etc.

A collocational analysis is useful for two reasons. First it provides a focus for our initial analysis which is particularly helpful when a large number of concordance lines needs to be sorted multiple times in order to reveal lexical patterns. Secondly, it gives us the most salient and obvious lexical patterns surrounding a subject, from which a number of discourses can be obtained. When two words frequently collocate, there is evidence that the discourses surrounding them are particularly powerful – the strength of collocation implies that these are two concepts which have been linked in the minds of people and have been used again and again – perhaps to the point where even one half of the pair is likely to prime someone who hears or reads that word to think of the other half. So with the 150 occurrences of *spinster* that did not include the strong collocates, we may still be primed to think of words like *elderly* or think about *sisters* living together, even when these words are not present. Collocates can therefore act as triggers, suggesting unconscious associations which are ways that discourses can be maintained. However, as pointed out at the end of the last chapter – we should also be aware that people are different. It is unlikely that everyone who sees or reads the word *spinster* will have exactly the same response – for example, a child, a linguist, someone who has English as a second language or someone who is themself a 'spinster' may all experience different reactions and associations when encountering the word *spinster*. Corpus data therefore gives us one way of understanding language, based on what is typical. Atypical responses are likely to lead to resistant discourses being formed around a subject. For example, in line 5 of Table 5.14 there is reference to the 'cruel stereotype of the sex-starved spinster'. Such a view acknowledges that the sex-starved spinster *is* a stereotype and therefore implies that there may be other, non-stereotyped ways of thinking. In fact, when looking at other concordance lines of *spinster*, we find that stereotypes are often referred to or challenged. Table 5.16 shows ten cases in the BNC where the term *spinster* is considered in a more reflexive way, in some cases challenging or criticizing the dominant negative discourses surrounding it. However, resistant discourses often have the effect of reproducing the hegemonic discourse. By being resistant they

114

have to state what they are against. Therefore, we still find negative terms: *sex-starved, despised, pitied, stark*, etc. This can make resistant discourses more difficult to be drawn out of a concordance. Clues that these concordance lines represent resistant discourses are found in the context: terms like *stereotype, portrayed, evokes, label, language, word* and *not*.

Table 5.16 Contesting discourses of spinster

1	men and the **stereotype** of the elderly	spinster	, in part reflect cohort effects; future
2	y **cruel stereotype** of the sex-starved	spinster	fantasising about rape.
3	eighteenth century the **stereotypical**	spinster	was "... one to be despised, pitied, a
4	sfactory alternative, for the life of the	spinster	is often **portrayed** in stark terms.
5	paraging **word** for lesbians, and with	spinster	, less disparaging but still pretty ne
6	I think "housewife" is like	spinster	and "spinster" is a **terrible label** to
7	ers were, in the **language of the day**,	spinster	– mainly former teachers or civil s
8		Spinsters	are **still** despised and mocked.
9	To be a	spinster	is **not quite the abnormality it**
10	Here, too, **the word**	spinster	**evokes** an ugly, lonely woman who

Therefore, collocates may also contain traces of resistant discourses, which are worth exploring in the remaining concordance lines. Interestingly, there do not appear to be any resistant discourses in the BNC surrounding the term *bachelor*, perhaps due to the fact that *bachelor* at least has some positive associations, whereas the mainstream discourse of *spinster* is more negative.

From looking at the collocates surrounding the words *bachelor* and *spinster*, we can also get an idea of discourses about marriage and gender per se. A dominant overarching discourse appears to be that it is generally good to get married (to a member of the opposite sex), whether one is male or female. In addition to this though, being male and unmarried is seen as unproblematic, and indeed an enjoyable state of being, as long as the man is relatively young. Freedom from responsibility, as well as the ability to 'play the field' if one is viewed as 'eligible' suggests that a young bachelor life is a happy one. An extended period of bachelorhood, however, is viewed as less preferable to marriage. Older bachelors are frequently characterized as being lonely and eccentric. However, there is no equivalent state of happy youthful spinsterhood. The concept of a young spinster (whether happy or not) is simply absent from the corpus data. Older spinsters are described as unattractive and also as living with relatives, possibly because they are unable to support themselves. An examination of other concordance lines in the corpus also reveals the presence of a resistant discourse surrounding spinsters, which challenges what is seen as negative stereotyping. Therefore, the analysis has not only been useful in revealing discourses concerning bachelors and spinsters, but it has also provided us with some of the ways that gender is constructed differently and how views on being unmarried are dependent on a number of factors including sex, age and perceived attractiveness.

Collocational networks

So far we have tended to consider collocates individually, or we have looked at groups of collocates together because they have tended to show similar sorts of discourse prosodies or because their meanings are similar, e.g. *elderly/lonely* or *days/life/living*. While this methodology, based on researcher interpretation did prove to be productive, there is another way to consider links between collocates. For example, one of the collocates of *bachelor* was *James*. Another was *Gilbey*. As we have already seen, this was due to references to the person James Gilbey. Unsurprisingly, *James* and *Gilbey* were both strong collocates of each other (achieving a score of over 5 with the log-log calculation), as well as being collocates of *bachelor*. By plotting links between collocates in this way, either in a table or a chart, we can start to see closer links between words which point at different types of discourses. Figure 5.4 shows the collocates of *bachelor* which also collocate with each other.

It can be seen that the words connected to the educational meaning of *bachelor* also tend to collocate with each other: *education,*

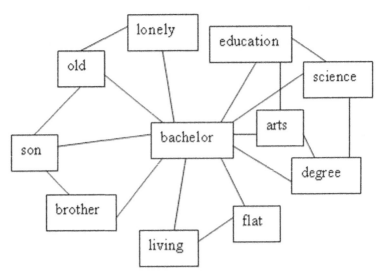

Figure 5.4 Collocational network of bachelor

arts, degree, science. Old and *lonely* also collocate together, as do *living* and *flat*. Some words which have no additional collocates – *confirmed, days, eligible* and *button* are not included in the network. This is not to say that they are not important, just that the discourses around them are negotiated through a more straightforward linear relationship between them and the word *bachelor*, rather than being part of a network of interrelated terms.

And it is possible to take collocational networks a step further, by considering second-order collocates. For example, in the BNC two collocates of the word *elderly* are *chronically* and *infirm. Chronically* and *infirm* do not collocate with each other, but the word *sick* is a collocate of both of these words. *Sick* is therefore a second-order collocate of *elderly* and suggests a further relationship between *chronically* and *infirm.* Figure 5.5 shows first and second-order, collocates of the word *elderly* (in order to restrict the number of collocates I only looked at words which had a MI score above 7.0). Second-order collocates are shown in circles.

This network is interesting in that it shows a host of associations connected with the term *elderly*. One set of words: *dementing, long-*

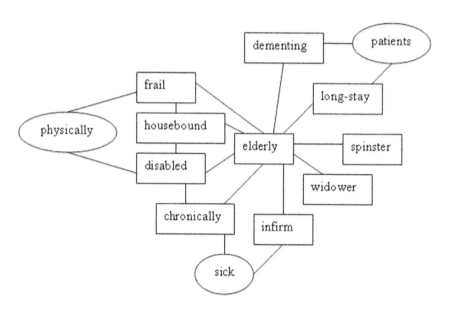

Figure 5.5 Collocational network of elderly

stay, patients implies people who have been permanently hospitalized, due to mental deterioration. Another set: *housebound, frail, disabled, physically, chronically, sick* and *infirm* suggests physical illness, not requiring institutionalization but implying inability to get around. The only two words which are not part of these deterioration discourses are *spinster* and *widower*. However, if we don't think of *elderly* when we think of the term *spinster* when it appears on its own, we are perhaps more likely to associate words like *frail, housebound, sick,* etc. when we see a phrase like *elderly spinster* due to the other associations of *elderly*. It is also interesting that while *spinster* and *widower* are strong collocates of *elderly*, *bachelor* does not appear in the network (it received a lower MI score – see Table 5.17). This suggests that we may be more likely to think of someone who is elderly in terms of an unmarried woman or a man whose wife has died rather than say, an unmarried man or a woman whose husband has died. Perhaps this is due to the somewhat dualistic nature of *bachelor* (it can mean someone living a more carefree younger existence). Why does *widower* collocate more strongly with *elderly* than *widow* does? Maybe not all widows are elderly – women tend to live longer than men anyway, so men who are widowed may tend to be relatively old, having outlived their wives who also tend to live a long time. There is further evidence for this in the fact that *young* and *widow* significantly collocate together, but *young* and *widower* do not.

Table 5.17 *Some collocates of elderly and their MI scores*

collocate	MI score
spinster	7.9
widower	7.1
bachelor	5.7
widow	4.8
woman	4.5
man	2.9

Conclusion

As we have seen, collocates are useful in that they help to summarize the most significant relationships between words in a corpus. This can be incredibly time-saving and give analysts a clear focus. Collocates are also useful in helping to spell out mainstream discourses – while a closer analysis of them can reveal resistant discourses too.

However, it is important that we do not over-interpret collocational data. We should check the context that collocates occur in by examining concordances in more detail. It is also important to consider issues of semantic preference or discourse prosody, which an initial collocational analysis is likely to overlook. However, as seen with our analysis of the phrases *bachelor days* and *confirmed bachelor*, carrying out additional collocational analyses in a general corpus can help to reveal discourse prosodies.

We should also be aware that different methods of calculating collocation tend to yield different results – the interplay between frequency and saliency needs to be taken into account. And an examination of the historical backgrounds and etymologies of words is also useful (it was only from considering other (non-corpus) sources that we were able to make the link between the meanings of *bachelor* as a type of degree and a married man). Finally, we also need to take into account issues of production and reception. We considered collocates of *bachelor* and *spinster* in a corpus of general British English. However, had we focused on a particular genre of text – for example, novels, newspapers or academic papers in the social sciences, the collocates (and discourses) that we uncovered are likely to have been different. Additionally, we can't assume that everyone will be primed to think of collocations in the same way. Even if we have had a wide enough exposure to English to be aware to some degree that a word like *spinster* collocates with *elderly* and therefore will shore up associations of old age whether we want it to or not, the way that we interpret and respond to these mental associations is likely to differ depending on dozens of social and individual factors. For example, our most recent encounter of the word *spinster* may have an increased weighting in the way that we interpret the word the next time we read or hear it.

In the following chapter we consider another way of examining saliency in texts – this time not by focusing on words which occur near other words, but simply by considering words which occur more often than we would expect them to by chance alone – keywords.

Step-by-step guide to collocational analysis

1. Build or obtain access to a corpus.
2. Decide on a search term (e.g. *bachelor*), bearing in mind that the terms can be expanded to include plurals or other forms, euphemisms, anaphora or relevant proper nouns.

3. Obtain a list of collocates. If you are able to use different algorithms to obtain your list, then it is worth trying this.

4. Decide how many collocates you want to look at – for example, anything scoring an MI score of above 3, or the strongest 30 collocates, whatever they are. You may also decide to 'clean' the collocates list by removing proper nouns or grammatical words.

5. Can the collocates be grouped semantically, thematically or grammatically – e.g. words like *elderly*, *old*, etc.? Use this as a basis for the order in which you analyse the words in more detail.

6. Obtain concordances of the collocates and look for patterns within the context. This should enable you to uncover dominant discourses surrounding the subject.

7. Consider contesting discourses – concordance lines which go against or question the dominant reading of a term.

8. Look at concordance lines of the search term that do not contain collocates. What discourse prosodies are present there? Do they support or contradict those found in the analysis of the collocates?

9. How do the collocates relate to each other? Try building a first or second-order collocational network.

10. Attempt to explain why particular discourse patterns appear around collocates and relate this is to issues of text production and reception and/or etymologies of particular words.

Notes

1. The terms *marriage* and *institution* have a strong MI collocation of 3.79 in the BNC.

2. Other terms and phrases, e.g. *bachelorette, man who never married* are also possible, but for the sake of simplicity, this chapter only considers *bachelor* and *spinster*.

3. Jones and Sinclair (1974) suggest that significant collocates are found within a span of 4:4, although Stubbs (2001b: 29) points out that there is no total agreement to this.

6 Keyness

Frequency revisited

As we saw in Chapter 3, a frequency list can help to provide researchers with the lexical foci of any given corpus. Investigating the reasons why a particular word (or cluster of words – wordlists don't have to be limited to single words) appears so frequently in a corpus can help to reveal the presence of discourses, especially those of a hegemonic nature. For example, in Chapter 3, an examination of the most frequent ten lexical lemmas in the holiday corpus provides clues about the overall focus of the leaflets (the top two lemmas: BAR and CLUB were used in ways which made much of the importance of being located within access to numerous places to drink). Obviously, the terms themselves don't yield this information; it is only with further explorations – collocational analyses, concordances, comparisons to other, similar terms that such conclusions can be drawn. Yet compiling a frequency list is an important first step in the analysis, giving the researcher an idea about what to focus on.

However, simple frequency lists also possess limitations. In order to demonstrate this, I want us to turn to a new research topic and text type: political debates on fox-hunting in the British House of Commons. In the UK, fox-hunting as it is recognized today had been practised since the seventeenth century (Scruton 1998). There have been numerous attempts to regulate or ban it, stretching back over half a century. In January 2001, according to the BBC, more than 200,000 people took part in fox-hunting in the UK, and it was described as 'one of the most divisive issues among the population'.[1] Tony Blair's Labour Party manifesto in 1997 promised a 'free vote in parliament on whether hunting with hounds should be banned'. In July 1999 he announced that he would make fox-hunting illegal and before the next general election if possible. A government inquiry on hunting with dogs concluded that 'This is a complex issue that is full of paradoxes' (Dept. for Environment, Food and Rural Affairs 2000: 1). The Inquiry did not attempt to answer the question of whether or not hunting should be banned but did consider the consequences of banning hunting and how such a ban might be implemented. After a number of parliamentary debates and votes, the ban was finally implemented in February 2005.

Crystal (1995: 378) notes that parliamentary language is rarely taken at face value: participants do not assume that Grice's conversational Maxims are being followed. Politicians are aware that they are playing a language game with huge consequences, and that they must appear to speak with authority and conviction. In order to survive these demands they often develop a style of speaking which is opaque, vague or empty.[2]

Therefore, in order to examine discourses surrounding the issue of banning fox-hunting I decided to build a corpus of parliamentary debates on the issue. I collected electronic transcripts of three debates in the House of Commons which occurred prior to votes on hunting. These occurred on 18 March 2002, 16 December 2002 and 30 June 2003. In general, the majority of Commons members voted for the ban to go ahead, although in each debate a range of options could be debated and subsequently voted upon. For example: a complete ban vs. hunting with some form of supervision. These three debates were not the only ones on banning hunting which had occurred, however, looking back at debates which had occurred as far back as 1997 would have made the factor of diachronic change a much more important consideration. Additionally, debates also took place in the House of Lords, which I also decided not to examine for the purposes of this chapter. One of the reasons why fox-hunting was debated so often in the House of Commons was because the House of Lords rejected an outright ban on a number of occasions, sending the Bill back to the Commons. Therefore the outcome of debates in the House of Commons was significantly different to that those in the House of Lords. Examining both sets of debates over a wider range of time is beyond the scope of this chapter.

Focusing then, on the three debates which I did collect, the first procedure that was carried out was to create a word list of the 'fox-hunting' corpus. The corpus size was 129,798 words. Tables 6.1 and 6.2 show the ten most frequent words and lexical items respectively from this corpus (derived via WordSmith).

Table 6.1 The ten most frequent words in the fox-hunting corpus

Rank	Word	Frequency
1	the	8,575
2	to	4,186
3	that	4,118
4	of	3,599
5	and	2,905
6	is	2,599
7	a	2,586
8	in	2,364
9	I	2,312
10	it	1,866

Table 6.2 The ten most frequent lexical words in the fox-hunting corpus

Rank	Word	Frequency
1	hon.	1,113
2	hunting	1,051
3	Mr.	711
4	bill	665
5	house	490
6	ban	442
7	right	433
8	friend	413
9	minister	387
10	people	373

An examination of these two word lists does not reveal anything initially interesting that relates to possible discourses of fox-hunting within the debate. As with many other frequency lists, the most frequent words tend to be grammatical items such as determiners, prepositions and conjunctions. Sometimes grammatical items in themselves *can* be indicative of particular discourses, for example if a conjunction like *and* is repeatedly used to stress a connection between two objects of discussion (e.g. sex *and* violence on television) then this may be worth noting. However, on the whole collocational and concordance analyses of high frequency grammatical words are not always the best way to approach a corpus-based analysis of discourse.

The most frequent lexical words (Table 6.2) are perhaps more interesting, although here we find words that we would perhaps have expected or guessed to appear. There are terms of address associated with the context of a parliamentary debate: *hon., Mr., friend, right* (the phrase *hon. friend* appears 396 times in the corpus while *right hon. friend* occurs 173 times). There are also other words associated with the context of parliament (*bill, house, minister*) and words connected with the subject under discussion (*hunting, ban*). Therefore, the most frequent lexical words in this case have only helped to confirm expectations surrounding the genre of the text, which isn't necessarily the most useful means of inquiry.

One way of finding out what lexical items are interesting in a frequency list is to compare more than one list together. If a word occurs comparatively more often in, say, a corpus of modern English children's stories, when compared to the British National Corpus, we could conclude that such a word has high saliency in the genre of children's stories and is worth investigating in further detail.

So thinking about comparative possibilities of the fox-hunting debate, it might be useful to consider that the debate has two sides and ultimately each speaker had to vote on the issue of banning fox-hunting. While it may have been the case that speakers who voted the same way actually approached the subject from very different perspectives and had different reasons for the way they voted, the fact that speakers voted, and that their contributions to the debate would be made with an idea of persuading others to vote the same way as them, suggests one area where conflicting discourses may be illuminated. Therefore, it was decided to split the corpus into two. The speech of all of the people who voted to ban fox-hunting was placed into one file, while the speech of those who voted for hunting to remain was placed in another. The frequencies of the top ten lexical words from these sub-corpora are presented in Table 6.3.

Table 6.3 The ten most frequent lexical words used by opposing groups in the fox-hunting debate

	Anti-hunting			Pro-hunting	
Rank	**Word**	**Frequency**		**Word**	**Frequency**
1	hon.	647		hunting	485
2	hunting	566		hon.	466
3	bill	445		mr.	395
4	house	329		people	222
5	mr.	316		minister	215
6	ban	264		way	193
7	right	256		member	182
8	friend	248		ban	178
9	new	235		right	177
10	way	223		friend	165

Although it was hoped that this table would reveal more interesting differences, what it has actually shown us are similarities!

Seven of the words (*Hon., hunting, mr., ban, right, friend, way*) appear in both lists, and almost all of the words are again connected to either the subject under discussion (hunting) or the context where the debates took place (parliament). Some of the frequencies may be more interesting to examine – for example, the pro-hunt voters refer to the word *ban* only 178 times, compared to the anti-hunt voters, who used the same word 264 times. And is it relevant that *hunting* was mentioned 566 times by the anti-hunt voters and 485 times by the pro-hunt voters?

As it turns out, the anti-hunt voters contributed more speech to the debates overall (71,468 words vs. 58,330 words), so as proportions, these frequencies are more similar than they originally look (for example, *ban* occurs as 0.36 per cent of the anti-hunt vocabulary and as 0.30 per cent of the pro-hunt vocabulary). Therefore, a measure which takes into account the relative size of both sub-corpora combined with the relative frequencies of each word would be more useful. Fortunately such a measure exists, in the concept of keyness.

Introducing keyness

Using WordSmith, it is possible to compare the frequencies in one wordlist against another in order to determine which words occur *statistically* more often in wordlist A when compared with wordlist B and vice versa. Then all of the words that do occur more often than expected in one file when compared to another are compiled together into another list, called a keyword list. And it is this keyword list which is likely to be more useful in suggesting lexical items that could warrant further examination. A keyword list therefore gives a measure of *saliency*, whereas a simple word list only provides *frequency*.

So how exactly is a keyword list compiled? WordSmith takes into account the size of each sub-corpus and the frequencies of each word within them. It then carries out statistical tests on each word (the user can specify the chi-squared or log-likelihood test) which gives each word a p (or probability) value. The p value (a number between 0 and 1) indicates the amount of confidence that we have that a word is key due to chance alone – the smaller the p value, the more likely that the word's strong presence in one of the sub-corpora isn't due to chance but a result of the author's (conscious or subconscious) choice to use that word repeatedly. Because every word in the two corpora is assigned a p value, as corpus users it is up to us to decide how low the p value needs to be before we can label a word as key. The same sort of problem occurs in the social sciences, particularly in experimental psychology – and in general a p value of about 0.05 (indicating 95 per cent confidence that the results didn't occur due to chance) or less is taken as a 'cut-off' point and therefore viewed as worth reporting. However, as Oakes (1998: 4) points out, 'In corpus analysis, much of the data is skewed.' Words *don't* just occur as random collections; for example, the presence of an article (e.g. *the* or *a*) is incredibly likely to mean that a noun or adjective will follow it. One way to overcome the issue of skewness is to use log-normal distributions (hence the log-likelihood test is useful). However, taking a p value of 0.05 as the cut-off point may not be as sensible as with other disciplines in the social sciences. For example, if we were to take a p value of 0.05 as the cut-off point in determining whether a word was key or not, we would find that *eliminated*, which occurs four times in the anti-hunting part of the debate and zero times in the pro-hunting part of the debate would be classed as key – for something to occur only four times to be key in a corpus of this size doesn't suggest that it is a particularly salient feature. Additionally, with a p value of 0.05 we would find that 797 words altogether would be key. As there were 6,955 original types

key words (keyness)

N	WORD	FREQ	AYE.LST %	FREQ	NO.LST %	KEYNESS	P
1	MICHAEL	133	0.19	0		158.8	0.000000
2	ALUN	129	0.18	0		154.1	0.000000
3	I	1,451	2.03	865	1.48	55.7	0.000000
4	CLAUSE	215	0.30	71	0.12	49.7	0.000000
5	BILL	445	0.62	220	0.38	39.0	0.000000
6	COMMONS	46	0.06	4		33.4	0.000000
7	NEW	235	0.33	99	0.17	32.9	0.000000
8	HOUSE	329	0.46	161	0.28	29.8	0.000000
9	CONCLUSION	45	0.06	5		29.2	0.000000
10	ISSUE	185	0.26	75	0.13	28.4	0.000000
11	DOGS	182	0.25	74	0.13	27.8	0.000000
12	CLEAR	112	0.16	38	0.07	24.7	0.000001
13	ATKINSON	0		15	0.03	24.0	0.000001
14	FISH	2		23	0.04	25.2	0.000001
15	MINISTER'S	10	0.01	41	0.07	27.1	0.000000
16	LIDINGTON	2		25	0.04	28.1	0.000000
17	GARNIER	3		28	0.05	28.7	0.000000
18	PEOPLE	151	0.21	222	0.38	32.0	0.000000
19	MR	316	0.44	395	0.68	32.3	0.000000
20	EMOOR	5		38	0.07	35.9	0.000000
21	CRIMINAL	2		38	0.07	47.3	0.000000
22	GRAY	8	0.01	64	0.11	61.7	0.000000

Figure 6.1 Keywords when p < 0.000001

of words in the corpus, this would mean that over 11 per cent of them would be classed as keywords, far too many to examine. Scott (1999) suggests then, that the notion of risk is less important than the notion of selectivity, so it is therefore more sensible to specify a much lower p value: WordSmith uses a default of p < 0.000001 which with our data gives us a more manageable total of 22 keywords (See Figure 6.1).

Here the first column (N) simply numbers the keywords in the order that they are presented (they are ordered here in terms of keyword strength). The second column (WORD) lists each keyword. The third column (FREQ.) gives the frequencies of each keyword as it occurred in the anti fox-hunting sub-corpus. The fourth column (AYE. LST %) shows this figure as a percentage of the whole sub-corpus. Where there is no figure at all, it is because the percentage is so small to be negligible. The fifth and sixth columns show the same figures for the pro fox-hunting sub-corpus. Due to the fact that the two sub-corpora are of different sizes, the best way to compare frequencies is to look at the percentage columns rather than the raw frequency columns. The seventh column assigns a keyness value to each word; the higher the score, the stronger the keyness of that word, whereas the final column gives the p value of each word. As p is set so low here, almost all of the figures in this column are 0.000000. Therefore the keyness value gives a more gradable account of the strength of each word in the table.

You may have noticed that the keyness score starts high (at 158.8) for the word *Michael*, and gradually decreases, to around 24 by the middle of the table. However, after that it starts to get higher again. By the last row of the table it has risen to 61.7. This is because the table is actually showing two sets of keywords (hence the fact that about half of the list is in a different colour to the other). The first part shows words which occur more frequently in the anti-hunt speeches when compared to the pro-hunt speeches, while the opposite is true for the second part of the list.

So is the keyword list any more helpful than a simple list of raw frequencies? Well one aspect of the list that perhaps isn't helpful is the number of proper nouns within it. Scott (1999) says that keyword lists tend to show up three types of words. First, there are proper nouns. Secondly the list will probably contain a number of 'aboutness' keywords. These tend to be lexical words: nouns, verbs, adjectives, adverbs and are generally those which are most interesting to analyse. Finally, there may be more high frequency grammatical words, which Scott says may be more indicative of style than aboutness. As the style of a text may play some role in the discourses within it, it is recommended that such high frequency words are not discarded at this point, although some users of WordSmith create 'stop lists' to remove grammatical words from the keywords procedure altogether. For example, a word like *to* may occur as key due to its appearance in phrases related to modality, like *refused to* or *is unwilling to*, which may be worth investigating further. Function words can also help to identify phraseologies which may have unfixed patterns in terms of form, but are more fixed in terms of function, e.g.: *refuse to, refused to, is refusing to*.

The reason why so many proper nouns occur in this keyword list is due to the fact that each speech in the transcription is prefaced with the speaker's name, and to the fact that speakers regularly refer to each other's speeches. The first and second keywords in the list, *Michael* and *Alun* occur because the person responsible for the Bill to change the laws on fox-hunting is called Alun Michael. In the second part of the keyword list the nouns *Atkinson, Lidington, Garnier* and *Gray* all refer to Members of Parliament who wanted fox-hunting to remain legal. The proper noun *Exmoor* refers to a region of the UK where hunting often takes place, and is therefore a place which is likely to be affected by a ban. Although in some cases it may be interesting to pursue the use of proper nouns further, at this point I am going to move on to look at some of the other types of words in the list.

Analysis of keywords

The majority of the keywords found are of the 'aboutness' variety, in both parts of the list. It should be noted again that the words at the extremes of the keyword list are the strongest in terms of them occurring *significantly* more often in one side of the debate than the other. Consider the word at row 21 of the table – *criminal*. Once the proper noun *Gray* has been discarded, the word *criminal* is the strongest keyword used by those who were opposed to a ban on hunting. It occurs 38 times in the collective speech of the pro-hunters and only twice in the speech of the anti-hunters. Why is this the case? As with ordinary frequency lists, this is unfortunately where the limitations of keyword lists come into play. We may want to theorize for the reasons why *criminal* is used so much by pro-hunters – looking at some of the other keywords may provide clues. However, without knowing more about the context of the word *criminal*, as it is used in both sides of the debate, our theories will remain just that – theories. Therefore, it is necessary to examine individual keywords in more detail, by carrying out concordances of them and looking at their collocates.

When a concordance of *criminal* was carried out on the corpus data, it was found that common phrases containing the word *criminal* included *the criminal law* (14), *a criminal offence* (10), *criminal sanctions* (6) and *a criminal act* (3). A collocation table (see Figure 6.2) provides more information – the modal verbs *would* and *should* occur as collocates of criminal, as do forms of the verb MAKE (e.g. *make* and *made*).

N	WORD	TOTAL	LEFT	RIGHT	L5	L4	L3	L2	L1	*	R1	R2	R3	R4	R5
1	CRIMINAL	42	1	1	1	0	0	0	0	40	0	0	0	0	1
2	THE	25	18	7	0	3	1	0	14	0	0	3	1	2	1
3	A	17	14	3	0	0	0	0	14	0	0	0	1	0	2
4	LAW	14	0	14	0	0	0	0	0	0	14	0	0	0	0
5	OF	12	8	4	2	0	1	5	0	0	0	0	0	1	3
6	TO	12	8	4	0	4	2	2	0	0	1	1	1	1	0
7	THAT	11	5	6	4	0	0	0	1	0	0	1	3	1	1
8	BE	10	8	2	1	1	0	6	0	0	0	0	1	0	1
9	OFFENCE	10	0	10	0	0	0	0	0	0	10	0	0	0	0
10	WOULD	10	5	5	1	2	2	0	0	0	0	0	3	1	1
11	IT	8	5	3	0	3	0	2	0	0	0	1	2	0	0
12	MAKE	8	6	2	0	0	2	1	3	0	0	0	0	1	1
13	AND	7	5	2	1	0	1	1	2	0	0	2	0	0	0
14	IN	7	2	5	1	1	0	0	0	0	0	3	0	2	0
15	SANCTIONS	7	1	6	0	1	0	0	0	0	6	0	0	0	0
16	WE	7	5	2	1	3	1	0	0	0	0	0	0	1	1
17	IS	6	2	4	2	0	0	0	0	0	2	0	1	1	0
18	PEOPLE	6	1	5	0	1	0	0	0	0	1	3	1	0	0
19	SHOULD	6	4	2	1	0	3	0	0	0	1	0	1	0	0
20	HUNTING	5	5	0	1	3	0	1	0	0	0	0	0	0	0
21	MADE	5	5	0	0	1	0	3	1	0	0	0	0	0	0
22	NOT	5	5	0	1	3	1	0	0	0	0	0	0	0	0

Figure 6.2 Collocation table of criminal

As the lemma MAKE seemed to be a relatively important collocate of *criminal*, a concordance of MAKE when it occurs within five places to the left or right of *criminal* was carried out on the pro-hunt section of the corpus (see Table 6.4). What seems clear from the table is that the pro-hunters are using a strategy of framing the proposed fox-hunting ban as criminalizing (making criminal) people (see lines 6 and 9) and that they are against this (the negator *not* appears as a collocate of *criminal* and occurs in lines 1, 10 and 11 of the table). Also, the table contains the words *wrong* (line 3) and *cruel* (line 6).

129

Table 6.4 Concordance of MAKE with criminal

1	With the greatest respect, we do not	make	the criminal law on the basis of opinion polls.
2	f all those of whom we disapprove or	make	criminal those activities that we do not wis
3	dom. It is quite wrong in principle to	make	criminal an activity just because a certain
4	consequences may follow if it were	made	a criminal offence. It would undoubtedly-I do
5	ggesting that their findings should be	made	part of the criminal law, foxhunting would c
6	be sufficiently cruel to justify our	making	it a criminal offence and sending people to pri
7	nt of people support hunting being	made	a criminal offence, while 49 per cent. said th
8	that they supported hunting being	made	a criminal offence, and 49 per cent. said that
9	attracting criminal sanctions, but to	make	criminal those people who otherwise want t
10	ent to it so it is not appropriate to	make	it a criminal activity. Secondly, most Member
11	approve of should not necessarily be	made	criminal. The first point that this debate sh
12	te a criminal offence. The Bill would	make	hunting a criminal offence unless it fell withi

Looking at the concordance of the word *criminal*, there are other concordance lines which suggest a similar pattern, but do not include the verb MAKE (a sample of this concordance is presented in Table 6.5). For example, the use of INVOKE in lines 2 and 4 and IMPOSE in lines 9 and 10. Here again, in order to get a better idea of the discourse prosodies associated with these terms, it is useful to refer to a corpus of general English.

Table 6.5 Concordance of criminal containing similar patterns to that of 'make criminal'

1	ack Benches. The Bill will turn into a	criminal	offence an activity now lawfully enjoyed by a
2	be particularly wrong to invoke the	criminal	law against people in my constituency who t
3	be found so to do. It is the use of the	criminal	law that would most appal me. I shall not hav
4	eman to say that the invocation of the	criminal	law in these circumstances is somehow akin t
5	Mr. Garnier: We are extending the	criminal	law. Does my hon. Friend think it in the least
6	he reason we do not normally use the	criminal	law in areas of this kind. Of course, we use t
7	sued by the new authority would be a	criminal	act attracting a fine of up to £5,000. The auth
8	his view, it should not be part of the	criminal	law. My hon. Friend the Member for North
9	ny law that we might pass. Imposing	criminal	sanctions on anybody is a serious matter. The
10	like to address the issue of imposing	criminal	sanctions on people who transgress any law t

Interestingly, in the British National Corpus, INVOKE collocates strongly with two sets of words – legal terms (*procedure, jurisdiction, law, legal*) and terms relating to supernatural forces: *spirits, command, powers* and *god*. Semantically then, INVOKE implies reference to higher powers (with a connection being made between the legal and the supernatural). When the pro-hunters talk about the 'invocation of the criminal law' are they making an implicit comparison to invoking spirits: something which has traditionally been tabooed as dangerous? This is a difficult question to provide a conclusive answer to here, but see Chapter 7 for a discussion of metaphor and corpora, and also Hunston (2002: 119–123). The lemma IMPOSE, on the other hand, is less problematic to interpret. It collocates in the BNC with *restrictions, sanctions, curfew, fines, ban, penalties, burdens* and *limitations*. It therefore contains an extremely negative discourse prosody – if we use *impose* in relation to *criminal law/sanctions*, then we are showing we disapprove of the *criminal law/sanctions*.

It can therefore be seen that once a keyword is made the subject of concordance and collocational inquiry, interesting patterns of discourse begin to emerge. Terms like *invoke* and *impose* are rhetorical strategies, used to strengthen a particular discourse position, in this case, that a ban on hunting would be wrong.

Let us consider another keyword, this time one which occurs more often on the side of the debate of those who want to ban hunting: the word *dogs*. This word occurs 182 times (0.25 per cent) in the speech of the anti-hunters and 74 times (0.13 per cent) in the speech of those who want hunting to remain legal. So this word is also of reasonably high frequency (referring to the ordinary frequency list we first made, it is the 24th most frequent lexical item in the corpus) although it is used significantly more often by those who want to ban hunting.

Another way of exploring the significance of a word in a corpus is to explore the clusters which occur around or near it. The most common three word clusters which occur within five places to the left or right of the word *dogs* are shown in Table 6.6.[3] As the word *dogs* occurs less frequently in the pro-hunt sub-corpus, the number of overall clusters in the right-hand part of the table is smaller. However, what is most clearly similar about both sides of the debate is that when the word *dogs* is used, it appears as part of the cluster *hunting with dogs* most often. In fact, quite a few of the less frequently occurring clusters are connected to hunting with dogs. For example, if we expand the clusters *on hunting with, of hunting with* and *ban on hunting*, we find that they occur as *on hunting with dogs, of hunting with dogs* and *ban on hunting with dogs*. Although *hunting with dogs* is the most frequent cluster under analysis here in both sides of the debate, it should be noted that proportionally it occurs more often in the speech of the anti-hunters than in the speech of the pro-hunters.

Table 6.6 Common clusters occurring within 5L and 5R of dogs

	Anti-hunting speech		Pro-hunting speech	
	cluster	F	cluster	F
1	hunting with dogs	89	hunting with dogs	25
2	on hunting with	17	use of dogs	9
3	of hunting with	16	the use of	9
4	with dogs is	16	of hunting with	5
5	ban on hunting	10	on hunting with	3
6	use of dogs	10		
7	the use of	9		
8	associated with hunting	8		
9	with hunting with	8		
10	cruelty associated with	7		
11	mammals with dogs	7		
12	wild mammals with	7		

The second most common cluster in the pro-hunting speeches is the phrase *use of dogs* which occurs nine times. Interestingly *use of dogs* occurs ten times in the anti-hunting speeches, meaning that this statement occurs proportionally more often in the speech of the pro-hunters (taking into account the relative sizes of the two sub-corpora). *Use of dogs* also appears to be connected to other clusters: particularly *the use of*. As a whole then, it appears that *dogs* appears in two common types of phrase across the corpus – the more popular (*on/of*) *hunting with dogs (is)* and the less common *(the) use of dogs*. These two clusters appear to be alternative ways of phrasing the same idea. We might want to ask why this is the case, and we may theorize that it could be because one is more specific (*hunting with dogs*) whereas the other is vague (*the use of dogs*). However, we need to take care. Maybe *the use of dogs* only appears vague because it occurs as part of a range of clusters such as *the use of dogs to hunt* or *the use of dogs in hunting*, etc. In order to examine this, a concordance of *the use of dogs* was carried out for the whole corpus (see Table 6.7 – the top half of the table contains all the examples from pro-hunters, the bottom half contains all the examples from anti-hunters). From looking at this table, it transpires that in general the phrase *the use of dogs* does not appear as part of statements such as *the use of dogs to hunt animals*. Indeed, the only case where this happens is in line 18, which is used by an anti-hunt speaker. Instead, we find *the use of dogs on rabbits and rats* in line 1 (quite a vague statement), and *the use of dogs to cull foxes* in line 2. Here, the use of *cull* is interesting. The verb lemma CULL collocates most strongly in the BNC with *from* and appears in phrases such as 'National newspapers cull their stories from all over the country'. *Cull* therefore appears to be close in meaning to *take* rather than *kill*; as with the phrase *use of dogs* the word *cull* also acts somewhat euphemistically.

Table 6.7 Concordance of the use of dogs

Examples from the pro-hunt side of the debate

1	ms of hunting, perhaps requiring	the use of dogs	on rabbits and rats would be perfectly sen
2	oes he propose a closed season for	the use of dogs	to cull foxes, but not for the shooting or sn
3	tee stage bans on hare hunting and	the use of dogs	below ground, as well as the original ban o
4	ed hunt? We would argue that the	the use of dogs	is the most selective and humane method
5	down to drafting a Bill in terms of	the use of dogs	. Then the practical difficulties begin. In C
6	d not have fox-hunting also rely on	the use of dogs	. The Minister for Rural Affairs will remem
7	ll. The legislation concentrates on	the use of dogs	. When we start to look at it in detail, we di
8	sion for various loopholes allowing	the use of dogs	. So, let us be clear that this debate is abo
9	fewer alternatives are available to	the use of dogs	"? Mr. Geoffrey Clifton-Brown (Cotswold):

Examples from the anti-hunt side of the debate

10	e for banning hare hunting, or that	the use of dogs	would not result in significantly less sufferi
11	h as ratting, it is equally clear that	the use of dogs	will always be likely to cause less sufferin
12	pest control and, secondly, whether	the use of dogs	will cause significantly less suffering than
13	ath more cruel than that involving	the use of dogs	. Alun Michael: The hon. Gentleman, who
14	-new clause 6-which would permit	the use of dogs	under ground and enable the Secretary of
15	deer hunting and hare hunting and	the use of dogs	under ground that were agreed by the Sta
16	registration of hunting involving	the use of dogs	under ground. However, he would replace t
17	ut there are circumstances in which	the use of dogs	is less cruel than the alternatives and in w
18	at should not be discounted to zero.	The use of dogs	to hunt animals is acceptable in certain cir

So a trend here is that one side of the debate uses a more explicit way of referring to the outcomes of fox-hunting, while the other chooses to be vague or use euphemistic references. At the moment, this finding only provides a clue to possible discourses that are being used in the debate, but it is one which is worth bearing in mind as the other keywords are examined.

What of the other keywords in the list? To examine each one in turn would take up more space than I am able to use, although all provide something interesting – each is a different piece of a puzzle which gradually helps to form a clearer picture. The word *people*, for example, which is key in the pro-hunt side of the debate is often used in attempts to reference a large uncountable mass in two ways. First, *people* refers to those who will be adversely affected by the Bill if it is passed (their livelihoods stopped, their communities threatened and their futures involving a prison term). Secondly, it refers to (a presumably greater number of) people who do not hunt, but are not upset or concerned by those who do.

133

However, the keyword list has only given us a small number of words to examine, and once the proper nouns (*Michael, Alun, Atkinson, Lidington, Garnier, Gray*) have been discounted, this leaves us with just sixteen words in total. We may also want to discount (or at least background for the moment) the keywords which relate to parliament (*Bill, Commons, House, Minister's*), which leaves us with only twelve keywords.

Now at this point we may decide that in fact, 12 keywords aren't enough to carry out an analysis on. So in order to address this issue, it is sometimes worthwhile increasing the p value and carrying out the keywords process again. For example, increasing the p value to $p < 0.001$ elicits 120 keywords, which can be reduced to 88 once the proper nouns have been discarded.

Although the keyness scores in this longer list are less impressive, what is interesting about working with a larger list, is that it becomes possible to see connections between words, which may not always be apparent at first, but are clearer once they have been subjected to a more rigorous mode of analysis. For example, keywords in the pro-hunt debate include the following words: *fellow, citizens, Britain, freedom, imposing, illiberal, sanctions* and *offence*. All of these keywords are connected in some way to the findings we have already looked at. So *sanctions, offence, imposing* and *illiberal* occur in similar ways to the word *criminal* which was examined above. Table 6.8 shows a concordance of the word *illiberal*. It should be seen that it is used as a direct reference to the proposed Bill (e.g. *licensing regime* line 1, *legislation* lines 2, 4 and 6, *Bill* line 4, 5 and 7.) It also occurs in three cases with the intensifying adverbs *deeply* and *profoundly* (lines 2, 4 and 5) and in four cases it appears as part of a longer list of negative adjectives (e.g. *difficult* line 1, *intolerant* and *arbitrary* line 3, *divisive* line 6, and *ineffectual* line 7).

Table 6.8 Concordance of illiberal (pro-hunt debate)

1	other place will amend the Minister's	illiberal	and difficult licensing regime into
2	r to read this stuff before he brings deeply	illiberal	legislation to the House? Mr. Gr
3	lating on this topic. The Bill is intolerant,	illiberal	and arbitrary. It will restrict freedo
4	do so on the ground that it is a profoundly	illiberal	Bill-the kind of legislation that brin
5	ite, prejudice and bigotry. This profoundly	illiberal	Bill, which should concern everyo
6	fabric of rural Britain and passed the most	illiberal	and divisive piece of legislation for
7	in me in voting against this unnecessary,	illiberal	and ineffectual Bill. Mr. Hogg: O

There isn't space to look at the keywords *sanctions, offence* and *imposing* in detail, but they too cover similar ground, contributing to the discourse of hunting as a civil right.

As a different yet related strategy, the keywords *fellow, citizens, Britain* and *freedom* are related to the keyword *people* which was discussed earlier. Consider the concordance in Table 6.9. We can see that the term *fellow citizens* is always preceded by a first person possessive pronoun (*my* or *our*). The use of this term looks like a strategy on the behalf of pro-hunters to appear to be speaking for and with the people of Britain, thereby implicitly labelling their discourse as the hegemonic one. Note also how in lines 10 and 11, the debater actually speaks for the people 'the people of Britain are beginning to catch on', 'for most of the 55 million people in England it is of peripheral interest'. Finally, in lines 13–16 the lemma RESTRICT and the word *individual* both collocate with *freedom*. There is an underlying nationalist discourse being drawn on here, in terms of: 'Britain is a good country because it is a place where people are free'. This discourse is used as an argument to allow fox-hunting to continue.

Table 6.9 Sample concordance of fellow citizens, Britain and people (pro-hunt)

1	able to me and, I believe, to most of my	fellow citizens	. The killing of an animal is justifiable only
2	a small but significant minority of our	fellow citizens	. I agree with one thing the Minister said.
3	al freedom, that it will rob some of our	fellow citizens	of their livelihood and take homes from a
4	7, when the pensions of millions of our	fellow citizens	are affected by a deeply serious crisis fr
5	at. Of course, I accept that some of our	fellow citizens	genuinely disapprove of hunting with hou
6	umber of my family and 407,000 of my	fellow citizens	, I took part in the march for liberty and liv
7	the Third Reich. Down the ages, we in	Britain	have fought against the persecution of min
8	an who ripped apart the fabric of rural	Britain	and passed the most illiberal and divisive p
9	that is being practised on the people of	Britain	tonight. Mr. Atkinson: There we have it.
10	se to offer the people of Britain, and the	people	of Britain are beginning to catch on.
11	rs speak, but for most of the 55 million	people	in England it is of peripheral interest. Mr.
12	ce to a largely urban nation, millions of	people	people recognise that to criminalise at a str
13	unjustifiable restrictions on individual	freedom	, would increase the suffering of foxes
14	unjustifiable restrictions on individual	freedom	, that it will rob some of our fellow citiz
15	t, illiberal and arbitrary. It will restrict	freedom	and do nothing to help animal welfare.
16	e unjustifiable restrictions on individual	freedom	trying to justify itself, but failing, in th

Finally, consider another keyword used by the pro-hunt speakers: *practices* (Table 6.10). This word is interesting because it is difficult to determine exactly what it means. It occurs as a plural, implying that there is a range of practices (the singular form *practice* is not a keyword incidentally). In Table 6.10 there are *veterinary practices, slaughter practices* and *livestock practices*, as well as *practices of slaughter, practices such as hare coursing* and *practices such as lamping* (shooting at night). The term *practices* is therefore used to refer to a multitude of techniques connected to animals. As with the

135

term *use of dogs*, I would argue that *practices* operates as a form of euphemism or vagueness, making it unclear to know exactly what is happening, so a direct response or criticism becomes more difficult.[4] The term also creates an association between non-lethal ways of dealing with animals, and those which involve killing them, making it more difficult to pinpoint and treat as separate cases those acts which involve slaughter as they only form part of a larger process.

Table 6.10 Concordance of practices (pro-hunt)

1	I mammals, but why on earth should those two	practices	be singled out for an outright ban? Wh
2	e place instead of hunting? They want to allow	practices	such as lamping. Lamping can work in
3	t clause 14, unless they are guilty of regarding	practices	that they believe to be cruel and lackin
4	uch as feed merchants, blacksmiths, veterinary	practices	, the horse industry, and village pubs a
5	ld be a good thing. We just heard about certain	practices	that are engaged in by certain of the h
6	t are engaged in by certain of the hunts. Those	practices	should be banned and the law should
7	is, however, public distrust and disquiet about	practices	such as hare coursing. I am open-min
8	er the law as it stands. We have to bring those	practices	within the remit of the law. For me, t
9	lfare organisations, who object strongly to the	practices	of slaughter involved in the preparation
10	ew I or anyone else may have on the slaughter	practices	involved in the preparation of these kin
11	h are illegal? We need to know which of those	practices	are more, and which less, cruel, and t
12	outh, involve cruelty. Most modern livestock	practices	would not pass the Minister's test of c

Therefore, examining these additional keywords helps to build on the findings we have already uncovered. A number of discourses are then starting to come into focus, particularly for the pro-hunt speakers at this stage. For example, use of terms like *criminal*, *sanctions*, *offence* and *imposing* suggest a discourse of civil liberties, whereas words like *Britain*, *fellow*, *citizens* and *people* suggest a discourse of shared British identity. It is not clear at this stage whether the keyword *practices* and the phrase *use of dogs* suggest another sort of discourse here. These euphemisms may simply be due to a stylistic choice, but they suggest that the speakers are at least aware that there are some aspects of their stance which may be best glossed over. The more explicit position taken by the anti-hunt speakers supports this hypothesis. Interestingly one of the keywords used in the anti-hunt sub-corpus is *barbaric* (Table 6.11) – a word which is so loaded that it hardly requires a great deal of close analysis to unearth a discourse position – collocates such as *cruel*, *obscene* and *bloodthirsty* make the position clear.

Table 6.11 Concordance of barbaric (anti-hunt)

1	overnments have legislated to ban cruel and	barbaric	sports, if one can call them sports,
2	ce. Licence or no licence, fohunting is cruel,	barbaric	, unnecessary and very ineffective. I
3	y to prevent it is to introduce a ban on these	barbaric	and bloodthirsty forms of hunting wi
4	ears will ensure the end of the obscene and	barbaric	sport of hunting wild mammals with
5	baiting or cock fighting was, and it is just as	barbaric	. One form of cruelty that is often ov
6	e introduction of a complete banning of such	barbaric	and bloodthirsty so-called sports.
7	It is not possible to make hunting "slightly"	barbaric	, or to allow animals to be "almost"
8	ears to give a little more credibility to what is	barbaric	and unacceptable. We are not tal
9	all I had to say 14 months ago. Hunting is a	barbaric	practice which we in the House sho
10	ts in Dartford think that ending the cruel and	barbaric	sport once and for all is a high prior
11	at they want-a total ban on such a cruel and	barbaric	sport – would it not have been better i

Using a reference corpus

So far our keywords analysis has been based on the idea that there are two sides to the debate, and that by comparing one side against another we are likely to find a list of keywords which will then act as signposts to the underlying discourses within the debate on fox-hunting. Our analysis so far has uncovered some interesting differences between the two sides of the debate. However, it also raises some issues. First, there is the matter of time it takes to collect and prepare the sub-corpora. Separating all of the speech in the different debates into different files depending on whether the speaker voted to ban fox-hunting or not was quite a lengthy process. Also, carrying out such a lengthy task is, in a sense, a risk – I might have had nothing worthwhile to write about at the end of it. As it happened, I carried out the process on a smaller pilot sample of data first to ensure that there would be at least a couple of interesting keywords to explore, before separating out all of the text. However, the task of creating these sorts of files can be off-putting, and in any case not always necessary. We may force ourselves to focus on different parts of a corpus when it may be more appropriate to look at the whole corpus as a whole. Not all texts consist of such clear-cut positions. For example, a corpus of newspaper articles on the same subject might be best considered as an undifferentiated mass, unless the articles came from two or more different newspapers or were written at different times.

And in focusing on difference, we may be overlooking similarities – which could be equally important in building up a view of discourse within text. For example, why do certain words *not* appear as keywords? Considering that *barbaric* occurred as a keyword in the anti-hunting speeches, another word that I had expected to appear as key in the anti-hunting debates was *cruelty*. However, this word occurred 124 times in the anti-hunting speeches and 106 times in the pro-hunting speeches. In terms of proportions, taking into account the relative sizes of the two sub-corpora, the anti-hunt speakers actually used the word *cruelty* proportionally *less* than the pro-hunters (0.17 per cent vs. 0.18 per cent). So while *cruelty* occurred slightly more often on one side of the debate, this was not a statistically significant difference – clearly the concept of cruelty is important to both sides. However, how would we know (without making an educated guess) that a word like *cruelty* is worth examining? One solution would be to carry out a different sort of keywords procedure; this time by comparing the entire set of debates against another corpus – one which is representative of general language use. This would produce a keyword list that highlights all of the words which occur in the fox-hunting debates more frequently than we would expect in 'normal' language. In this case it was decided to implement the Freiberg-Lancaster/Oslo-Bergen (FLOB) corpus which consists of one million words of written British English taken from the 1990s. Although the FLOB corpus contains written texts and the debates were spoken, a good proportion of the debate consists of prepared speech, so in a sense it could be argued as having elements of written language within it. A comparison of the hunting debates with the FLOB corpus reveals a different set of keywords; the 20 strongest being *hon.*, *hunting*, *that*, *bill*, *ban*, *I*, *friend*, *Mr.*, *foxes*, *member*, *clause*, *fox*, *minister*, *cruelty*, *we*, *gentleman*, *house*, *my*, *dogs* and *is*.

Comparing this list to Figure 6.1 (which showed keywords when the two sides of the debate were examined), it is clear that some of these words are key in the debates when compared to FLOB because they occur very frequently on one side of the debate (for example, *I*, *clause*, *bill*, *house* and *dogs* are key in both lists due to their prevalence of use by anti-hunting speakers). However, other words do not appear in both lists, for example *foxes* and *cruelty*. A further line of investigation therefore could be to examine words which are key across the debate when compared to a reference corpus, rather than simply looking at words which are only key on one side of the debate.

Examining the word *cruelty* in more detail, it becomes apparent that although it occurs with a reasonably comparable frequency on each side of the debate, the ways that it occurs are quite different for different speakers. The anti-hunters tend to use it in conjunction with words like *ban*, *prevent*, *unnecessary*, *tackle* and *eradicate* (Table 6.12). Their speech also tends to assume that cruelty already exists, e.g. 'The underlying purpose of the Bill is to ban all cruelty associated with hunting with dogs.' However, those who are pro-hunting question this position – using collocates such as *test*, *tests*, *prove*, *evidence* and *defining* (Table 6.13). Therefore rather than accepting the presence of cruelty, pro-hunting speakers problematize it: e.g. the full text in line 1 of Table 6.13 is: 'Cruelty is subjective and comparative, and the Bill entirely fails adequately to define cruelty or utility.'

Table 6.12 Concordance (sample) of cruelty (anti-hunt)

1	romise, no uncertainty, no delay; a **ban** on the	cruelty	and sport of hunting in the lifetime of this
2	ael: I see it very clearly in a Bill that **bans** the	cruelty	associated with hunting in all its forms. I h
3	ate about banning cruelty and **eradicating** the	cruelty	associated with hunting. I have tried to be
4	law, to be enforceable and to **eradicate** all the	cruelty	associated with hunting with dogs, and I i
5	rtant issue for many who want to see an **end** to	cruelty	and for those who want things to remain a
6	listen to an organisation that exists to **prevent**	cruelty	to animals and I remind the hon. Member
7	enshrining in law the principle of **preventing**	cruelty	as well as the principle of recognising utili
8	ke effective and enforceable law. It will **tackle**	cruelty	, but it also recognises the need to deal wi
9	ise, is uncompromising in seeking to **root out**	cruelty	. It will not allow cruelty through hunting
10	mingly, twice, to bring an end to **unnecessary**	cruelty	to wild mammals. There can seldom in pa

Table 6.13 Concordance (sample) of cruelty (pro-hunt)

1	and the Bill entirely fails adequately to **define**	cruelty	or utility. As my hon. Friend the Mem
2	eedless or avoidable suffering" when **defining**	cruelty	. The phrase playing the fish" is no euph
3	al act. The arbitrary application of the **tests** of	cruelty	and utility to fohunting is illogical when
4	ul unless those who hunt can meet the **tests** of	cruelty	and utility described by the Minister. Th
5	. The whole House has heard the **definition** of	cruelty	, as given by the Minister, relating to ne
6	ften than not, focuses on cruelty or **perceived**	cruelty	. I commend the former Home Secretary
7	. It will not be for the authorities to **prove** that	cruelty	takes place; if the Bill is enacted, hunti
8	r described as incontrovertible **evidence** of the	cruelty	of deer hunting, he must tell us what it i
9	s. If the Minister is so concerned, where is the	cruelty	**test** in the autumn for shooting or snari
10	he Minister said that those would not pass the	cruelty	or utility **tests**. How can he know that?

Comparing a smaller corpus or set of texts to a larger reference corpus, is therefore a useful way of determining key concepts across the smaller corpus as a whole. Indeed, for many studies where the text or set of texts under scrutiny is relatively uniform, using a reference corpus may be all that is needed. However, in order to address the problem of overfocusing on differences at the expense of similarities, it is recommended that the corpus being analysed is used in the creation of more than one keyword list.

Finally, using a reference corpus may be useful in revealing those words that are *under*-represented in the data. When comparing a smaller corpus with a reference corpus, WordSmith also gives a list of all the *negative* keywords – words which did occur in the small corpus, but much less frequently than would be expected by chance alone when compared to the reference corpus. This list doesn't take into account words which appeared zero times in the small corpus – so

139

a word must be present at least once for it to be a negative keyword. However, negative keywords can still help to show topics or words of style which are not favoured in a corpus, which in itself can be illuminating.

So what were the negative keywords – words which occurred less often in the fox-hunting debate than we would expect, when compared to the FLOB Corpus of general British English? The strongest 20 negative keywords were *just, into, family, seemed, English, development, himself, a, each, non, were, million, European, like, felt, looked, book, too, hand* and *young.*

It is notable that four of these negative keywords relate to rather impressionistic notions of perception or comparison: *felt, looked, seemed, like.* The fact that the fox-hunting debate contains fewer of these words than in general British English suggests something about the nature used in the language of the fox-hunting debate. Both sides are concerned to present their accounts using more concrete and certain language. (This would make the use of vagueness in phrases like *use of dogs* or the word *practices* all the more relevant.) However, at this point this is a tentative theory and would need much more exploration.

Key clusters

Another way of spotting words which occur frequently in two comparable sets of texts but may be used for different purposes is to focus not on keywords per se but on key *clusters* of words. Using WordSmith, it is possible to derive wordlists of clusters of words, rather than single words. Then two of these lists can be compared against each other, in order to see which combinations of words occur more frequently in one text or corpus when compared with another – a list of *key clusters.* WordSmith also allows the user to specify the size of the cluster under examination – generally, the larger the cluster size we specify, the fewer the number of key clusters that are produced.

Taking a cluster size of three, a list of key clusters was obtained by comparing the speech of the pro-hunters with those who were against hunting. This list (not shown as a table) contained some interesting clusters. For example, *a complete ban* and *a total ban* were key clusters used by anti-hunters. One aspect of the language of the pro-hunters was the fact that they tended to use a number of supportive phrases to show that they agreed with each other: *a good point, friend is right, and learned friend.* However, I want to focus mainly on clusters containing the word *cruelty,* because as we have seen, this was a high frequency word which occurred on both sides of the debate (and it was key when compared to the FLOB corpus). And while *cruelty* itself was not a keyword when the two sides of the debate were compared with each other, it did appear in a number of key clusters, suggesting that although it appeared with similar frequencies, its actual uses when embedded in discourse were more marked.

For the anti-hunt speakers, *cruelty* occurred as key in the following cluster: *cruelty associated with* (10 vs. 0 occurrences) and *the cruelty associated* (6 vs. 0 occurrences). In the pro-hunt speech, *cruelty* occurred as key in *there is cruelty* (0 vs. 5 occurrences) and *is cruelty in* (0 vs. 5 occurrences).

Table 6.14 Concordance of cruelty associated with (anti-hunt)

1	erlying purpose of the Bill is to ban all	cruelty associated with	hunting with dogs. The well-est
2	her provisions of the Bill, it will ban all	cruelty associated with	hunting with dogs. The first gr
3	n. Friends. The Bill will ensure that all	cruelty associated with	hunting with dogs will be banne
4	m of the Bill is to deal with the issue of	cruelty associated with	hunting with dogs. The question
5	o be enforceable and to eradicate all the	cruelty associated with	hunting with dogs, and I invite
6	see it very clearly in a Bill that bans the	cruelty associated with	hunting in all its forms. I have ju
7	ut banning cruelty and eradicating the	cruelty associated with	hunting. I have tried to be clinic
8	on offer today is a complete ban on the	cruelty associated with	hunting with dogs and a compl
9	rt the principle of the Bill to outlaw the	cruelty associated with	with hunting, I am unhappy with
10	art is the key purpose of preventing the	cruelty associated with	hunting with dogs. That is why i

Looking first at *cruelty associated with* (Table 6.14), it can be seen from the concordance that this phrase is used as part of a particular pattern in almost all cases. There is a reference to the Bill under discussion, then the intention to ban (or outlaw, prevent or eradicate) cruelty associated with hunting (usually with dogs). The language used here assumes that there *is* cruelty associated with hunting with dogs: lines 5 to 10 state it as a given fact by using the definite article *the*. Additionally, in lines 1, 2, 3 and 5 the word *all* appears as a pre-modifier to the phrase, indicating that the types of cruelty are multiple. Only in line 4 is cruelty not presented as a given but as something more questionable, e.g. 'to deal with the issue of cruelty … '.

How about the phrases *there is cruelty* and *is cruelty in* which are key in the pro-hunt speech? Both of these clusters occur as part of a longer four-word cluster *there is cruelty in* (see Table 6.15).

Table 6.15 Concordance of there is cruelty in (pro-hunt)

1	, Coastal (Mr. Gummer,) who said that	there is cruelty in	any form of field sport. Of course the
2	e there is. There is cruelty in shooting.	There is cruelty in	fishing. There is particular cruelty in
3	f field sport. Of course there is.	There is cruelty in	shooting. There is cruelty in fishing.
4	e is particular cruelty in coarse fishing.	There is cruelty in	any form of killing animals. There is
5	cruelty in any form of killing animals.	There is cruelty in	slaughterhouses. We eat meat for our

Interestingly, this concordance has a less clear pattern – the speakers simply state that there is cruelty in a range of different activities – field sport, fishing, shooting, killing animals and slaughterhouses. However, in carrying out a dispersion plot (see Chapter 3) of *there is cruelty in* (Figure 6.3) it is apparent that all of the cases of this cluster appear in one single file and in the same place – there is only one thick black vertical line in the plot showing where the five cases of this cluster appear.

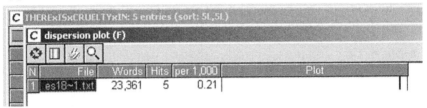

Figure 6.3 Dispersion plot of there is cruelty in

Therefore, this cluster appears to be key because it appears as part of a single statement, rather than it being representative of the speech of the pro-hunting debaters. The relevant part of this speech is shown below:

> Many hon. Members have spoken about cruelty. I agree with my right hon. Friend the Member for Suffolk, Coastal (Mr. Gummer,) who said that **there is cruelty in** any form of field sport. Of course there is. **There is cruelty in** shooting. **There is cruelty in** fishing. There is particular cruelty in coarse fishing. **There is cruelty in** any form of killing animals. **There is cruelty in** slaughterhouses. We eat meat for our pleasure. We wear leather shoes for our pleasure. Any form of killing animals is cruel, but the question is how cruel it is.
>
> (Extracted from pro-hunting sub-corpus)

Therefore, what this speaker appears to be arguing is that the extent of cruelty is more important than the presence of cruelty, a statement which fits in with the earlier findings relating to the more questioning use of the word *cruelty* by the pro-hunting speakers.

The fact that the key cluster *there is cruelty in* can only be attributed to one speaker, and one small part of his speech, would perhaps make us question its relevance to the whole debate. For keyness to be meaningful does it actually need to be evenly distributed throughout a text or corpus? If its relative frequency is simply due to a single case of repetition, is it worth commenting on? WordSmith does allow users to carry out a statistical measure of the 'spread' of keywords across a corpus (when a corpus consists of multiple files), using a function called *key keywords*. It is also possible to examine dispersion plots to obtain similar results (although this must be done for each keyword separately and gives a more impressionistic measure of dispersion). We may want to argue then, that as the cluster *there is cruelty in* occurs in such a restricted way, its saliency as 'key' across the whole text can be questioned.

However, it could also be argued that there is a strong rhetorical impact of having this cluster occur five times in such close proximity. It is extremely salient in terms of style. Crystal (1995: 378) notes that ancient rhetorical structures consisting of lists 'convey a sense of ... power and provide a climax of expression which can act as a cue for applause'. Therefore, perhaps we should not simply dismiss this particular cluster because its frequency is due to repetition in one speech. However, when reporting the analysis of keyness, it is worth mentioning dispersion, particularly in cases like this where dispersion brings up something unexpected. Again, this requires a more close analysis of words and phrases in the corpus, rather than simply recounting frequencies from wordlists.

Key categories

A further way of considering keyness is to look beyond the lexical or phrasal level, for example by considering words that share a related semantic meaning or grammatical function. While a simple keyword list will reveal differences between sets of texts or corpora, it is sometimes the case that lower frequency words will not appear in the list, simply because they do not occur often enough to make a sufficient impact. This may be a problem, as low frequency synonyms tend to be overlooked in a keyword analysis. However, text producers may sometimes try to avoid repetition by using alternatives to a word, so it could be the case that it is not a word itself which is particularly important, but the general meaning or sense that it refers to. For example, it could be the case that the notion of 'largeness' is key in one text when compared to another, and this is demonstrated by the writer using a range of words such as *big, huge, large, great, giant, massive*, etc. – none of which occur in great numbers, but taken as a cumulative whole, would actually appear as key. Thinking grammatically, in a similar way, one text may have more than its fair share of modal verbs or gradable adjectives or first person pronouns when compared to another text. Finding these *key categories* could help to point to the existence of particular discourse types – they would be a useful way of revealing discourse prosodies.

143

In order for such analyses to be carried out, it is necessary to undertake the appropriate form(s) of annotation (see Chapter 2). As with all forms of automatic annotation, there is a possibility for human error which needs to be taken into account. Therefore, ideally, the annotation should be hand-checked and corrected before key categories are derived.

The automatic semantic annotation system used to tag the fox-hunting corpus was the USAS (UCREL Semantic Analysis System) (Wilson and Thomas 1997). This semantic tagset was originally loosely based on McArthur's (1981) *Longman Lexicon of Contemporary English*. It has a multi-tier structure with 21 major discourse fields, subdivided, and with the possibility of further fine-grained subdivision in certain cases. In some cases, tags can be assigned a number of plus or minus codes to show where meaning resides on a binary or linear distinction. For example, the code T3 refers to 'Time: Old, new and young; age', so the word *kids* is assigned T3− placing it at one end of a linear scale, whereas a word like *pensioner* would receive T3+. Once the semantic annotation had been carried out, word lists (consisting of words and semantic tags) of the two sides of the fox-hunting debate were created and compared with each other to create a keyword list. From this list, the relevant key semantic tags were singled out for analysis. There isn't enough space to look at all of the key tags in detail, so I want to concentrate on a couple of findings here.

Two key tags which occurred significantly more often in the pro-hunt speeches were S1.2.6 'sensible' and G2.2 'ethics – general'. Looking at a concordance of words that were tagged as S1.2.6 (Table 6.16 shows a small sample from the total number of cases) it is clear that this contains a list of words relating to issues of sense: *sensible, reasonable, common sense, rational, ridiculous, illogical* and *absurd*. The prevalence of this class of words is due to the way that the pro-hunt speakers construct the proposed ban on hunting (as ridiculous, illogical and absurd) and the alternative decision to keep hunting (as reasonable, sensible and rational). While this way of presenting a position would appear to make sense in any argument, it should be noted that the anti-hunt speakers did *not* tend to characterize the debate in this way. They did not argue, for example, that their position was sensible, reasonable, etc. and that of their opponents was ridiculous and absurd. It is also worth noting that one feature of hegemonic discourses is that they are seen as 'common-sense' ways of thinking. To continually refer to your arguments in terms of 'common-sense' is therefore quite a powerful rhetorical strategy. With this sort of analysis, we are not only seeing the presence of discourses in texts, but we are also uncovering evidence of how they are repeatedly presented as the 'right' way of viewing the world.

144

Table 6.16 Concordance (sample) of words tagged as S1.2.6 'sensible' (pro-hunt)

1	he Bill makes illegal only the perfectly	reasonable	sensible and respectable occupations
2	continuation of hunting. I appeal to all	reasonable	hon. Members to support me in seeki
3	inal law rather than fiddle around in an	absurd	way with this absurd Minister on this
4	rmed roast. The debate has not shown a	rational	analysis of the facts: misplaced co
5	be justified by scientific evidence. The	ridiculous	new clause 13 wrecks it further, and i
6	this matter. Most people with common	sense	will say, "Why don't they reach a dea
7	eds your protection. Mr. Gray: Calm,	sensible	and rational people across Britain a
8	ss. Why not? That would be a logical,	sensible	and coherent approach. As I have to
9	method of control in that time is utterly	illogical	Mr. Gray: My hon. Friend makes an
10	ng-during that time. This ludicrous and	illogical	new clause is the result of a shabby d

What other key categories of meaning did the pro-hunters tend to focus on? The G2.2 tag was affixed to a set of words that included *moral, rights, principles, humane, morality, ethical, legitimate, noble* and *fair*. It appears that the pro-hunt speakers are more likely to argue their position from an explicitly ethical standpoint – a somewhat surprising finding considering that the ethical position of ending cruelty to animals would appear to be a more obvious stance for the anti-hunt protesters to have taken. However, a closer examination of a concordance of words which receive the G2.2 tag (Table 6.17) reveals that the pro-hunt speakers are pre-occupied with issues of morality because they wish to question the supposed absolutist ethical standpoint of the anti-hunters. Therefore, their frequent references to ethics are based around attempts to problematize or complicate the ethical position of the anti-hunters: again, this finding complements and widens the analysis of the word *cruelty* above.

Table 6.17 Concordance (sample) of words tagged as G2.2 – 'ethics: general' (pro-hunt)

1	e should be careful about imposing our	morality	on other people, someone on the Lab
2	ople to make up their own minds about	morality	. One of the issues that I dealt with as
3	In any event, they are surely moral and	ethical	issues to be considered by individu
4	g, vivisection and slaughter? There are	moral	gradations here and no moral absolut
5	the Bill that it is based on no consistent	ethical	principle. I was rather pleased when
6	ere is a complete absence of consistent	ethical	principles in the contents of the Bill.
7	at not an issue? Is hunting not the more	humane	method of controlling the fox pop
8	omeryshire (Lembit Öpik). There is no	moral	justification for the Government's po
9	questions involved, will he explain the	moral	difference between a gamekeeper us
10	en. Predators do not consider the moral	rights	and wrongs as we do as human bein

What about the other side of the debate? One semantic category which occurred more often in the speech of those who are opposed to hunting was S1.2.5 'Toughness; strong/weak'. This category consists of

145

words such as *tough, strong, stronger, strength, strengthening, robust, weak* and *feeble* (Table 6.18 shows a small sample of these cases). On this side of the debate then, the pro-hunt stance is viewed as weak, whereas the proposed Bill is frequently characterized as tough, strong or robust. So here we have a significant difference in the ways that the two sides of the debate try to position themselves as correct. While the pro-hunt debate frames itself in terms of what is *sensible*, the anti-hunt debate uses *strength* as its criteria. At this point we would want to ask why this is the case, which would lead to a more detailed analysis of the relevant concordances.

Table 6.18 Concordance (sample) of words tagged as S1.2.5 5 'Toughness; strong/weak' (anti-hunt)

1	to the Bill, we would have incredibly	strong	legislation with which to tackle hunti
2	lleagues to unite today in getting good,	strong	legislation through the House. I hope
3	n. However, although the current Bill is	strong	in that respect, it does not set the th
4	hon. Lady's argument is not especially	strong	. The Bill is good in that it takes us
5	stands is far from imperfect. It is a very	strong	Bill. It deals with the issue of cruelty
6	the other Government amendments to	strengthen	the Bill are agreed, I can give the Ho
7	practicable in their area. The measure is	tough	but fair, and it will be simple to
8	The tests, as I have said, are	tough	but fair. Supporters of hunting say th
9	eve in while being seen by the public as	tough	and fair and being strong enough to
10	upport it appear to be unable to see the	weakness	of their case. Having given every op

A semantic tagging of the corpus then, helps to reveal some of the more general categories of meaning which are used in the construction of discourse positions on the different sides of the debate. The pro-hunt speakers talk in terms of what is sensible, whereas the anti-hunt speakers talk in terms of what is strong. On their own, individual words like *strong, tough, sensible* and *rational* did not appear as keywords – it was only by considering them as a single part of a wider semantic category that their importance became apparent. Widening the scope of keywords beyond the lexical level can therefore be a fruitful endeavour.

Possible uses of keywords

So having looked at how the concept of keyness could be used in the analysis of discourses of legal debates, in what other situations could keyness be called upon to explore discourses in texts?

Keyness works particularly well when something is compared against something else. A keywords analysis can therefore be used to compare two (or more) sides of an argument – as in political debates,

146

or it could simply be used to compare the linguistic styles of different speakers. For example, Culpeper (2001) analysed the speech of six characters in the Shakespeare play *Romeo and Juliet* by comparing keywords in the speech of each character against the speech of every other character, while Baker (2005) carried out a similar approach with characters in the American situation comedy series *Will & Grace*. A keyword analysis can also be carried out on texts which are from different genres (e.g. comparing the language of the fox-hunting debates in the House of Commons with the media coverage surrounding it) or which are intended for different audiences (for example erotic narratives which are intended for either gay men or lesbians; Baker 2005). Keywords taken from comparing two sets of party political texts were examined by Fairclough (2000) in order to examine diachronic change between traditional Labour and the values of the 'New' Labour party headed by Tony Blair in the UK. New Labour keywords included *partnership*, *new*, *deliver*, *deal*, *business* and *promote* suggesting a more managerial style of government which focused on business interests and competition.

Keywords may also be derived from large comparable corpora containing different language varieties. For example, by comparing the FLOB corpus of British English with the FROWN corpus of American English we are provided with a list of keywords which shows some of the underlying differences between the two language varieties. Once proper nouns and keywords due to different spelling conventions (e.g. *color/colour*) are removed, we are left with a list of 'cultural keywords' and some interesting questions – why does American English seem to contain more references to taboo and 'disaster' terms (*plague*, *death*, *nuclear*, *poverty*, *parasite*, *drug*, *incest*, *cancer*) and words connected to identity (*black*, *white*, *male*, *women*, *gender*)? And why does British English contain more time and order-oriented keywords (*afterwards*, *yesterday*, *again*, *last*, *secondly*)?

However, keyness does not necessarily require texts to be considered in relationship to other 'equivalent yet different' texts. By using a large reference corpus as the comparison, a text or smaller corpus can be examined for the words, clusters or categories which make it unique when compared to 'general language'. For example, Johnson *et al* (2003) investigated keywords in a corpus of British newspaper articles across a five-year period. All of the articles contained reference to the concept of *political correctness* in some way. They found that the strongest keywords differed over time as focus around political correctness shifted from a range of minority identities and the media in 1994 to racism in 1999.

Scott (2002) took a more complex look at key keywords in *The Guardian* newspaper examining their associates: 'clumps' of key keywords which tend to occur together. He found that clumping was useful in determining different senses of individual key keywords – for example, the key keyword *spin* had several sets of associates: one set which referred to politics {*doctor, Mandelson*} and another which referred to sport {*cricket, bowling, England*}. Such associates are useful in teasing out different types of meanings and associations between words, particular those that are used in a variety of contexts.

And as we have seen in this chapter, keywords not only point to the existence of discourses, but they help to reveal the rhetorical techniques that are used in order to present discourses as common sense or the correct ways of thinking.

Conclusion

A keyword list is a useful tool for directing researchers to significant lexical differences between texts. However, care should be taken in order to ensure that too much attention is not given to lexical differences whilst ignoring differences in word usage and/or similarities between texts. Carrying out comparisons between three or more sets of data, grouping infrequent keywords according to discursive similarity, showing awareness of keyword dispersion across multiple files by calculating key keywords or dispersion plots, carrying out analyses on key clusters and on grammatically or semantically annotated data, and conducting supplementary concordance and collocational analyses will enable researchers to obtain a more accurate picture of how keywords function in texts. Although a keyword analysis is a relatively objective means of uncovering lexical salience between texts, it should not be forgotten that the researcher must specify his/her cut-off points in order to determine levels of salience: such a procedure requires more analysis to establish how cut-off points can influence research outcomes.

When used sensitively, keywords can reveal a great deal about frequencies in texts which is unlikely to be matched by researcher intuition. However, as with all statistical methods, how the researcher chooses to interpret the data is ultimately the most important aspect of corpus-based research.

Notes

1. http://news.bbc.co.uk/1/hi/uk/449139.stm.
2. One interesting aspect of the parliamentary debates I examined for this

chapter, was the amount of repetition, both in terms of lexis and the sorts of arguments that appeared. It could be argued that the lengthy and multiple parliamentary debates on fox-hunting, actually appeared to have had little effect on the voting behaviour of the Members of Parliament; most MPs would have already made up their minds long before arriving at the debate. Instead the debates could be understood more clearly in terms of the legitimation of legal change. It is beyond the remit of this chapter to provide a full review of research into parliamentary language, but see Ayala (2001), Shan (2000), Van der Valk (2003) and Blas-Arroyo (2003) as well as the journal *Language and Politics*.

3. Note here that we are looking for three word clusters five spaces to the left or right of the word *dogs*, so while these clusters may actually contain the word *dogs*, they may also not. For example, if the sentence 'the use of dogs to hunt' appears lots of times in the corpus, then the cluster 'the use of' will come up as a frequent cluster as it occurs within a five space window of *dogs*.

4. As a related point, in tabloid newspapers and debates in the House of Lords about changes to the laws relating to anal sex, gay sex is regularly referred to as *practices* (Baker 2005). It is clear that *practices* is therefore used in other contexts to gloss over something which the speaker either finds unpleasant or thinks the hearer is likely to.

7 Beyond Collocation

Introduction

So far we have considered ways of analysing discourse by focusing mainly on lexical items – for example a collocational analysis looks at relationships between pairs of words, whereas a keywords analysis examines words which occur in a text or corpus more often than we would expect them to by chance alone. Our concordance-based analysis of news stories also tended to focus on patterns of language which occurred around the subject of refugees, although here we started to place lexical items and phrases into groups in order to reveal discourse prosodies.

However, I want to use this chapter to focus on aspects of discourse analysis which are more concerned with grammatical rather than lexical patterns – although it should be clear that the two are linked. It isn't as easy to use a corpus to analyse grammar – particularly because patterns tend to be more complex and varied when we move beyond looking at single words. However, that isn't to say that corpus-based inquiry of discourse should remain at the lexical level, just that we may need to devote slightly more time to our analyses. In this chapter I will be considering a number of ways that a more grammar-based analysis can be of value to researchers looking at discourse via corpora. I aim to discuss nominalizations, modality, attribution and metaphor. These are features mentioned by Fairclough (1989: 111, 122) as ways of focusing on what is in a text, what particular choices have been made and what discourse types the text is drawing upon.

In order to illustrate how corpora can be used to enable the analysis of these phenomena I have also chosen not to examine a social grouping (such as refugees) or topic (fox-hunting) as I have done in the last chapters, but instead I want to look at a single term, the lemma ALLEGE and its forms. The analysis of the lemma ALLEGE was inspired by my reading of an article on a news website about an alleged rape. Due to the fact that the article makes potentially libellous claims, it is not possible to reproduce it here, although in Figure 7.1 I have written a similar article which changes details such as people's names and professions, as well as locations, but maintains the lexical-grammatical structures that I am interested in looking at. I wish to use this article as a starting point for the analysis, although I am more interested in an investigation of ALLEGE rather than a full analysis of the article itself. The article therefore acted as a springboard, raising a number of questions about ALLEGE, which I then decided to investigate in more detail using data from the British National Corpus. I was particularly interested in the last paragraph of the article which contains a statement from a spokeswoman representing a man accused of rape, and how the language used in that statement differs from the rest of the article. Compared to the remainder of the article, I felt that there was something unusual about this statement and therefore a more detailed analysis of ALLEGE in a corpus might help to illuminate what, if anything, this was. A corpus analysis would also help us to establish whether or not the patterns of language found in the article are typical (possibly allowing us to make more wide-reaching claims), or atypical of general English usage.

Holly Scott's director faces rape case

Holly Scott's director Tom North has been accused of raping a former actress who was in a drink and drugs-induced haze.

North, who directed Holly Scott's latest film, Step Back, is being sued in Miami for £10.5 million after the alleged attack in Casablanca last year.

Papers have been filed by actress Susan Arden in Miami seeking compensation for punitive damages, pain and suffering and mental damages, her lawyer Josh West said.

Earlier this month Holly denied on Radio KAT that she had had an affair with the director. Ms Arden alleged that the attack happened in a motel, hours after a wrap party. The 27-year-old said North approached her during the party and asked for sex, which she declined.

She alleged that the next morning he went to her motel and raped her for 20 to 25 seconds while she was in a drug and alcohol-induced haze … Ms Arden said that she had drunk six glasses of wine before the attack …

A spokeswoman for North, Jenny Smythe, called the lawsuit baseless. "These are ludicrous allegations. Tom hasn't been charged with anything," she said.

Figure 7.1 *Article regarding alleged rape*[1]

The use of specific types of language surrounding talk about rape has been discussed by Kitzinger and Thomas (1995), Ehrlich and King (1996) and Ehrlich (1999), who have drawn their data from interviews and disciplinary tribunals. Kitzinger and Thomas (1995) argue that a discourse-based approach to sexual harassment reveals the futility of attempting to devise watertight definitions because the assertion of one construction of reality over another is one of the techniques employed by any dominant group in order to maintain its position of power. Ehrlich and King (1996) look at questioning strategies in a rape case, concluding that 'rape trials will often protect the sexual prerogative of a man at the expense of a women's sexual autonomy', whereas Ehrlich (1999) uses community of practice theory (Eckert and McConnell-Ginet 1992) in order to account for the differential linguistic behaviour of women involved in a sexual harassment tribunal. Clearly, choice of words and the way that they are used is an important aspect of the way that rape cases are talked and written about. The verb *allege* and its related forms, is therefore a key aspect in the discursive construction of stories about rape. In the following section I examine its various forms in more detail, considering collocations around different grammatical forms.

Nominalization

Nominalization involves a process being converted from a verb or adjective into a noun or a multi-noun compound (e.g. discover → discovery, solve → solution, careless → carelessness). Fowler (1991: 80) writes 'Nominalization ... offers extensive ideological opportunities.' This is due to the fact that nominalizations often involve reductions or deletions in some way. For example, Fairclough (1989: 103) shows how a newspaper headline like 'Quarry load-shedding problem' contains nominal forms which serve to obscure agency – neither the problem-causer nor the load-shedder is explicitly identified in the headline.

As I am interested in *allege* and its related forms, it is perhaps a good idea to start by looking at the term's incidence in various parts of the British National Corpus. In the BNC, the words *allege, alleging, alleged, alleges, allegedly, allegation* and *allegations* collectively occur proportionally much more frequently in the 'World Affairs' text domain. They also occur much more often in written-to-be-spoken texts than written or spoken texts (see Table 7.1). A closer look at the nature of these written-to-be-spoken texts in the corpus reveals that they mainly involve radio or television news reports. The lemma

153

ALLEGE is therefore strongly associated with a variety of forms of news reporting. Clearly, allegations are newsworthy subjects.

Table 7.1 Combined frequencies per million words of allege, alleging, alleged, alleges, allegedly, allegation and allegations in various text domains and genres in the BNC

Text type	Frequency per million words
World Affairs	207.86
Social Science	91.76
Commerce and Finance	56.08
Leisure	54
Applied Science	33.22
Belief and Thought	32.26
Arts	30.37
Natural and Pure Sciences	16.65
Imaginative	7.87
Written-to-be-spoken	170.96
Written books and periodicals	78.8
Written miscellaneous	27.94
Spoken context-governed	22.17
Spoken demographic	1.43

Looking back at the news article, forms of the lemma occur four times:

1. North ... is being sued ... after the **alleged** attack in Miami ...
2. Ms Arden **alleged** that the attack happened in a motel ...
3. She **alleged** that the next morning he went to her motel and raped her ...
4. These are ludicrous **allegations**.

In the final example ALLEGE is nominalized and also stated in the plural – referring to more than one allegation. The first three examples are written in the main narrative voice of the article, whereas the final example is a case of reported speech by a spokeswoman for the man who is accused of rape. Note that it is only in the third case that the word *raped* is actually paired with the term *alleged*. In the first two cases, a less specific word: *attack* is used, whereas in the final case, which is reported speech, the nature of the allegations that have been made is left unspecific.

References to someone alleging that someone has been raped can be nominalized in a number of ways. For example:

She alleged that she was raped.

154

This contains no nominalization at all. However:

> She made allegations that she was raped.
> She made allegations.
> She alleged rape.

All contain single cases of nominalization – the word *allegations* in the first and second examples and the word *rape* in the third. Finally, the phrase:

> She made allegations of rape.

contains two cases of nominalization.

Searching with grammatical tags

So what can the BNC tell us about the ways that ALLEGE is normally used? What are the frequencies of the different word forms in general British English? This requires us to carry out several corpus searches, again using BNCweb (see Chapter 5). For some forms, this is simple enough – searches on the noun and adverb forms: *allegation, allegations* and *allegedly* are all reasonably straightforward. However, there is a problem when we consider a word like *alleged*. This word can be a verb, as in 'she alleged something', or an adjective as in 'The alleged rape'. If we are looking at nominalization, it is important that we distinguish between the verb and adjectival forms of the word *alleged*. A simple search on *alleged* in the BNC reveals that there are 3,058 cases. However, it would be a laborious process to have to interpret that many concordance lines as being either adjective or verb usages. Fortunately, the BNC is grammatically tagged so the work has already been done for us. The tag AJ0 stands for adjective, so we can find only the adjectival uses of *alleged* by carrying out a search on alleged=AJ0. The search for verb uses of *alleged* is slightly more complex, however. The BNC distinguishes between the past tense form of verbs and the past participle form. For example: 'She alleged=VVD rape' contains a past tense verb while 'She has alleged=VVN rape' is an example of *alleged* as a past participle. For this analysis we are not particularly interested in distinguishing between the past tense and the past participle so we simply need to carry out two separate searches on alleged=VVD and alleged=VVN and then combine the totals. The tags VVD and VVN refer to the different verb forms respectively.

However, the categorization of grammatical forms of *alleged* in the BNC is made even more complicated by the presence of portmanteau tags. Because the grammatical tagging of the BNC was carried out automatically by a computer program, it can not claim to be 100 per cent accurate (usually automatic tagging is around 97 per cent, although this figure can be higher or lower depending on the complexity and predictability of the text being tagged). In order to take into account the problem of inaccurate decisions, the BNC uses portmanteau tags which enable a decision to be hedged. For example, if the tagger is unable to decide between VVD and VVN, it will assign the tag VVD-VVN. Table 7.2 shows the frequencies of the decisions made in tagging the word *alleged* in the BNC.

Table 7.2 Frequencies of grammatical forms of the word alleged

Tag	Frequency
AJ0	1687
VVD	337
VVN	429
AJ0-VVD	38
AJ0-VVN	37
VVD-AJ0	15
VVN-AJ0	307
VVD-VVN	117
VVN-VVD	91

As we are only interested in the difference between adjectives and verbs, we can probably quite safely label the cases of VVD–VVN and VVN–VVD as simply being verbs. The other portmanteau tags (e.g. AJ0–VVN) are more problematic, there being 397 cases of these in total. If we have time, we could examine the contexts of these cases and make decisions on whether they are actually used in the verb or adjectival form. Or we could discount them from our current analysis.

Theoretically, we could encounter a similar sort of problem when searching on words which end in –s. In many cases, such words could be a countable plural noun (as in 'The dogs barked' or the –s form of a verb as in 'She dogs my every move'). Fortunately, the word *alleges* is always a verb as the plural noun form is *allegations* not *alleges*, so we don't need to worry about searching with grammatical tags.

Table 7.3 shows the frequencies of the different forms of the lemma in the BNC. It can be seen that the nominal form is the most frequent overall – with the plural *allegations* being much more popular than the singular. What is the function of referring to more than one allegation? Perhaps it makes the nature of the accusation both unspecific and also more serious. In reporting, both of these functions can be quite helpful linguistic strategies – the former as a means of increasing reader speculation and also in terms of protection from libel, in case the accusations are disproven at a future point – by being non-specific

156

it may be difficult to bring a court case against the newspaper. In terms of making the story more serious, the fact that the accusations are multiple (*allegations* rather than *an allegation*) is also likely to increase reader speculation and interest, as well as making the person being accused appear like a recidivist or multiple-offender; the story therefore becomes more newsworthy.

The adjectival form *alleged* is also quite popular in the corpus. This term occurs 1,687 times (not counting cases of portmanteau tags) and although the adjective *alleged* is not a nominal, it occurs within noun phrases such as *alleged vote rigging, alleged fraud, alleged victim*, etc. Therefore, if we include the adjectival forms as a type of nominal, ALLEGE tends to occur in a nominal form 3,800 times as opposed to its verb form of 1,531 times.

Table 7.3 Frequencies of different grammatical forms of ALLEGE in the BNC

Type	Word	Total
Nominals	allegation 370 allegations 1,743	2,113
Adjectives	alleged 1,687	1,687
Verbs	allege 116 alleges 151 alleging 290 alleged 974	1,531
Adverbs	allegedly 1,039	1,039

Collocations of grammatical forms

What do the forms of ALLEGE usually collocate with? Table 7.4 shows the strongest overall collocates of the four different forms (verb, adverb, adjective and noun) using mutual information.

Table 7.4 Strongest collocates of the different grammatical forms of ALLEGE in the BNC

	Strongest 10 Collocates
ALLEGE Verb	gilfoyle, prosecution, assaulted, breaches, infringement, bias, carr, prosecuting, negligence, undue
allegedly Adverb	abducted, tortured, corrupt, sacked, failing, murdered, offences, bomb, arrested, committed
alleged Adjective	contmenor, accomplices, infringements, irregularities, embezzlement, blasphemy, perpetrators, collaborators, breaches, atrocities
allegation(s) Noun	unsubstantiated, refuted, groundless, malpractice, refute, unfounded, infidelity, corruption, untrue, substantiate

From the table it can be seen that ALLEGE (verb) collocates strongly

157

with terms relating to legal processes, e.g. *prosecution* as well as some words related to types of crime or misdemeanour – *negligence, assaulted, bias, infringement, breaches*. The adverbial form *allegedly* also collocates with verbs suggesting crimes: *abducted, tortured, murdered, committed*, etc.

The adjectival form *alleged* collocates with words specifying groups of people who are accused: *accomplices, perpetrators, collaborators* as well as crimes or misdemeanours: *infringements, embezzlement, blasphemy, atrocities*. On the other hand, the nominal form *allegation(s)* collocates with a set of words which are related to denying something: *unsubstantiated, refuted, groundless, refute, unfounded, untrue, substantiate*. This suggests that the contextual uses of ALLEGE have quite different typical discourse functions which are dependent on whether they appear as a nominal, verb or adjective form. The nominalized *allegation(s)* form has a discourse prosody for denial which is not found with any of the other forms of ALLEGE. Such a finding is congruent with the case of the news article under analysis. There the only case of *allegations* was used by a representative of the accused, in order to deny the accusation, while the cases of *alleged* were connected more strongly to 'crime' words like *attack* and *rape*. So far then, the article's use of language conforms to typical expectations and patterns in terms of its use of ALLEGE.

It is also relevant to mention again that the first three cases of ALLEGE are all written in the article's main narrative voice, whereas the fourth example is a case of reported speech from a spokesperson who refers to *allegations*, but does not pair this with the term *rape* or any other noun. The final example is also the strongest case of nominalization being used; the first three examples used verb and adjectival forms of ALLEGE.

From our findings in the BNC, this suggests that two different discourse strategies are being used within the article which reveal different degrees of certainty about the rape. Both strategies are careful not to imply that a rape actually happened – the main narrative voice of the newspaper presents a more objective 'reporting' stance (most likely for its own protection against possible cases of libel in the future), while the spokeswoman is more vigorous in denying the rape:

> A spokeswoman for North, Jenny Smythe, called the lawsuit baseless. "These are ludicrous allegations. Tom hasn't been charged with anything," she said.

So her use of the nominalization *allegations* – a word which, as we've seen, shows a semantic preference for the concept of denial in general English, coupled with the adjective *ludicrous*, serves to strongly refute the truth of the claim.

But is *ludicrous* a typical adjective which is used in connection with the term *allegations*? In the BNC *ludicrous* only co-occurs once in the same sentence as *allegations* – so it is possible, but fairly atypical. The strongest adjectival collocates which appear within five places to the left or right of *allegations* in the BNC are shown in the box below:

> unsubstantiated, groundless, unfounded, probing, untrue, widespread, electoral, serious, false, sexual, fresh, senior, recent, specific, similar, original, true, financial, certain, political, british, new, other

Looking at concordances containing these words, we see that there are three main patterns when adjectives occur with the word *allegations*. The first is in the form [allegations of (adjective) X] such as *allegations of sexual misconduct*. The second is the form [allegations about/against (determiner) adjective X] such as *allegations against senior officials*. We can discount the adjectives that appear in these two types of patterns as the adjectives do not directly describe allegations but are used to refer to something else. The third pattern takes the form [adjective *allegations*] or [*allegations are* adjective]. Here, allegations *are* being directly described. Looking at the adjectives which occur in this third pattern, we have the following:

> unsubstantiated, groundless, unfounded, untrue, widespread, serious, false, fresh, recent, specific, similar, original, true, certain, new, other

We can further classify these adjectives based on their meaning (see Table 7.5).

Table 7.5 Types of adjectives used to describe allegations

certainty	unsubstantiated, groundless, unfounded, untrue, false, true
age	recent, fresh, new, original
type	other, similar, specific, certain
severity	serious, widespread

So the largest set of adjectives used to describe allegations are those which relate to certainty – and again, most of these words indicate denials.

A further line of enquiry would be to investigate the word *ludicrous* which was used by the spokeswoman in the article to describe the allegations, to obtain an idea of what other things are commonly ascribed as ludicrous. The only noun collocate of *ludicrous* in the BNC is *situation*. Most of the other collocates are adverbs: *almost, rather, most, too, so, how, even* which relate to the scale of which something is described as ludicrous. More interestingly, there is also one strong modal verb collocate: *would*, which occurs in phrases like 'it would be ludicrous if they did'. This suggests that *ludicrous* contains a preference for occurring in hypothetical constructions – again linking the word to the idea of something that *hasn't* happened. And looking at some of the lower-frequency words which co-occur with *ludicrous*, we find that a number of them also refer to abstract ideas rather than concrete facts: *notion, observation, proposition, statement, suggestion.* The pairing of *ludicrous* and *allegations* is therefore a particularly powerful language strategy as both words contain strong associations of untruth or unreality embedded within them.

Modality

So far the analysis of ALLEGE in the BNC has shown how it has a strong association with news reporting and how the nominalized form has a strong discourse prosody for denial, while the non-nominalized forms do not. However, what else can the corpus tell us about ALLEGE? Modality relates to speaker or writer authority and is based around the use of a range of modal auxiliary verbs: *could, should, would,* etc. Different modal verbs can be used to express different levels of authority, which can be linked to the ways that certain groups are discursively constructed. For example, in a sample of the BNC, the modal verb *should* (which tends to denote strong obligation) tends to collocate with 'person' words like *tenant, pupils* and *applicants* whereas the modal verb *might* (denoting possibility) collocates with *authorities, military* and *teachers*. Such a strong presence or absence of certain modal verbs is therefore an indication of power relationships and status – relatively powerful groups seem to be paired with modal verbs which give them more freedom and choice, while more controlling modal verbs are used with less powerful groups.

One line of exploration into the term ALLEGE would be to determine how often its various word forms occur with modal verbs. Using the BNC, I again carried out searches on the noun, adjective, verb and adverb forms of ALLEGE and then counted the number of times modal verbs appeared within three spaces to the left and right of them. Concordances were examined in order to remove from the data cases where words like *may, can* and *will* were not used as modal verbs, e.g. 'He alleged on May 14.' The results are shown in Table 7.6 below.

Table 7.6 Frequencies of modal verbs with ALLEGE

	Total in BNC	All forms ALLEGE	Noun forms allegation, allegations	Adjective form alleged	Verb forms allege, alleged, alleges, alleging	Adverb form allegedly
would	245,813	30	**11**	5	7	**7**
could	160,165	25	**11**	4	7	3
will	244,050	23	**11**	7	3	2
should	109,156	19	5	**8**	6	0
may	112,768	18	7	3	**8**	0
might	59,127	10	5	2	3	0
need	3,250	5	0	3	2	0
must	69,932	5	3	1	0	1
can	231,722	5	3	0	0	2
shall	19,814	3	1	1	1	0
ought	5,838	2	1	0	1	0
Total		145	58	34	38	15

What does this table show us? It is probably not a good idea to compare the figures across the different columns as the fact that we have different overall frequencies of noun forms, verb forms, etc. makes comparisons somewhat fruitless (we would need to convert these figures to relative percentages in order to do that).

However, comparing figures within individual columns, we can start to get an idea of some of the preferences surrounding modal use in conjunction with different forms of ALLEGE. The figures in bold print in each column represent the most popular modal choices for that form. The most popular modal constructions are summarized below:

- Noun forms: *allegations would, could* or *will* (quite a wide range of modality).
- Verb forms: *may, would* or *could allege* (more uncertain).
- Adjective form: *alleged ... should/will* (firm certainty/obligation).
- Adverb form: *would allegedly* (not very certain).

Although there are no clear-cut patterns here, it appears that there are some overall trends. In general British English, the modal verbs *would, will, can* and *could* are most popular in overall language usage, while

161

modals like *shall*, *ought* and *need* are much less common. It is useful to bear this in mind when looking at modal use in connection with different forms of ALLEGE. Here, it appears that *could* appears more often in conjunction with ALLEGE than we would perhaps expect it to (judging by its total frequency), and *can* occurs with ALLEGE less often than expected. In terms of the noun forms, we find modal verbs such as *would*, *could* and *will* occurring often – quite a wide range of modality being expressed. The adjective form *alleged* tends to be connected to two of the most certain modal verbs: *should* and *will*. On the other hand, the verb and adverb forms are used more with uncertain modals: *may*, *would* and *could*. We can link this back to our findings regarding nominalization – where ALLEGE is nominalized, modality tends to be represented with more certainty than with verb or adverb forms. Why does this appear to be the case? There are a number of possible theories we could form at this point. First, recall how the nominalized forms of ALLEGE tended to also strongly correlate with words related to denial. This suggests that the forms of denial are made more categorical by the use of stronger, more certain modal verbs. However, it might be that the stronger modals are not connected to denial but are instead simply a function of writers and speakers not needing to hedge their words because nominalizations allow agency to be obscured. We would need to carry out more detailed analyses of individual concordance lines in order to confirm or refute these hypotheses.

It should also be noted that modality is actually relatively infrequently used in connection with ALLEGE – there are many more cases of the lemma appearing with no modal verbs in the vicinity.

Attribution

Within the reporting of allegations of rape it is possible to name a number of actors – for example, the person who is supposed to have been raped, the person who carried out the rape, the person making the allegation (often, but not necessarily the same as the person being raped) and the person who the rape is reported to (e.g. the police). At the same time, certain actors may be foregrounded or referred to often, at the expense of backgrounding or not referring at all to others. The presence (or absence) of different types of actors in narratives of rape can have consequences which relate to both the focus of the story and the way that the agency of those involved is represented.

In the news article both the person who is accused of raping, and the person who claims to be raped are mentioned several times and in a variety of ways (e.g. 'a former actress', 'actress Susan Arden', 'she' and 'Ms Arden' all refer to the same person). One aspect of the story that appears interesting is that the alleged rapist and victim are only referred to by name together in the same sentence once. In all the other sentences, one receives more focus, while the other is backgrounded.

How does this relate to allegations of rape in the BNC? Table 7.7 shows all of the cases where ALLEGE and RAPE collocate in the BNC.

Table 7.7 Concordance of ALLEGE and RAPE in the BNC

1	by the" News of the World" of **rape**	allegations	against Banbury CID officers).
2	a result of her claims, another **rape**	allegation	, relating to the autumn of 1991,
3	three charges of making bogus **rape**	allegations	, pointed out her conduct.
4	r a different name, to make a further	allegation	of **rape** and another sex offence."
5	But if a wife's	allegation	of **rape** is true, her motive for bring
6	y, because my postbag suggests that	allegations	of **rape** can arise from previously n
7	he brutality of the Iraqis, focusing on	allegations	of mass **rape** of expatriate women.
8	His case, involving an	allegation	that he **raped** another student after
9	Also	alleging	**rape** and torture, Amnesty urged th
10	Although Bracton	alleged	that the **rape** of non-virgins was[2]
11	FP report of April 3 said that a letter	alleging	**rape** and the destruction of villages
12	ath a pensioner the day after charges	alleging	he **raped** and indecently assaulted h
13	It was	alleged	she was **raped** in the taxi near Trent
14	ther's home in Ayr at the time he was	alleged	to have **raped** her.
15	and had a mistress at the time of the	alleged	**rape**, the jury has been told.
16	y than men to believe the evidence of	alleged	**rape** victims.
17	eal of publicity, and every case of an	alleged	**rape** of a Serbian woman by an
18	to discourage women from reporting	alleged	**rape**".
19	time lag between the occasion of the	alleged	**rape** and the reporting of it to the
20	in the furore resulting from a case of	alleged	**rape** involving his nephew, Willia
21	22 ruled that the sexual history of an	alleged	**rape** victim might be offered as
22	or an independent inquiry into the	alleged	**rape**.
23	eports on Dec. 7, the victim of the	alleged	**rape**, Farhana Hayat, had named Irf
24	Sergeant Norton was acquitted of the	alleged	**rape** of an 18 year old girl at Chelte
25	THE father of an	alleged	**rape** victim told a jury yesterday of
26	tioned by detectives investigating the	alleged	**rape** of a 27-year-old teacher.
27	is six fifteen and still to come, should	alleged	**rape** victims be granted anonymity?
28	been demands today for the names of	alleged	**rape** victims to be published if the a
29	should have been named as should all	alleged	**rape** victims when their case comes
30	ish to question in connection with an	alleged	double **rape** of a teenager.
31	year in Detroit alone, at least 3,370	alleged	victims of **rape** were treated in hos
32	e legal evidence on the identity of the	alleged	**rapist**.
33	ght it's been permitted to name the	alleged	**rapist**.
34	This is the man who	allegedly	**raped** a 38 year old woman.
35	ial of a landscape gardener man who	allegedly	**raped** two teenage girls is expected
36	r-old girl, who became pregnant after	allegedly	being **raped** by the father of a frie
37	ld Crown Court has heard how a man	allegedly	kidnapped and **raped** his wife; the
38	ligence Agency, he was detained for	allegedly	**raping** and savagely beating a prost
39	or Hanson, a convicted **rapist** there	allegedly	attacked a woman while on home le

Looking at this table it appears that there are a number of different

163

ways that people involved in allegations of rape can be referred to. Their names can be used, e.g. line 24:

Sergeant Norton was acquitted of the   alleged   rape of an 18 year old girl at Chelte

They can also be referred to by a description which does not include their name, e.g. line 8:

His case, involving an   allegation   that he raped **another student** after

Or they can be referred to by an abstract or hypothetical reference, e.g. line 27:

is six fifteen and still to come, should   alleged   **rape victims** be granted anonymity?

Finally, an actor may simply be deleted altogether, e.g. line 32 has no mention of the person who was allegedly raped:

32   e legal evidence on the identity of the   alleged   rapist.

Collating the different types of attribution, Table 7.8 shows how many times different actors are referred to in the sentences in the BNC which contain forms of the lemma ALLEGE and RAPE. Note that I needed to expand some of the concordance lines in Table 7.7 in order to locate this information.

Table 7.8 *Presence and description of actors connected to allegations of rape in sentences in the BNC*

	accused	victim	accuser	hearer of accusation	Totals
Named	8	1	4	0	13
Referred to but not named	16	25	0	4	45
Abstract or hypothetical reference	2	8	0	2	12
Not referred to	12	4	34	32	82

The table shows that people involved in allegations of rape tend not to named, but are more likely to be referred to via descriptions such as 'a woman' or 'a policeman'. The most important (in terms of whether they appear in the sentence) actor is the victim, while the accused is the next most important. The person who makes the accusation and the person who hears the accusation tend to appear much less often.

When someone is likely to be named, it is the accused rapist, rather than the victim.

However, one problem with corpus data of this type is that a single sentence may obscure or represent a particular actor, but when we regard a sentence as simply one part of a larger text, we may find that elsewhere in the text, the obscured actor *is* actually referred to (this can be referred to as *backgrounding*). If we only carry out a search on sentences which contain the lemmas ALLEGE and RAPE, we may miss additional information which comes later or earlier in the text. For example, consider the following sentence in text K4W in the BNC: 'The jury in the trial of a landscape gardener who allegedly raped two teenage girls is expected to reach a verdict today.' We may categorize this sentence as referring to the alleged rapist but not by name. However, the sentence which directly comes next is 'Stanley Hornibrook, 42, of Wimpole Road, Stockton, has denied seven offences of indecent assault, four of rape … ' Therefore, the alleged rapist *is* named, but just not in the sentence containing the lemmas ALLEGE and RAPE. So in Table 7.9, the presence or absence of different types of actors is examined for whole texts which contain the lemmas ALLEGE and RAPE in a sentence, not just the sentences where these terms occur.

Table 7.9 Presence and description of actors connected to allegations of rape in whole texts the BNC

	accused	victim	accuser	hearer of accusation	Totals
Named	12	5	6	12	35
Referred to but not named	10	16	8	5	39
Abstract or hypothetical reference	5	7	2	1	15
Not referred to	1	0	12	10	23

Some of the numbers in this table are smaller than in Table 7.8 because we analysed all of the sentences separately before. Now that we are looking at texts, it becomes apparent that some sentences come from the same text, reducing the number of cases of actors being referred to overall. From Table 7.9 we see a couple of differences from our original analysis of the corpus. People involved in allegations of rape do tend to be named more often than we had first thought once we consider the entire text. We also find that accusers and hearers of accusations tend to feature more regularly once we look at the full text. However, it still appears to be the case that on the whole, victims tend to have their identity obscured more often than people who are accused of rape. In

165

fact, if we examine whole texts rather than sentences, we find slightly more cases of those who are accused having their full name printed than being referred to via a description.

How does this information relate back to the article we are examining? Here we have both the suspected rapist 'Tom North' and the alleged victim/accuser 'Susan Arden' being named in full. This is relatively unusual for patterns surrounding allegations of rape as it is more typical for the identity of the person making the accusation to be obscured. We may want to ask why the article has directly named the people involved and what bearing this is likely to have on the forthcoming trial, the careers of those named and the popularity of the news website which reported the case. Perhaps the fact that the people involved are celebrities means that their names are more likely to be used.

Let us look again at the quote by the spokeswoman for Tom North:

> A spokeswoman for North, Jenny Smythe, called the lawsuit baseless. "These are ludicrous allegations. Tom hasn't been charged with anything," she said.

Here, while the spokeswoman dismisses the charge of rape in very strong terms, her quote 'these are ludicrous allegations' does not include an actor. The allegations are not attributed to anybody. The statement could be rephrased as 'She has made ludicrous allegations' or 'The allegations made by Susan Arden are ludicrous'. By obscuring the accuser/victim, this strategy removes the focus away from the person being accused and may also help to protect Tom North – as his denial appears less personal and direct. It is also interesting that the spokeswoman does not make it clear what the allegations actually are. She could have said 'These *rape* allegations are ludicrous'. Therefore the nature of the supposed crime is also obscured by her language use.

Metaphor

So far we have seen that the word choice *allegations* is of particular salience to the news article, because it carries a strong association with denial. In the article it was used in a direct quote by a spokeswoman for the person who the allegations are being made about, but it was not used by the actual narrative voice of the article, with the more neutral term *alleged* occurring three times instead. We have used a reference corpus to look at collocations of the word *allegations*, as well as patterns or modal use and the presence or absence of various types of actors associated with allegations of rape.

Another way of understanding some of the hidden associations of the word *allegations* is to consider it in terms of metaphor. The news article doesn't contain any metaphors surrounding the word *allegations*. However, sometimes it is useful to investigate the ways that a word can be used metaphorically. As already suggested, words may prime people to think of their strong collocates, even when they are not present. The same may be true of metaphors. If we often see a particular word used in a metaphorical way, then we may be primed to think of the word in terms of that metaphor, even when it does not appear in that sense.

Metaphors are a particularly revealing way of helping to reveal discourses surrounding a subject. As Fairclough (1989: 119) points out, when we describe x in terms of y, all the 'ideological attachments', connotations, associations and their meanings carried by y are projected onto x. For example, if we recall the analysis of newspaper texts in Chapter 4, refugees were variously described in metaphorical expressions that referenced water and package metaphors, e.g. 'a flood of refugees'. In this sense, they were characterized as an out of control problem with no sense of agency, as well as being depersonalized. The metaphor of refugees as water, then, contributed to an overtly negative discourse. Looking at the presence of metaphors in a corpus, and noting their relative frequencies to each other, should provide researchers with a different way of focusing on discourse. Cognitive metaphor theory proposes that common linguistic associations are expressions which reflect the way that our brains actually work – not only do we talk about x in terms of y, but we *understand* x in terms of y (Lakoff and Johnson 1980; Gibbs and Steen 1999). However, we can understand metaphors in terms of dual levels. As Koller (2004: 9) points out 'A bi-level view of metaphor holds that metaphoric expressions witnessed in actual texts are just different realisations of productive underlying metaphors.' For example, the metaphorical expression 'I'm just wild about Harry' references an underlying LOVE IS MADNESS metaphor (Lakoff and Johnson 1980: 49).

Unfortunately though, there isn't a simple way of carrying out a metaphor-based analysis on a corpus. Deignan (1999: 180) points out the difficulties of using corpus-based techniques to uncover metaphors: '... there is no automatic way of discovering the linguistic realizations of any conceptual metaphor, because a computer cannot tell the researcher anything about speaker meaning. Concordances will show the researcher words in their context, but he or she has to process this information.' Until a linguistic metaphor database is widely available, it looks as if a bottom-up approach is the most likely option.

167

Charteris-Black (2004: 35–6) uses a qualitative, two-stage approach to corpus-based metaphor analysis. In stage one, the researcher carries out a close reading of a sample of texts in order to identify candidate metaphors. Words that have a tendency to be used in a metaphoric sense are noted as being 'metaphor keywords'. In stage two, corpus contexts are examined to determine whether these keywords are metaphoric or literal. To demonstrate this technique, Charteris-Black carried out a close reading of texts arising from the Twin Tower bombing on 11 September 2001. He found that a salient phrase was George W. Bush's vow to fight a 'crusade against terror', a term which could either be used in a literal or metaphorical sense. Charteris-Black then looked at the phrase *crusade against* in three reference corpora in order to see how it was commonly used. He found that strong collo- cates were words like *corruption, slavery* and *communism*, suggesting that *crusade against* was frequently used as a metaphor, i.e. a term from the domain of religious struggle being used in non-religious domains such as social reform. Charteris-Black (2004: 37) notes that 'this methodology was used ... because I believe it is only possible to develop software that searches for certain types of metaphor and not for metaphors that have become conventionalised ...' A similar 'close reading' approach was taken by Koller (2004) in her analysis of gendered metaphors in business media discourse. Koller found that the discourse was most frequently conceptualized around traditionally masculine metaphors concerning war and fighting.

However, some attempts have been made to automatically derive metaphors from corpora. For example, Sardinha (2002) carried out a corpus-driven analysis of metaphors in a corpus of dissertations. He first derived a list of the top 100 lexical keywords and examined their collocates. He then ran the collocational pairs he found through a program called WordNet[3] which compares word pairs and reports the amount of distance or similarity between them in terms of their meaning – his hypothesis being that sentences which contain metaphors will contain words which have dissimilar meanings – so if *flood* and *refugees* prove to be strong collocates of each other, this may suggest that a metaphorical construct is repeatedly occurring (unless of course we have a more literal case of a flood causing people to become refugees). Therefore, strong collocates which were scored as being dissimilar in terms of meaning were examined in more detail, and indeed, Sardinha found that many of these did prove to be the result of metaphorical constructs.

So, following from Charteris-Black and Sardinha, an examination of collocates is therefore a good starting place in order to derive metaphors surrounding a word. I examined the top 100 collocates of

168

the noun *allegation(s)* and focused particularly on collocates which seemed to have little or no semantic connection with each other. Abstract concepts are often constructed via metaphors which reference concrete entities, and it is probably the case that *allegation(s)* will have metaphors in common with similar terms like ACCUSATION or CLAIM. One group of collocates which initially looked quite hopeful in terms of metaphors were a set of words like *satanic, torture, fraud, coup* and *sexual*. However, these collocates tended to occur with *allegation(s)* as literal meanings – e.g. *allegations of sexual misconduct*. There were three word forms which were more helpful. These were *groundless, probing/probe* and *withdraw/withdrew*. I include a couple of examples of concordance lines of these words in Table 7.10.

Table 7.10 Metaphorical collocates of allegation(s)

1	I consider the levelling of **groundless**	allegations	to be a shameful response to the hos
2	area, but which had concluded that the	allegations	were **groundless**. On Jan. 24 Brig.
3	The Office of Fair Trading is **probing**	allegations	that the companies are charging rip-
4	n and the County Council's **probe** into	allegations	at Redoaks. You're listening to B B
5	. Gentleman is rising to **withdraw** that	allegation	, because it was totally groundless
6	estified against Muawad **withdrew** his	allegation	, saying it was "politically motiva

With the word *groundless* in examples 1 and 2 in the table, there is a possible metaphorical construction which links allegations either to the ground, to buildings or to weight. Examples 3 to 6 suggest a different sort of metaphor – to do with penetration or piercing, which may reference a primary metaphor to do with arguments being war.

While this method has provided us with two types of metaphors surrounding allegations (which require further analysis at this point), it is unlikely that this is the full picture. As we have already seen, word pairs need to occur relatively frequently to be marked as being significant collocates. However, words may contain strong semantic prosodies which are overlooked by simple collocation techniques. Therefore, an alternative procedure of deriving metaphorical expressions would be to examine a concordance (or thinned concordance containing a smaller number of concordance lines taken randomly) of *allegation(s)*. In doing this, it appears that certain grammatical patterns are more likely to reveal metaphorical expressions than others. For example, the following patterns were particularly relevant cues for the presence of metaphorical expressions:

- [noun] *of allegations*;
- [verb] *by allegations*;
- *allegations as* [adjective/noun].

169

However, other patterns may also exist for different search terms, e.g. *allegations are* [adjective]. It should be noted that such an approach is limited — it is phraselogical and moreover will only uncover metaphorical expressions which actually contain the word *allegations*. Anaphoric constructions, e.g. the following example from the BNC: 'I hope that the hon. Gentleman is rising to withdraw that allegation, because **it was totally groundless** and misleading' will not be uncovered by this form of analysis.

After examining the concordance data, the relevant concordance lines of metaphors surrounding *allegations* were put into groups, which are shown in Tables 7.11 to 7.16.

Table 7.11 *Allegations as something heavy/connected to the ground*

1	the security forces and lend **weight** to	allegations	of unprovoked use of lethal force
2	whether by reason of the **gravity** of the	allegations	or other exceptional circumstance.
3	a of demanding £4 million to **drop** the	allegations	
4	bsts, the government rejected the other	allegations	as "**groundless**".
5	e on previously neutral countries. Such	allegations	**paved** the way for justification of th

Within this table, there are a range of quite different types of metaphors, which reference more primary metaphors. For example, the phrase 'lend weight to allegations' can be traced back to a primary metaphor of HEAVY IS IMPORTANT. The phrase 'allegations as "groundless"' suggests a primary metaphor of ARGUMENTS ARE BUILDINGS (Lakoff and Johnson 1980: 46), while the phrase 'allegations paved the way' suggests a primary metaphor of AN ARGUMENT IS A JOURNEY (Lakoff and Johnson 1980: 90).

Table 7.12 *Allegations as water or connected to water*

1	itnesses as perjurors.Yet new **waves** of	allegations	continued.They were rejected in Ro
2	o discernable decline in the **stream** of	allegations	of torture and extra-judicial killing
3	sterday after being named in kinky sex	allegations	**splashed** across a Sunday newspap
4	belief that, no matter how bizarre, the	allegations	are **water**-tight?
5	plot by the boy's father. The	allegations	**surfaced** last week as Jackson bega

In Table 7.12, we can further recategorize metaphors connected to water. For example, the phrases 'waves of allegations' and 'stream of allegations' reference a primary metaphor connected to nature as being unpredictable (and potentially dangerous). Note how the refugees in Chapter 4 were also characterized as out-of-control water. The idea of allegations as water-tight suggests a metaphor of AN ARGUMENT IS A CONTAINER (Lakoff and Johnson 1980: 92).

170

Table 7.13 *Allegations as violence or war*

1	st as museum curator, and **besieged** by	allegations	of being an "indoor naturalist", a so
2	akes it difficult for anybody to **defend**	allegations	, irrespective of whether that was t
3	ing that President Bush has to **fend** off	allegations	of a long-ago affair as he gears up
4	hose credibility has been **damaged** by	allegations	relating to the Blue Arrow affair.
5	Meanwhile, RADIO 5 have **hit** back at	allegations	in The Sunday Times that the statio

The metaphors in Table 7.13 reference a primary metaphor of ARGUMENT IS WAR (Lakoff and Johnson 1980: 4).

Table 7.14 *Allegations as penetration/penetrated*

1	If the Secretary of State **withdraws** his	allegation	, I will withdraw my accusation
2	ith the Operation Cheetah **probe** into	allegations	of corrupt land deals have been sent
3	e Professor Oswald if he **retracted** his	allegations	.
4	As police **probe**	allegations	that the controversial Arsenal strike
5	blic school yesterday as police **probed**	allegations	of inde-cent assault.

In Table 7.14 allegations can be penetrated: 'probe allegations' which links into the water-tight (container) metaphor. But they can also be things that penetrate – 'withdraws his allegations' (linking to the violence/war set of metaphors).

Table 7.15 *Allegations as waste products*

1	Minister Andras Benkei described the	allegations	as "**rubbish**", but the Hungarian
2	press in January, Clinton dismissed the	allegations	as "old stories" and" **trash**",

In Table 7.15 we might want to note the fact that there are quote marks around the words 'rubbish' and 'trash' in these two cases. However, this appears to be due to the fact that they are reported speech, although the quotes also serve to distance the author from these opinions.

Table 7.16 *Allegations as fire, disease, something that can fly, or a horse/pony*

1	th her.These concerns were **fuelled** by	allegations	made by P. and B., who respective
2	osition Alliance (ADOC), **sparked** by	allegations	that a coup was being prepared agai
3	a reformed alcoholic, was **plagued** by	allegations	that she had used marijuana and coc
4	maintained.Now there have been some	allegations	**flying** around that there are people
5	maintained.Now there have been some	allegations	**flying around that there are**
6	t all Roy Hattersley can do is **trot out**	allegations	of electioneering and say he'll "c

In Table 7.16, the flying metaphor in lines 4 and 5 seems connected to the 'waves of allegations' and 'stream of allegations' in Table 7.12 – the sense that the allegation is unpredictable – we do not know where it is going. It also links to the metaphors in Table 7.11 – the idea of allegations being 'groundless'. So if heavy is important, then something up in the air will be seen as flimsy or unimportant.

For line 6 of Table 7.16, it is perhaps more questionable that we are witnessing a 'horse' metaphor here. In order to gather evidence for this, I consulted the British National Corpus to examine other cases of the word *trot*. Its strongest collocates are *canter, brisk, pony, wins, broke, hot* and *horse* and it normally occurs in texts about horses or ponies. If we wanted to be safe, we could say that this was a metaphor of allegations as an animal (or something else) that moves, but the strong collocation of *trot* with *pony* and *horse* (and no other animals) means that I can be fairly confident in stating that this is a metaphor of allegations as horses.

With many of these cases of metaphors, one way of making sense of them would be to inquire about other situations in the corpus where they are used. So in what contexts does 'trot out' occur in the BNC? Table 7.17 provides some more examples.

Table 7.17 Metaphorical expressions of trot out in the BNC

1	y Lyle, an affable philosopher, who will	trot out	an occasional quotation, from Shake
2	. would expect the older Wordsworth to	trot out	the arguments of the Established C
3	contributor agreed that it was possible to	trot out	any number of excuses for the lack
4	y work. Cos she was expecting me to	trot out	something like, yes both my parents
5	ewspapers had been able several times to	trot out	their favourite banner headline."Bri

Looking at other uses of *trot out* in the BNC (when used as a metaphorical expression), it seems that the phrase is often used to refer (somewhat sarcastically) to the ideas or speech of someone. What the expression seems to be suggesting is that the idea is somehow well-rehearsed or repetitive in nature. Therefore the corpus not only helps to uncover the possible metaphors surrounding a word or concept, but it can also be useful in revealing how that metaphor works in a range of other cases, enabling researchers to gain a greater understanding of its meaning.

And not only does the concordance analysis help to provide further examples of the metaphors found by looking at the strongest collocates, it has also expanded on the number of metaphors we had already found. Now we see *allegations* referred to in terms of heavy weight, water, violence, penetration, waste, fire, disease, flight and horses. Some of these metaphors appear to be more frequent than others – and in a few cases only one example of a particular metaphor was found. However, at a more general level, these themes also referenced a series of primary metaphors.

Because the term *allegations* is found in a range of general metaphorical patterns in British English it is not possible to say that any single metaphor dominates the way that we think of the term. However, what is interesting about the majority of metaphors concerning *allegations*, is that they tend to be used in fairly negative ways. We therefore have further evidence to suggest that the use of the term *allegations* by the spokeswoman in the news article is particularly salient. Metaphors associated with this word tend to have a negative discourse prosody.

Further directions

In this chapter we have only considered four linguistic phenomena: nominalization, modality, attribution and metaphor. We also considered how these aspects of language were used in a single text when compared with their 'norms' in a reference corpus. However, there are other ways that we could have approached nominalization, modality, attribution and metaphor. For example, we could have looked at a specialized corpus of texts. To go back to some of the earlier chapters in this book, we could have looked in more detail at patterns surrounding the agency or attribution of holidaymakers engaging in drinking behaviour, or we could have more closely considered metaphors of refugees.

We could have also expanded our analysis of the term *allegations* to consider a wider range of lexical, semantic and grammatical features. For example, how does word choice affect agency or passivization? For example, is the lemma ALLEGE more likely to occur in passive sentences or with obscured agency than sentences which contain the lemmas CLAIM, ACCUSE or REPORT? So does the act of reporting tend to occur in an active sense: 'she reported a rape' whereas alleging is something which people have done to them: 'he was alleged to have raped'? The article about Tom North is interesting because the first three paragraphs are written as passive sentences. In the first two (agentless passive) sentences, the focus is on Tom North, who is the recipient of allegations of rape. It is only in the third sentence, where we find out who has made the allegations: Susan Arden – this time the agent is present.

We may also want to consider co-ordination. How do co-ordinators like *despite, in spite of, due to, because* and *although* function in relationship to ALLEGE? What sort of expectations are set up in the use of these relative co-ordinating phrases? An examination of the corpus reveals that they are often used in cases where people are involved in denying allegation, yet at the same time there is an embedded implication that part of the allegation may be true, e.g.: 'All three denied the allegations although Viehweger resigned on Sept. 28'.

There are some techniques in critical discourse analysis which are more difficult to carry out on corpora. For example, Fairclough (1989) asks questions about the modes of sentences (whether they are declarative, questions or imperatives) as well as pronoun use. Examining a corpus to see whether certain words, lemmas or phrases regularly appear in particular sentence modes would require expanding concordance lines in order to examine full sentences. Similarly, if we are interested in looking at pronoun usage, we would need to be able to interpret different uses of the word *we* – distinguishing between the inclusive and exclusive forms. Being able to access pre-tagged corpora which are able to show us all of the linguistic categorizations that we are interested in is ideal, but often such corpora are not forthcoming. Hand-tagging a sample of the corpus, or using concordance searches creatively are two ways to get round the problem of deriving more interesting analyses from 'raw' data. However, at present, a great deal of corpus-based discourse analysis is still focused at the lexical level. The challenge to future researchers is to find ways to make grammar- and semantic-based analysis of corpora a more feasible proposition.

Notes

1. This extract is taken from a real news article but names and identifiable details have been changed for legal reasons.
2. Note that this concordance line is not referring to an alleged rape as such: 'Although Bracton alleged that the rape of non-virgins was also punishable, this does not appear to have been the practice of the courts.' It was therefore excluded from the analysis.
3. www.cogsci.princeton.edu/~wn/.

8 Conclusion

This book has identified some of the most useful methodological techniques of corpus-based research (frequencies, collocations, keywords, concordances, dispersions) and shown how they can be effectively used in the analysis of discourse.

I hope I have also illustrated some of the overarching theoretical positions within corpus linguistics: the view that the automatic techniques carried out on carefully chosen, large collections of naturally occurring texts will help to identify language norms and peculiarities as well as rare cases, reducing human bias (to a significant extent) and providing a more rigorous analytical framework for researchers.

What are the main points about language and discourse that our corpus-based analyses have revealed?

- Corpus-based discourse analysis is not simply a quantitative procedure but one which involves a great deal of human choice at every stage: forming research questions, designing and building corpora, deciding which techniques to use, interpreting the results and framing explanations for them. This is not simply true of discourse analysis, but all forms of analysis that use corpora.

- Corpus-based discourse analysis takes the researcher beyond simple lists of frequencies. Discourse analysis in particular benefits from the inclusion of full texts in corpora (rather than samples), enabling the user to specify dispersion analyses, showing how the presence of lexis or other linguistic features develops across the course of a single text or set of texts.

- Attitudes and consequently discourses are embedded in language via our cumulative, lifelong exposure to language patterns and choices: collocations, semantic and discourse prosodies.

- We are often unconscious of the patterns of language we encounter across our lifetime, but corpora are useful in identifying them: they emulate and reveal this cumulative exposure.

However, I want to return to some of the issues that have been raised at various points throughout the book. In working through the list of concerns I had collected, it became clear that they could be grouped around two main areas: corpus building and corpus analysis.

Corpus building

As discussed in the earlier chapters in the book, the design and availability of corpora are paramount to its analysis. Diachronically, language and society are constantly changing (at a somewhat accelerated rate in the last ten or so decades). Therefore, discourses are changing as well. There is an urgent need to build more up-to-date corpora in order to reflect this passing of time. The British National Corpus, containing data collected from 1992 and earlier, which has played a major role in the writing of this book, was outdated almost from the time that it became publicly available, and at several points in writing this book, I have questioned the viability of using it as a 'benchmark' for general contemporary English. Perhaps some aspects of language use do not change as rapidly as others, and if we bear that in mind, the BNC, used wisely, may continue to function as a benchmark of British English for years to come. However, the contents of the BNC are a testament to the way that people wrote and spoke in the early 1990s. As Burnard (2002: 68) points out 'It is a rather depressing thought that linguists of this century may continue to study the language of the nineties for as long as those of the preceding one were constrained to study that of the sixties.' Ideally something like the BNC should be built every ten years (the likelihood of this at the present is perhaps small, although lessons gained through previous experience, coupled with innovations in corpus collection and mark-up techniques may make the task less arduous if there *is* ever a next time). At one million words each, adding new members to the Brown family of corpora would prove to be more viable (and less expensive) and there are a number of projects in development at the time of writing, including for example the Lancaster1931 Corpus (Leech and Smith 2005). Blommaert (2005: 37) points out that a major problem of critical discourse analysis is its closure to a particular timeframe: 'the absence of a sense of history in CDA'. Every discourse, according to Blommaert (*ibid.* 136) is a discourse *on* history (where we see references to a variety of historical time frames) and discourse *from* history (articulating a set of shifting positions in history). Using corpora of texts that were created decades or centuries ago will help researchers to explore the ways that language was once used, shedding light on the reasons behind current meanings, collocations and discourse prosodies of particular words, phrases or grammatical constructions. Additionally, historic or longi-tudinal corpora allow us to chart how discourses have been formed, contested and modified over time. We can track the appearance of new lexis and subsequently the creation of new ideas. Comparing a range of corpora from different historic time periods will give us a series of linguistic 'snap-shots' which will allow discourses to appear to come to life – in the same way that the photographic film process works. However, the process of locating historical texts and converting them into electronic form is not likely to be as straightforward as building a modern-day corpus. Ideals concerning representativeness may also need to be compromised in terms of what is available.

Another of Blommaert's criticisms of CDA is also relevant here: 'There is no reason to restrict critical analyses of discourse to highly integrated, Late Modern and post-industrial, densely semiotised First-World societies.' (*ibid*. 35). I am ruefully aware that this book has utilized corpora (both general and specialized) that are made up only of British texts. In part, this has been due to my own preoccupations, coupled with availability (or lack) of certain types of corpus data, and the fact that my own ability to work with other languages is not great. However, as well as the need to continue creating up-to-date general corpora, it is also important that we do not neglect other societies (both past and present) which communicate in languages other than English. Although corpus linguistics is becoming rather less UK-centric than it once was, Blommaert's densely semiotized First-World societies are still somewhat over-represented in terms of corpus building (particu-larly in Europe, although North America is catching up with the creation of the American National Corpus). The release of the EMILLE (Enabling Minority Language Engineering) corpora (several hundred million words in Indic languages), suggests that it is feasible to build super-corpora based around non-romanized writing systems.[1]

It is also the case, as discussed earlier in the book, that there are more written corpora in existence than spoken corpora. Spoken data is more difficult to obtain, even in its raw audio-recorded state (particularly when collecting private conversations) and it cannot be easily converted to electronic form. However, spontaneous spoken data can be particularly useful in helping to identify how discourses are constructed and maintained at grass-roots level. Compared to written language, spoken data can be a more organic, unedited, untidy affair, full of inconsistencies and unconscious verbal tics (one reason why inter-views and focus groups can yield good data). Techniques of accurately and rapidly transcribing spoken data are therefore required in order to enable the creation of larger, more up-to-date spoken corpora.

And finally, another aspect of corpus building which is particularly relevant for discourse analysis is the fact that context is so important. Corpora that include both the 'electronic text-only with annotations' form and the original texts would be useful for making sense of individual texts within them. For example, in the case of newspaper or magazine articles it would be useful to make references back to the original page(s) so we could note aspects such as font size and style, colours, layout and visuals. With spoken texts, the inclusion of links back to digitized sound files would allow the reader to make more sense of a spoken utterance – *how* something is said often being more important than what is said. Unfortunately the act of reading a spoken transcript, no matter how well annotated, rarely gives the same impression as actually hearing it.

There are doubtless other points of interest worth making in relationship to corpus building, but I would like to move on now in order to consider some areas of concern regarding discourse *analysis* and corpora.

Corpus analysis

First, it is important to note that a corpus-based analysis will not give researchers a list of discourses around a subject. Instead, the analysis will point to patterns in language (both frequent and rare) which must then be interpreted in order to suggest the existence of discourses. Also, the corpus-based analysis can only show what is in the corpus, although it may be a far-reaching analysis, it can never be exhaustive (but to be fair, this rider applies to most if not all forms of analysis). However, because corpora are so large, we may be tempted to think that our analysis *has* covered every potential discursive construction around a given subject. It is important that we do not overstate our claims, particularly because non-diachronic corpora offer snapshots of language in use at best, the situation regarding discourse is always likely to change again in the future.

While the issue of overgeneralizing relates to all forms of data analysis, a second point of concern is perhaps more specific to corpus-based analysis. The techniques outlined in this book have tried to offer ways of reducing very large amounts of data into manageable portions, in order to make analysis a humanly possible task. However, even with this reduction, there still can be too much to make sense of. Lists of frequencies, keywords, collocates or concordance tables can still run to many hundreds of lines and it may be tempting to focus on aspects of the analysis which help to support our hunches. Transparency in reporting research outcomes is therefore necessary: the reader should be able to challenge or fine-tune the researcher's findings if they wish. Including full word lists or key word lists as Appendices to research, for example, would be helpful in enabling readers to determine whether the researcher has focused on one aspect of the data while backgrounding others.

The problem of cut-off points in corpus-based analysis is particularly relevant here. Why only look at the strongest 20 keywords when keyword number 21 reveals something relevant? Humans tend to like round numbers: 10, 50, etc. and our cut-off points often reflect this. However, such cut-off points are often a subjective aspect of the analysis (reflecting word count limits on publications or the researcher's own patience and endurance). More work needs to be carried out on determining the best compromise between saliency and quantity in terms of cut-off points, e.g. if a corpus is x words in size, then it would be useful to look at the strongest y keywords.

A linked issue to that of cut-off points is that the wide variety of alternative statistical techniques available to the corpus user might mean that data can be subtly 'massaged' in order to reveal results that are interesting, controversial or simply confirm our suspicions. A collocation list derived via log-likelihood doesn't reveal much of note? Never mind, try again using mutual information. Again, selectivity can deplete claims to impartiality (which some social scientists have argued is a moot point in any case). While there will always be a variety of measures to take into account, one way of lessening the issue of data massage would be to pick the technique which you think works best with the corpus data and then stick to it throughout your particular piece of research. So if you use log-log with a range of −4 to +4 to carry out a collocational analysis of the word *allegations*, you should use the same parameters for carrying out collocations of other words in the corpus. Fiddling with techniques looks sloppy at best and suspicious at worst, whereas sticking to the same measure at least offers internal consistency. And again, trying to explain your choices is always a good idea, e.g.: 'I chose to use the mutual information statistic for carrying out collocations because it tends to favour low frequency lexical words which reveal a range of semantic or discourse prosodies, however other algorithms may produce different results …'.

What else have our analyses revealed? That frequency is not always a perfect measure of a hegemonic discourse and that in a general corpus, we should perhaps not attribute equal weight to the variety of sources and range of author types – newspaper texts are likely to be more far-reaching than privately spoken conversations. When building specialized corpora to analyse, I tried to take this into account by ensuring that the individual texts at least came from a similar source. So when looking at refugees I only looked at newspaper data. This, of course, limits what we can say about the pervasiveness of any discourses that are suggested by the analysis, but at least we do not have to allow for text type as a factor.

When using a general corpus, issues surrounding the varying types of production and reception for all of the texts within, can become highly problematic. These concerns are something which corpus linguistics can only tangentially address, they move the focus away from a straightforward linguistic analysis towards the sort of research we would be more likely to find in anthropology, sociology, media and cultural studies. However, it is useful to show awareness of such issues, even if it is not possible to carry out wide-scale analyses of reception and production.

How can we address this problem? One option could therefore be to recognize that general corpora consist of a multitude of voices and to therefore use such data sparingly, instead carrying out the analysis of discourses on more specialized corpora, where issues of production and reception can be more easily articulated. I would not discount the use of general corpora altogether, as I also stated in Chapter 1, the corpus perspective is one view of language, while it may not be the only standpoint available to us – it is still an incredibly useful one.

A second solution could be to carry out a quantitative analysis, cross-tabulating the different kinds of texts in a general corpus alongside the different discourses that are elicited. For example, after analysing discourses surrounding a particular subject, e.g. 'refugees', we may hypothetically find that tabloid newspapers tend towards what could be termed racist discourses, broadsheet newspapers attempt to present a more neutral stance, whereas the more private texts in the corpus (letters, diary entries, spoken conversations) contain the most extreme discourse stances of all (both negative *and* positive). Such an analysis would obviously take time to carry out and in considering different genres in the corpus as separate like this, the researcher may find that the cake has been sliced too thinly, meaning that there is not enough data in certain categories to warrant saying anything of merit.

A third possibility could simply be to argue from a perspective that society is inter-connected and all texts influence each other. The view that political, religious, media and business leaders have sole access to the powerful discourses is not the case. If such discourses *are* so powerful, we would expect them to occur across a range of text types and genres. Therefore discourses encountered in private conversations are likely to be fuelled by discourses in newspapers or religious speeches. The discourses we examine in texts intended for a very

180

small audience may therefore be reflective of larger sources. They also may be more 'honest' stances – people are often less likely to be careful or hedge their opinions when writing or talking to a small informal audience (or no audience in the case of diary entries). And while these discourses would trickle-down – say from the media to personal conversations, the reverse would also be true – public language is often inspired by the personal and private.

Returning to another concern that I first raised in Chapter 1, corpora give somewhat decontextualized information about written or spoken language; the average corpus is unlikely to reveal anything about, say, the relationship between an image and the writing surrounding it, or the way that a hand gesture can show that a speaker is being serious or joking. Annotation systems may be developed in order to deal with such issues, but on the whole, corpora are collections of texts (and where they are annotated, it tends to be at the grammatical, morpho-logical or semantic level). Hypotheses derived from corpora, therefore, should be tested further, via close examination of single texts in their original form. Sometimes, it really is necessary to go back to the original text, as in Chapter 3 when I analysed holiday leaflets. Corpus analysis is useful for telling us what is 'normal' or not normal in a text population – it can tell us where we should dig, but the spadework is still going to be a human endeavour! Additionally, a corpus can only reveal its own contents to us. It does not tell us much about the world outside.

For example, many of the keywords produced in the examination of parliamentary debates in Chapter 6 were words which were stylistically unique to the genre. We would therefore need to know more about the types of explicit and implicit language restrictions, conventions and norms that occur in parliamentary language in order to explain that this was the case. We may be able to deduce some of this from a closer examination of certain keywords or linguistic patterns, but the corpus cannot explicitly tell us this itself. Further research into the history of the British Parliament and its relationship to law, British society and other ways of producing discourses would also be essential for a fuller analysis of the discourses of fox-hunting in Britain.

The parliamentary debates also only revealed discourses of fox-hunting that Members of Parliament felt were relevant or suitable to bring up in that particular context. So one discourse that was *not* drawn on very often in the parliamentary debates concerned the belief that the topic of fox-hunting reflected a significant division between upper-class people and the rest of the UK. The fox-hunting debate, then, has been constructed elsewhere as 'really being about social class' and not fox-hunting at all. However, the analysis of keywords in the parliamentary debate did not bring up any words that referred to this social class discourse of fox-hunting. Carrying out a specific search in the corpus (e.g. on the word *class*), it becomes clear that both sides do refer to the class discourse, although only a very small number of times. The word *class* occurs ten times across the debate and in six of these cases (three on each side of the debate) it is used to reference the social class discourse. Therefore, the word *class* was not shown up as key because it did not occur significantly more often on one side of the debate when compared to the other, and it did not occur particularly often when the whole debate was compared to the FLOB corpus of general British English. One way of revealing this relative backgrounding of the class discourse in the parliamentary debates would be to compare it to a corpus on fox-hunting taken from different sources. e.g. radio or television debates or internet bulletin board discussions. Such a comparison may have revealed class to be a 'negative' keyword in the parliamentary debates, allowing us to focus on it and the reasons why it occurred so infrequently.

Another issue concerns the corpus linguist's love of comparison, difference and categories. If we compare text a and text b, we are likely to focus on what is different between them. The human obsession with difference is perhaps another cognitive bias, a means of helping us to make sense of the world. However, if we begin an analysis by assuming that two things *are* different we may overlook the fact that they actually may be similar in more ways than they differ. This, of course, should not preclude the analysis, but it is worth bearing in mind. So when comparing the keywords used by pro- and anti-fox-hunting debaters in the House of Commons, it was also worth carrying out another comparison which put the whole debate against a corpus of general English. In doing this, it was found that in many ways, the debaters shared a lot in terms of the way they spoke and what they spoke about. Some of these linguistic phenomena were due to the fact that the debate was about fox-hunting and it is difficult to argue for or against the subject without mentioning fox-hunting, while other words used by both sides related to the genre or context of the debate – words connected to Parliament. However, surprisingly, that analysis revealed that the word *cruelty* was used significantly frequently on both sides of the debate (although in very different ways, it turned out). Identifying the ways that differences and similarities interact with each other is therefore an essential part of any comparative corpus-based study of discourse.

And a corpus-based analysis is only as effective as the analytical techniques that are available to us. Using WordSmith and BNCweb I was able to conduct fast analyses of frequencies, keywords and collocations. If I wanted to compare grammatical and semantic categories there are automatic taggers which can attach this kind of information throughout the corpus. However, in order to explore more complex linguistic phenomena such as metaphor and attribution I had to engage with the corpus by employing less mechanistic procedures. There are a set of related problems here: the fact that when we investigate discourses of a given subject in a corpus, it is easier to focus on direct references (e.g. we look for the word *refugees*) rather than patterns around anaphora (words like *them* or *those*). Also, presence tends to take precedence over absence in a corpus, because we often may not know what is missing. This can have consequences for research which examines lexical choice (some terms may simply be missing from a corpus or text) or agency (various actors may be excluded or backgrounded, cf. Van Leeuwen 1996). And consequently, certain discourses may not be present. The key point here is that some forms of analysis appear to be more 'convenient' than others. The development of corpus tools and techniques which allow for more sophisticated automatic analyses is therefore another area where further work could gainfully be carried out.

Finally, I return to the problem of interpretation brought up in Chapter 1. A corpus-based analysis of discourse affords the researcher with the patterns and trends in language (from the subtle to the gross). People are not computers though, and their ways of interacting with texts are very different, both from computers and from each other. Corpus-based discourse analysis should therefore play an important role in terms of removing bias, testing hypotheses, identifying norms and outliers and raising new research questions. It should not replace other forms of close human analysis, but act in tandem with them. The corpus is therefore an extremely useful instrument to add to the workbox of techniques available to discourse analysts. But it should not mean that we can now throw away all of our existing tools.

Notes

1. Michael Barlow maintains a website which contains links to corpora in a range of languages. See www.athel.com/corpus.html.

183

References

Andor, J. (2004), 'The master and his performance: An interview with Noam Chomsky', *Intercultural Pragmatics*, 1:1, 93–111.

Armistead, N. (1974), *Reconstructing Social Psychology*. Harmondsworth: Penguin.

Atkinson, D. (1999), *Scientific Discourse in Sociohistorical Context*. Mahwah New Jersey: Erlbaum.

Ayala, S. P. de (2001), 'FTAs and Erskine May: Conflicting needs? – Politeness in Question Time' *Journal of Pragmatics* 33, 143–69.

Bahktin, M. (1984), *Problems of Dostoevsky's Poetics*. Minneapolis: University of Minnesota Press. First published 1929.

Baker, P. (2005), *Public Discourses of Gay Men*. London: Routledge.

Baker, P. and McEnery, T. (2005), 'A corpus-based approach to discourses of refugees and asylum seekers in UN and newspaper texts.' *Language and Politics* 4:2.

Baldry, A. (2000), *Multimodality and Multimediality in the Distance Learning Age*. Campobasso: Palladino.

Becker, H. (1972), 'Whose side are we on?', in J. D. Douglas (ed) *The Relevance of Sociology*. New York: Appleton-Century-Crofts.

Berry-Rogghe, G. L. E. (1973), 'The computation of collocations and their relevance in lexical studies', in A. J. Aitken, R. Bailey and N. Hamilton-Smith (eds), *The Computer and Literary Studies*. Edinburgh: Edinburgh University Press.

Bhaskar, R. (1989), *Reclaiming Reality*. London: Verso.

Biber, D. (1988), *Variation in Speech and Writing*. Cambridge: Cambridge University Press.

Biber, D. and Burges, J. (2001), 'Historical shifts in the language of women and men: gender differences in dramatic dialogue' in D. Biber and S. Conrad (eds) *Variation in English: Multi-Dimensional Studies*. London: Longman, 157–70.

Biber, D., Conrad, S. and Reppen, R. (1998), *Corpus Linguistics: Investigating Language Structure and Use*. Cambridge: Cambridge University Press.

Biber, D. and Johansson, S., Leech, G., Conrad, S., and Finegan, E. (1999), *Longman Grammar of Spoken and Written English*. London: Longman.

Blas-Arroyo, J. L. (2003), 'Perdóneme que se lo diga, pero vuelve usted a faltar a la verdad, señor González': Form and Function of Politic Verbal Behaviour in Face-to-Face Spanish Political Debates. *Discourse Society*, 14, 395–423.

Blommart, J. (2005), *Discourse*. Cambridge: Cambridge University Press.

Borsley, R. D. and Ingham, R. (2002), 'Grow your own linguistics? On some applied linguistics' views of the subject.' *Lingua Franca* 112, 1–6.

Brown, G. and Yule, G. (1983), *Discourse Analysis*. Cambridge: Cambridge University Press.

Brown, P. (1973), *Radical Psychology*. London: Tavistock.

Bryan, M. T. (1988), SGML – *An Author's Guide to the Standard Generalized Markup Language*. Wokingham: Addison-Wesley.

Buchanan, D. R. (1992), 'An uneasy alliance: combining quantitative and qualitative research methods', *Health Education Quarterly*, 19: 117–35.

Burnard, L. (2002), 'Where did we go wrong? A Retrospective look at the British National Corpus,' in B. Kettemann and G. Marko (eds) T*eaching and Learning by Doing Corpus Analysis*, Amsterdam: Rodopi, 51–70.

Burr, V. (1995), *An Introduction to Social Constructionism*. London: Routledge.

Caldas-Coulthard, C. R. and Moon, R. (1999), 'Curvy, hunky, kinky: Using corpora as tools in critical analysis.' Paper read at the Critical Discourse Analysis Meeting, University of Birmingham 1999.

Caldas-Coulthard, C. R. and van Leeuwen, T. (2002), 'Stunning, shimmering, iridescent: Toys as the representation of gendered social actors.' In L. Litosseliti and J. Sunderland (eds) *Gender Identity and Discourse Analysis*. Amsterdam: John Benjamin, 91–108.

Cameron, D. (1998), 'Dreaming the dictionary: Keywords and corpus linguistics.' *Keywords* 1, 35–46.

Cameron, D. (2001), *Working with Spoken Discourse*. London: Sage.

Charteris-Black. J. (2004), *Corpus Approaches to Critical Metaphor Analysis*. Basingstoke Hants: Palgrave Macmillan.

Chilton, P. (2004), *Analysing Political Discourse: Theory and Practice*. London: Routledge.

Cicourel, A. V. (1964), *Method and Measurement in Sociology*. New York: Free Press.

Clear, J., Fox, G., Francis, G., Krishnamurthy, R. and Moon, R. (1996), 'Cobuild: the state of the art'. *International Journal of Corpus Linguistics* 1, 303–14.

Cotterill, J. (2001), 'Domestic discord, rocky relationships: semantic prosodies in representations of marital violence in the O.J. Simpson trial.' *Discourse and Society*. 12:3, 291–312.

Crystal, D. (1995), *Cambridge Encyclopedia of the English Language*. Cambridge: Cambridge University Press.

Culpeper, J. (2001), *Papers from the SALA symposium Conversation in life and in literature Uppsala, 8–9 November 2001*. 'Computers, language and characterisation: An analysis of six characters in Romeo and Juliet'. Uppsala: ASLA, 11–30.

Danet, B. (1980), '"Baby" or "fetus": language and the construction of reality in a manslaughter trial.' *Semiotica* 32: 1/2, 187–219.

Deignan, A. (1999), 'Corpus-based research into metaphor', in Lynne Cameron and Graham Low (eds) *Researching and Applying Metaphor*. Cambridge: Cambridge University Press.

Denzin, N. K. (1988), 'Qualitative analysis for social scientists', *Contemporary Sociology* 17: 3, 430–2.

Department for Environment, Food and Rural Affairs. (2000), *The Final Report of the Committee of Inquiry into Hunting with Dogs in England and Wales*. Norwich: The Stationery Office.

Derrida, J. (1978), *Writing and Difference*. Chicago: University of Chicago Press.

Derrida, J. (1981), *Dissemination*. Chicago: University of Chicago Press.

Downing. J. (1980), *The Media Machine*. London: Pluto.

Dunning, T. (1993), 'Accurate methods for the statistics of surprise and coincidence'. *Computational Linguistics* 19: 1, 61–74.

Eckert, P. and McConnell-Ginet, S. (1992), 'Think practically and look locally: language and gender as community-based practice'. *Annual Review of Anthropology* 21, 461–90.

Ehrlich, S. (1999), 'Communities of practice, gender and the representation of sexual assault.' *Language in Society* 28:2, 239–56.

Ehrlich, S. and King, R. (1996), 'Consensual sex or sexual harassment: negotiating meaning', in V. L. Bergvall, J. M. Bing, and A. F. Freed (eds) *Rethinking Language and Gender Research: Theory and Practice*. London: Longman, 153–72.

El Refaie, E. (2001), 'Metaphors we discriminate by: Naturalized themes in Austrian newspaper articles about asylum seekers'. Journal of Sociolinguistics, 5, 352–71.

Eysenk, H. J. (1953), *The Structure of Human Personality*. New York: Wiley.

Fairclough, N. (1989), *Language and Power*. London: Longman.

Fairclough, N. (1995), *Media Discourse*. London: Hodder Arnold.

Fairclough, N. (2000), *New Labour, New Language?* New York: Routledge.

Fairclough, N. (2003), *Analysing Discourse: Textual analysis for Social Research*. London: Routledge.

Firth, J. R. (1957), *Papers in Linguistics* 1934–1951. London: University Press.

Flowerdew, J. (1997), 'The discourse of colonial withdrawal: a case study in the creation of mythic discourse.' *Discourse and Society* 8, 453–77.

Flowerdew, L. (2000), 'Investigating referential and pragmatic errors in a learner corpus.' In L. Burnard and T. McEnery (eds) *Rethinking Language Pedagogy from a Corpus Perspective*. Frankfurt: Peter Lang, 145–154.

Foucault, M. (1972), *The Archaeology of Knowledge*. London: Tavistock.

Fowler, R. (1991), *Language in the News*. London: Routledge.

Francis, W. N. and Kučera, H. (1982), *Frequency Analysis of English Usage: Lexicon and Grammar*. Boston: Houghton Mifflin.

Gergen, K. (1973), 'Social psychology as history', *Journal of Personality and Social Psychology* 26, 309–20.

Gibbs, R. W. Jr. and Steen, G. J. (1999), *Metaphor in Cognitive Linguistics*. Amsterdam: John Benjamins.

Gibson, O. (2003), 'Sales dip may push Mirror under 2m: Morgan accepts war stance could reduce circulation to 70-year low.' *The Guardian*. April 2, 2003.

Gilbert, N. and Mulkay M. (1984), *Opening Pandora's Box: A Sociological Analysis of Scientists' Discourse*. Cambridge: Cambridge University Press.

Gill, R. (1993), 'Justifying justice: broadcasters' accounts of inequality in radio.' In E. Burman and I. Parker (eds) *Discourse Analytic Research*. London: Routledge, 75–93.

Goldfarb, C. (1990), *The SGML Handbook*. Oxford: Clarendon Press.

187

Gramsci, A. (1985), *Selections from the Cultural Writings 1921–1926*. ed. D. Forgacs and G. Nowell Smith, trans. W. Boelhower, London: Lawrence and Wishart.

Hacking, I. (1990), *The Taming of Chance*. Cambridge: Cambridge University Press.

Hajer, M. (1997), *The Politics of Environmental Discourse: Ecological Modernization and the Policy Process*. Oxford: Oxford University Press.

Hall, S., Critcher, C., Jefferson, T., Clarke, J. and Roberts, B. (1978), *Policing the Crisis: Mugging, the State, and Law and Order*. London: Macmillan.

Hardt-Mautner (1995a), *Only Connect: Critical discourse analysis and corpus linguistics, UCREL Technical Paper 6*. Lancaster: University of Lancaster.

Hardt-Mautner, G. (1995b), 'How Does One Become a Good European: The British Press and European Integration.' *Discourse and Society* 6:2, 177–205.

Harré, R. and Secord, P. F. (1972), *The Explanation of Social Behaviour*. Oxford: Blackwell.

Hermes, J. (1995), 'Easily Put Down: How Women and Men read Women's Magazines.' *Reading Women's Magazines: An Analysis of Everyday Media Use*. Oxford: Polity Press, 29–65.

Hoey, M. (1986), 'The discourse colony: a preliminary study of a neglected discourse type', in *Talking about Text*, Discourse Analysis Monograph no. 13, English Language Research, University of Birmingham, 1–26.

Hoey, M. (2005), *Lexical Priming. A New Theory of Words and Language*. London: Routledge.

Holloway, W. (1981), '"I just wanted to kill a woman", Why? The Ripper and male sexuality.' *Feminist Review* 9, 33–40.

Holloway. W. (1984), 'Gender differences and the production of the subject'. In J. Henriques, W. Hollway, C. Urwin, C. Venn and V. Walkerdine (eds) *Changing the Subject*. London: Meuthuen, 227–63.

Holmes, J. (2001), 'A corpus based view of gender in New Zealand English'. In M. Hellinger and H. Bussman (eds) *Gender Across Languages. The Linguistic Representation of Women and Men*. Vol 1. Amsterdam: John Benjamins, 115–36.

Hunston, S. (1999), 'Corpus evidence for disadvantage: issues in critical interpretation', Paper read at the BAAL/CUP seminar 'Investigating discourse practices through corpus research: methods, findings and applications', University of Reading, May 1999.

Hunston, S. (2002), *Corpora in Applied Linguistics*. Cambridge: Cambridge University Press.

Johansson, S. (1991), 'Times change and so do corpora', in K. Aijmer and B. Altenburg (eds.) *English Corpus Linguistics: Studies in Honour of Jan Svartvik*, London, Longman, 305–14.

Johns, T. (1997), 'Contexts: the background, development and trialling of a concordance-based CALL program' in A. Wichmann, S. Fligelstone, McEnery, T. and Knowles, G. (eds.) *Teaching and Language Corpora*, London: Longman, 100–15.

Johnson, S., Culpeper, J., and Suhr, S. (2003), 'From "politically correct councillors" to "Blairite nonsense": discourses of political correctness in three British newspapers.' *Discourse and Society* 14:1, 28–47.

Jones, S. and Sinclair, J. (1974), 'English lexical collocations.' *Cahiers de Lexicologie*, 24, 15–61.

Käding, J. (1897), *Häufigkeitswörterbuch der deutschen Sprache*, Steglitz: privately published.

Kahneman, D. and Tversky, A. (1973), 'On the psychology of prediction.' *Psychological Review*, 80, 237–51.

Kaye, R. (1998), 'Redefining the Refugee: The UK Media Portrayal of Asylum Seekers.' In K. Koser and H. Lutz (eds) *The New Migration in Europe: Social Constructions and Social Realities*. London: Macmillan Press, 163–82.

Kennedy, G. (1998), *An Introduction to Corpus Linguistics*. London: Longman.

Kenny, D. (2001), *Lexis and Creativity in Translation: A Corpus-based Study*. Manchester: St Jerome Publishing.

Kilgarriff, A. and Tugwell, D. (2001), 'WASP-Bench: an MT Lexicographers' Workstation Supporting State-of-the-art Lexical Disambiguation'. *Proceedings of MT Summit VII*, Santiago de Compostela, 187–90.

Kitzinger, C. and Thomas, A. (1995), 'Sexual harassment: A discursive approach', in Wilkinson, S. and C. Kitzinger (eds.) *Feminism and Discourse: Psychological Perspectives*. London: Sage, 32–48.

Koller, V. (2004), *Metaphor and Gender in Business Media Discourse. A Critical Cognitive study*. Houndmills: Palgrave MacMillan.

Kress, G. (1994), 'Text and grammar as explanation' in U. Meinhof and K. Richardson (eds.) *Text, Discourse and Context: Representations of Poverty in Britain*. London: Longman, 24–46.

Kress, G. and van Leeuwen, T. (1996), *Reading Images: The Grammar of Visual Design*. London: Routledge.

Kytö, M. and Rissanen, M. (1992), 'A language in transition: the Helsinki Corpus of English texts', *ICAME Journal* 16, 7–27.

Lakoff, G. and Johnson, M. (1980), *Metaphors We Live By*. Chicago University Press. Chicago.

Law, I, Svennevig, M. and Morrison, D. E. (1997), *Privilege and Silence. 'Race' in the British News during the General Election Campaign, 1997. Research Report for the Commission for Racial Equality*. Leeds: University of Leeds Press.

Layder, D. (1993), *New Strategies in Social Research*. Cambridge: Polity Press.

Leech, G. (1991), 'The state of the art in corpus linguistics', in K. Aijmer and B. Altenberg (eds) *English Corpus Linguistics: Studies in Honour of Jan Svartvik*. London: Longman, 105–122.

Leech, G. (2003), 'Modality on the move: the English modal auxiliaries 1961–1992.' In: Roberta Facchinetti, Manfred Krug and Frank Palmer (eds.) Modality in Contemporary English. Topics in English Linguistics 44. Berlin and New York: Mouton de Gruyter, 223–40.

Leech, G. and Smith, N. (2005), 'Extending the possibilities of corpus-based

189

research on English in the twentieth century: a prequel to LOB and FLOB.' *ICAME Journal 29.*

Löbner, S. (2002), *Understanding Semantics.* London: Arnold.

Lorenz, G. (1998), 'Overstatement in advanced learners' writing: stylistic aspects of adjective intensification' in S. Granger (ed.) *Learner English on Computer.* London: Longman, 157–76.

Louw, B. (1997), 'The role of corpora in critical literary appreciation' in A. Wichmann, S. Fligelstone, McEnery, T. and Knowles, G. (eds.) *Teaching and Language Corpora*, London: Longman, 140–251.

Marsh, A. (1976), 'Who hates the blacks?' *New Society*, 23 September, 649–52.

McArthur, T. (1981), *Longman Lexicon of Contemporary English.* London: Longman.

McEnery, T., Baker, P and Hardie, A. (2000), 'Swearing and Abuse in modern British English' In B. Lewandowska-Tomaszczyk and J. Melia *PALC 99 Practical Applications in Language Corpora.* Hamburg: Peter Lang, 37–48.

McEnery, A. and Wilson, A. (1996), *Corpus Linguistics.* Edinburgh: Edinburgh University Press.

McIlvenny, P. (1996), 'Heckling and Hyde Park: Verbal audience participation in popular public discourse. *Language in Society* 25:1, 27–60.

McNeill, P. (1990), *Research Methods.* Second Edition. London: Routledge.

Morgan, N. and Pritchard, A. (2001) *Advertising in Tourism and Leisure.* Oxford: Butterworth-Heinemann.

Morrish, L. (2002) '"That's so typical of Peter – as soon as there's a cock-up he tries to sit on it.": British Broadsheet Press versus Peter Mandleson 1996–2001." Paper given at the *9th Annual American University Conference on Lavender Languages and Linguistics.*

Morrison, A and Love, A. (1996), 'A discourse of disillusionment: Letters to the Editor in two Zimbabwean magazines 10 years after independence', *Discourse and Society* 7, 39–76.

Mynatt, C. R., Doherty, M. E., and Tweney, R. D. (1977), 'Confirmation bias in a simulated research environment: an experimental study of scientific inference.' *Quarterly Journal of Experimental Psychology*, 29, 85–95.

Newby, H. (1977), "In the Field: Reflections on the Study of Suffolk Farm Workers", in Bell, C. and Newby, H. (eds), *Doing Sociological Research.* London: Allen and Unwin.

Oakes, M. (1998), *Statistics for Corpus Linguistics.* Edinburgh: Edinburgh University Press.

Omoniyi, T. (1998), 'The discourse of tourism advertisements: Packaging nation and ideology in Singapore'. *Working Papers in Applied Linguistics*, 4, (22), 2–14.

Parker, I. (1992), *Discourse Dynamics: Critical Analysis for Social and Individual Psychology.* London: Routledge.

Parker, I. and Burman, E. (1993), 'Against discursive imperialism, empiricism and constructionism: thirty two problems with discourse analysis.' In Burman E. and I. Parker (eds) *Discourse Analytic Research. London:* Routledge, 155–72.

Partington, A. (1998), *Patterns and Meanings.* Amsterdam: Benjamins.

Partington, A. (2003), *The Linguistics of Political Argument: The Spin-doctor and the Wolf-pack at the White House.* London: Routledge.

Piper, A. (2000), 'Some people have credit cards and others have giro cheques: "Individuals" and "people" as lifelong learners in late modernity' *Discourse and Society* 11, 515–42.

Potter, J. and Wetherell, M. (1987), *Discourse and Social Psychology.* London: Sage.

Preyer, W. (1889), *The Mind of the Child.* New York: Appleton. Translation of original German edition of 1882.

Quirk, R. (1960), 'Towards a description of English usage', *Transactions of the Philological Society*, 40–61.

Rayson, P., Leech, G., and Hodges, M. (1997), 'Social differentiation in the use of English vocabulary: some analyses of the conversational component of the British National Corpus' *International Journal of Corpus Linguistics* 2, 133–50.

Renouf, A. (1987), 'Corpus development' in J. Sinclair (ed.) *Looking Up. An Account of the Cobuild Project in Lexical Computing.* London, Collins, 1–40.

Rey, J. M. (2001), 'Changing gender roles in popular culture: Dialogue in *Star Trek* episodes from 1966 to 1993', in D. Biber and S. Conrad (eds) *Variation in English: Multi-Dimensional Studies.* London: Longman, 138–56.

Rich, A. (1980), 'Compulsory heterosexuality and lesbian existence.' *Signs: Journal of Women in Culture and Society* 5, 631–60.

Ringbom, H. (1998), 'Vocabulary frequencies in advanced learner English: a cross-linguistic approach.' in S. Granger (ed.) *Learner English on Computer.* London: Longman, 41–52.

Sardinha, T. B. (2002), *Metaphor in Corpora: A Corpus-driven Analysis of Applied Linguistics Dissertations.* Paper given at the International Conference on Metaphor in Language and Thought. PUCSP.

Sarup, T. R. (1986), *An Introductory Guide to Post-structuralism and Postmodernism.* Hemel Hempstead: Harvester Wheatsheaf.

Saussure, F. de (1974), *Course in General Linguistics.* London: Fontana.

Schmid, H.-J. and Fauth, J. (2003), 'Women's and men's style: Fact or fiction? New grammatical evidence.' Paper presented at the Corpus Linguistics Conference, Lancaster, March 2003.

Scott, M. (1999), *WordSmith Tools Help Manual.* Version 3.0. Oxford: Oxford University Press.

Scott, M. (2002), 'Picturing the key words of a very large corpus and their lexical upshots – or getting at the Guardian's view of the world' in B. Kettemann and G. Marko (eds.) *Teaching and Learning by Doing Corpus Analysis*, Amsterdam: Rodopi, 43–50.

Scruton, R. (1998), *On Hunting.* London: Yellow Jersey Press.

Shalom, C. (1997), 'That great supermarket of desire: attributes of the desired other in personal advertisements', in Harvey, K. and Shalom, C. (eds.) *Language and Desire*, London: Routledge, 186–203.

191

Shan, S. (2000), 'Language, gender and floor apportionment in political debates' *Discourse and Society* 11:3, 401–18.

Sherrard, C. (1991), 'Developing discourse analysis.' *Journal of General Psychology* 118: 2, 171–79.

Sigley, R. and Holmes, J. (2002), '*Girl*-watching in corpora of English.' *Journal of English Linguistics* 30: 2, 138–57.

Sinclair, J. (1991), *Corpus, Concordance, Collocation.* Oxford: Oxford University Press.

Sinclair, J. (1996) 'The search for units of meaning'. *Textus* 9, 75–206.

Sinclair, J. M. (1999), 'A way with common words' in H. Hasselgård and S. Oksefjell (eds) *Out of Corpora: Studies in Honour of Stig Johnasson.* Amsterdam: Rodopi. 157–79.

Slembrouck, S. (1992), The Parliamentary Hansard 'Verbatim' Report: The Written Construction of Spoken Discourse. *Language and Literature* 1:2, 101–19.

Snyder, M. and Gangestad, S. W. (1986), 'On the nature of self-monitoring: Matters of assessment, matters of validity.' *Journal of Personality and Social Psychology*, 54, 972–79.

Stubbs, M. (1983), *Discourse Analysis: the Sociolinguistic Analysis of Natural Language.* Chicago: University of Chicago Press.

Stubbs, M. (1996), *Text and Corpus Analysis.* London: Blackwell.

Stubbs, M. (2001a), 'Texts, corpora and problems of interpretation: A response to Widdowson.' *Applied Linguistics* 22: 2, 149–72.

Stubbs, M. (2001b), *Words and Phrases: Corpus Studies of Lexical Semantics.* London: Blackwell.

Stubbs, M. (2002), 'On text and corpus analysis: A reply to Borsley and Ingham.' *Lingua Franca* 112, 7–11.

Stubbs, M. and Gerbig, A. (1993), 'Human and inhuman geography: on the compute-assisted analysis of long texts,' in M. Hoey (ed) *Data, Description, Discourse.* London: HarperCollins, 64–85.

Sunderland, J. (2004), *Gendered Discourses.* Basingstoke: Palgrave.

Swann, J. (2002), 'Yes, but is it gender?' In L. Litosseliti and J. Sunderland (eds) *Gender Identity and Discourse Analysis.* Amsterdam: John Benjamin, 43–67.

Taine, H. (1877), 'On the acquisition of language by children.' *Mind* 2, 252–9.

ter Wal, J. (2002), *Racism and Cultural Diversity in the Mass Media.* Vienna: European Research Center on Migration and Ethnic Relations.

Tognini-Bonelli, E. (2001), *Corpus Linguistics at Work* (Studies in Corpus Linguistics: 6). Amsterdam/Atlanta, GA: John Benjamins.

Tversky, A. and Kahneman, D. (1973), Availability: A heuristic for judging frequency and probability. *Cognitive Psychology*, 5, 207–32.

Vallone, R. P., Ross, L., and Lepper, M. R. (1985), 'The hostile media phenomenon: Biased Perception and Perceptions of Media Bias in Coverage of the "Beirut Massacre"'. *Journal of Personality and Social Psychology*, 49, 577–85.

Van Der Valk, I. (2003), 'Right-Wing Parliamentary Discourse on Immigration in France' *Discourse Society*, 14, 309–48.

van Dijk. T. (1987), *Communicating Racism: Ethnic Prejudice in Thought and Talk*. London: Sage.

van Dijk, T. (1991), *Racism and the Press*. London: Routledge.

van Dijk, T. (2001), 'Critical discourse analysis', in D. Schiffrin, D. Tannen and H. E. Hamilton. (eds) *The Handbook of Discourse Analysis*. London: Blackwell, 352–71.

Van Leeuwen, T. (1996), 'The representation of social actors' in C. R. Caldas-Coulthard and M. Coulthard (eds.) *Texts and Practices*. Routledge, London, 32–70.

Westermarck, E. (1921), *The History of Human Marriage*. London: Macmillan and Co.

Wickens, P. (1998), 'Comparative analysis of the use of projecting clauses in pedagogical legal genres.' Paper read at the 25th International Systemic-Functional Congress, University of Wales, Cardiff, July 1998.

Widdowson, H. G. (2000), 'On the limitations of linguistics applied.' *Applied Linguistics* 21:1, 3–25.

Williams, P. and Chrisman, L. (eds) (1993), *Colonial Discourse and Post-colonial Theory: A Reader*. London: Longman.

Wilson, A. and Thomas, J. (1997), 'Semantic annotation', in R. Garside, G. Leech and A. McEnery (eds) *Corpus Annotation: Linguistic Information from Computer Texts*. London: Longman, 55–65.

Wodak, R. and Meyer, M. (2001), *Methods of Critical Discourse Analysis*. London: Sage.

Wools, D. and Coulthard, M. (1998), 'Tools for the trade' *Forensic Linguistics* 5, 33–57.

Zwicky, A. (1997), 'Two lavender issues for linguists.' In A. Livia, and K. Hall, (eds), (1997). *Queerly Phrased*. Oxford: Oxford Studies in Sociolinguistics, 21–34.

Index

Lightning Source UK Ltd.
Milton Keynes UK
UKOW05f0343011116
286602UK00006B/135/P

9 780826 477255